MOTIVATING YOUR CHILD

*Tools and Tactics to Help Your Child
be a Self-starter*

Elizabeth Hartley-Brewer

VERMILION
London

First published in the United Kingdom in 1998 by Vermilion,
an imprint of

Ebury Press
Random House UK Ltd
Random House
20 Vauxhall Bridge Road
London SW1V 2SA

Random House Australia (Pty) Ltd
20 Alfred Street
Milsons Point, Sydney
New South Wales 2061, Australia

Random House New Zealand Limited
18 Poland Road, Glenfield
Auckland 10, New Zealand

Random House South Africa (Pty) Limited
Endulini, 5a Jubilee Road
Parktown 2193, South Africa

Random House UK Limited Reg. No. 954009

A CIP catalogue record for this book is available from the British Library.

ISBN 0 74 932311 6

Printed and bound in Great Britain by Cox & Wyman Ltd, Reading, Berks

Papers used by Vermillion are natural, recycable products made from wood
grown in sustainable forsests.

For all discouraged children.

Do not train boys to learn by force and harshness but lead them by what amuses them so they may better understand the bent of their minds.

Plato

Acknowledgements

Writing this book has been one of the hardest things I have ever done, testing my own motivation on occasions. Putting my theory into practice, I sought honest feedback from a number of friends and colleagues as the book took shape, to spur me on. I would like to thank Gillian Pugh, Gerda Hanko, Titus Alexander, Dominic Regan and John Coleman, who had the difficult job of commenting on particular chapters or sections without the benefit of seeing them in the context of the completed book, as well as Victoria Hipps and Sarah Sutton for their editorial guidance. Their comments, guidance and suggestions for further reading were invaluable.

Particular thanks are due, first, to Charles and Elizabeth Handy for agreeing to my request to meet to discuss motivation within organisations and families; and, second, to Dr Howard Hall, Principal Lecturer in Sports Psychology at De Montfort University, Bedford, who was very generous with his time explaining his work and that of other researchers in his field. I have not been able to include all that Dr Hall covered, so any omissions are my responsibility.

I will remain eternally grateful to my family. I thank my two children, Stephen and Georgia, for tolerating my preoccupation, for their love and for their sensible reactions and straight talking that have taught me so much; and my stepdaughter, Julia, whose unquenchable wit and vitality lifts all our spirits. My husband, Michael, has also shown remarkable patience. His clarity of thought and own writings on management issues have been most useful.

Finally, I would like to say a warm thank you to all those friends who agreed to let me use their stories.

Author's Note
Throughout the text the child is referred to as 'he', except when a specific child is being referred to; however, all the content of this book applies equally to boys and girls.

The examples given on p107 appeared first in the *Independent* and are reproduced with their kind permission.

Contents

PART THREE
Rediscovering Motivation: Getting Them Back on Track

The Great Balancing Act

Being a parent of young children at the turn of the twentieth century is hard, and it is not likely to get any easier. We have to make ends meet in an increasingly harsh and competitive world; we have to manage a variety of family arrangements and new roles; we have to compromise constantly, juggling our needs, wishes and opportunities with those of our partners and children. And all the while we are held responsible for an ever greater number of personal and social ills. Children's underachievement is just one of these.

The stakes are rising for all of us as competition stiffens for places in sought-after nurseries, schools, colleges and, finally, for jobs. The pressure starts early, as children's future behaviour, life chances, talents and fulfilment are significantly determined, we are told, by us in their early years. Of course we want them to get ahead, so we naturally want to get it right. It is a heavy responsibility for us to bear and an even harder one for us to carry out successfully.

In parallel with underachievement, and at the opposite end of the achievement spectrum, we are seeing a growing band of prodigies – virtuosi violinists aged 10, international swimmers over the hill by the age of 16, single-minded tennis starlets, mathematical genii hothoused from five, budding linguists who start preschool. With the right learning techniques, we are told, the sky is the limit for our children. If our child is not displaying notable talent in some area or another by the end of primary school, we can easily think we have failed in our duty to explore and exploit his potential. Guilt and pressure can become relentless.

The parent of a three-year-old mini-gymnast was overheard asking the class coach, after only four weeks of attendance, whether her daughter was any good. 'If she's not got any talent, I don't want to waste my time bringing her here,' she explained with no thought whatsoever for her child's enjoyment. Ferrying children from one after-school or weekend activity to another to try to find an area in which they will excel takes not only time but also a great deal of money. There is a growing social and economic divide between the do-nothing children and the do-everything ones. While many children certainly do underachieve, having few opportunities to discover unexplored talents which can help them grow in confidence and pride, others are in danger of being over-extended – managed, monitored and chivvied all day long. Social and educational one-upmanship is in danger of stifling the very creativity and motivation the new opportunities are designed to promote.

For many of us whose children merely plod along somewhere in the middle, it can be hard to know which way to turn. Of course we want our children to develop their talents, but when does encouragement develop into pushiness and secret glory-seeking on our part? When do high expectations and the pursuit of excellence – something all schools are now asked to aim for – lead to burn out? Is our child's lack of enthusiasm for some activity a genuine preference, or a result of low confidence and self-belief which need to be worked through? We are in danger of creating a world in which so much is expected that no one has time to rest, neither parents nor children. If we don't ask ourselves some fundamental questions, this search for fulfilment could create as many problems as it solves.

Why Motivation is an Increasing Issue for Parents

There is nothing new about motivation. For as long as human beings have lived, it has been a fact of life. The readiness to strive, to try new things, to give our best and to consider the quality of our work, is an eternal facet of human personality. The quotation at the beginning of the book from the writings of the Greek philosopher, Plato, shows that people asked questions about how children best learn in ancient times. But not many children were educated in 400BC when Plato was writing: only boys, and only the sons of citizens, not slaves.

It is very different for parents today. Every family is affected by schooling. More testing and measuring of children's academic progress in school makes us more aware of how they are doing and how they compare with other children whom we know. Home-school contracts encourage parents to get involved in learning and homework. The increase in selective schools in the private and state sector means more children are sitting exams, and having extra coaching in preparation. Outside school, a greater number of activities are on offer for children, making it possible for them to explore and develop a huge variety of skills and talents. Media coverage of children with exceptional talents whets parents' appetites for success, and provides role models for children.

Social and economic factors have their impact too. Fewer unskilled jobs, especially full-time ones, mean qualifications are increasingly important for those entering the world of work. At the same time, pockets of high unemployment, often hitting young people especially hard, can make studying seem pointless. Fragile and fragmented families can affect younger children's willingness and ability to learn and develop themselves, causing particular distress to those parents who are successful themselves.

Many parents, therefore, consider it increasingly important for their children to make their mark in some way during their school years, while more of these children are finding it harder to apply themselves and fulfil their potential. The long tail of underachievement is getting longer and some children are finding that striving to meet everyone else's expectations can sometimes be at the cost of their mental health. Their self-esteem and sense of self-worth become undermined. Youth suicide, self-harm, eating disorders and chronic fatigue syndrome are just some of the signs of distress when things go wrong.

In trying to encourage our children to explore and fulfil themselves, we inevitably raise the possibility of killing their enthusiasm stone dead. For the more we interfere with our children's talents, the more we stop whatever activity it is being their thing. We are inclined to apply our – usually inappropriate – standards to their performance, coming across as critical and negative. If we make it clear that a particular goal is our treasured target for them, they are likely to choose that very thing to turn against if they become angry or resentful and want to make a stand. We must beware of taking over their soul. It is almost certainly easier for a parent to destroy a child's passion than to create it.

What is the Message of this Book?

The message contained in this book is relevant to all parents, not simply to those facing problems.

Children are people, not puppets, pigeons or performers. A parent's prime responsibility is to nurture the whole child – and to encourage self-motivation. Parents cannot have influence for ever. Nevertheless, our early role is vital. With an eye always on our child's evolving autonomy and his need to believe in and manage himself, from the first day of his life – we can help to create a motivational climate and energy for him that models good practice and creates a continuing momentum as we gradually withdraw, leaving him in full control. The same approach also works when a child loses heart and direction. The effective motivator does not rely on 'secret plans and clever tricks', to quote Roald Dahl's children's story *The Enormous Crocodile*, but instead works openly to build a child's:

- self-belief
- self-efficacy
- self-direction

Self-belief means you have a clear and positive sense of your 'self' and are able to view yourself in a favourable light, in many different ways. Children who lack self-belief are filled with a generalised self-doubt. Self-efficacy exists when you feel capable because you believe and expect you can carry something out effectively. Children who lack a sense of self-efficacy feel hopeless and incompetent. Self-direction means being able to work independently on tasks and problems. Children who lack the ability to direct themselves feel helpless and become dependent on others to take them forward.

Parents who demand too much and in the wrong way can do as much harm as those who demand too little. We have to aim for a healthy balance, for our sanity and for our children's longer-term success and emotional health. This is not a book for parents who desperately want their child to excel and are looking for some quick fixes. Neither does it provide quick or easy answers for those who have drifted away from their child emotionally, who only realise the consequence of this when any problems with motivation become serious. Certainly, there are ways to help rebuild relationships and regenerate motivation, but they are neither quick nor necessarily easy.

Maintaining a healthy balance is often easier said than done. We may be blind to our personal style and the extent of its impact. Sometimes, when the point of balance needs to shift, it takes us a while to recognise this. Outside influences and pressures may become too strong to resist. At other times, we may have neither the emotional nor the financial resources to reflect or give much at all. Nonetheless, if we are able to think a little more deeply about our own motives, goals and tactics; acknowledge and respect our children's feelings and perceptions, dreams and fears; and keep to some fundamental principles of good practice which enshrine the three guiding 'self' beacons above, we are more likely to steer a successful middle course.

The middle course is achieved when parents show interest, but aren't intrusive; offer direction, but aren't directive; encourage talents, yet leave the child in control; contain, but don't confine; establish routines, but build in flexibility; support and encourage, but don't control and push; offer choices, but avoid being manipulated.

The effective motivator realises that self-motivation depends on building quality relationships. The effective motivator trusts, respects, listens, encourages responsibility wherever possible, allows choices, nurtures competence and shares the trials and tribulations of effort, success and setbacks.

The parent who is most likely to have a relaxed and self-motivated child:

- works with, not against, the personality and character of the child
- starts from where the child is, not where others want him to be
- encourages curiosity
- ensures experience of success
- offers the chance to try himself out
- focuses on the positive
- values a wide variety of skills
- helps the child to help himself
- does not make approval conditional on success
- does not compete
- takes no 'ownership' of his efforts and achievements
- provides a stable, predictable and trusting environment

All these issues are explored and developed later on in the book. It offers practical guidance and wider understanding on the subject of motivation and children. It offers suggestions both to parents who have children going through difficult times and to those wanting to establish a positive motivational environment from the beginning. Although it is not a psychology book, we must understand that words and actions, interpretations and assumptions, make a difference. Emotions and feelings, particularly about ourselves, lie at the heart of learning and striving. Managing motivation is about managing relationships. It is therefore important to understand something about the reasons behind the behaviours we see.

Part One of this book develops our understanding of motivation. It looks at what different people mean when they use the term; develops a model of motivation which sees it as a process and identifies five stages within it; and also surveys a few of the key theories about motivation which have been important in fields such as sport, education and industry. This first part also explores the part played by self-esteem in generating self-motivation and how this relates to our three motivational beacons: self-belief, self-direction and self-efficacy. Finally, it considers what we as parents bring into the equation: how our style and personal history influence the motivational environment.

Part Two presents the principles linked to each of the three beacons. The importance of each one is explained, before exploring how to put it into practice.

Children – happily or unfortunately – grow. Strategies that are useful and successful for children at one stage of childhood become less relevant and effective at other times. This is partly because children get wiser as they age. Perhaps more importantly, children at different ages and stages of development have different social and emotional needs. As they grow, different issues arise and parents have to respond differently. Adolescence is, of course, notoriously problematic. It is a time when motivation is frequently replaced by distraction and disenchantment, to the considerable distress and confusion of parents. Throughout Part Two, the general principles are also applied more specifically wherever possible to children of different ages.

Part Three looks at some common motivational problems and offers suggestions for getting children back on track. It also tries to deepen understanding of the nature of some of the problems. Most problems are progressive. If we understand why things might have gone wrong at the 'serious' end, we can become more aware of general good practice which should prevent problems surfacing.

I should like to state at this point that *Motivating Your Child* is not intended for parents who fear their child may have a serious learning problem or deeper psychological difficulties. If this is your concern, it would be advisable to seek appropriate professional help.

PART ONE

UNDERSTANDING MOTIVATION: THEORIES AND CONCEPTS

1

What is Motivation?

Motivation is something most of us feel we don't have enough of. We know it is important; it helps us to feel fulfilled and it helps us to feel responsible for ourselves and in control. It is fundamental to personal development, contentment and success. Without it, either our potential remains untapped or we end up where chance directs us, not having taken control of our own life. In either case, we can be left with a sense of disappointment, a feeling of 'if only. . .' which can eat away at our self-respect.

As parents, if our children do not seem motivated, we can worry that they might not do themselves justice, that they might get led astray or even waste their lives. We are certainly likely to feel guilty, wondering whether their lack of purpose has something to do with us, despite finding ready excuses in unsuitable friends, poor teachers, absent partners, television or hormones. On a purely practical level, life is so much less stressful and more pleasurable if our children are motivated.

Motivation is fundamental, as it relates to the whole of human endeavour. We confront it in our work, leisure and pleasure. It influences, and is influenced by, our key relationships. We know through any experience with depression, when motivation evaporates, that it is also linked to our emotions. Yet, despite being so central, it remains frustratingly intangible. Even though the term is widely used in many different fields – in sport, in schools, in the workplace, in the creative arts – it is also surprisingly hard to define, describe and explain. Different people make sense of it in very different ways, as we shall see. It even contains within itself a crucial confusion, one summarised neatly by Charles Handy, the internationally acclaimed writer on business organisations and management. In an informal discussion over breakfast, I asked him how he defined motivation and what the term meant for him. 'I don't like the word,' he said. 'For one thing, it does not make clear whether it is something that is done to people, or whether people do it to themselves.' Something that is done to someone implies a degree of manipulation and control. This is at odds with the goal of self-motivation, when people manage themselves. This difference is very important, and parents forget it at their peril. Feeling obviously more comfortable with words such as 'passion', 'fire' and 'hungry spirit', the last being the title of his latest book, Handy explained what he saw as the limits to outside influence. While a powerful and sensitive person can create the conditions within which people can release, sustain and express their passion, an outsider cannot, he said, put the fire, or inspiration, inside someone. This has to spring from within.

I would like to add that if motivation is to be likened to fire, a source of energy that sustains commitment, it requires fuel. Parents provide some of that fuel: but, just like real fires, too much fuel that cuts out the life-giving oxygen will smother the fire and extinguish it. We must be constantly aware of the difference between child-directed and parent-driven motivation. Get the two confused and our interventions can backfire. It will help to understand more about the language of motivation.

The Language of Motivation

Motivation as:

- inspiration
- perspiration
- aspiration
- explanation
- self-exploration

Motivation as Inspiration

For some people, motivation is mainly about energy and enthusiasm, passion and purpose. Inspiration is the key; it is the essence of self-motivation. It expresses something very personal about what someone likes or wants: what makes them them. The passion creates both the drive necessary to stick at tasks when they become difficult and the desire to perform tasks well. Effective leaders nurture, preserve and protect this passion.

It would be great if all children were inspired. The trouble is, they are often not. Children's lives are full of things they have to do that we cannot expect them to get passionate about. For example, few children exult over homework. It is a rare child who gets excited about keeping his bedroom tidy, or is inspired by every subject that he has to learn in school. There are also common times during childhood when things that children were passionate about lose their appeal and times when personal problems can leave a child feeling empty and directionless. Where passion and inspiration coexist, parents have few problems. The issue, for parents and professionals alike, is not only how to stimulate and impassion children but also how to foster resilience and determination when passion falters or when there is little scope for inspiration.

Motivation as Perspiration

The common definition of motivation is the degree of effort made to achieve ends or goals. Words like 'willpower', 'diligence', 'perseverance', 'fortitude', 'tenacity' and 'self-discipline' come to mind. Some people in education today think that too much emphasis has been placed on self-gratification: allowing children to wait for inspiration which makes their task easier. Doing something when we are inspired and enjoy the activity does not involve real effort or real discipline; the kind of discipline we need when we are required to undertake unwelcome tasks. As a result, these critics believe that children have become feather-bedded, and have lost the ability to work at things simply because they have to be done, whether they are enjoyable or not. For them, the energy referred to in the definition of motivation is not passion but perspiration and effort.

This understanding of motivation is, however, limited. Of course, a measure of self-discipline, or steadfastness, is important to anyone in achieving their aims, whether or not they are fuelled by passion. But motivation is a subtle and complex process that involves many skills, experiences and understanding. As John Hunt, an organisation theorist, has written, 'Motivation is not an engine built inside an individual. . . it is the individual responding to a whole range of experiences. . . '. The model of motivation introduced in the next chapter illustrates some of this complexity.

Using terms such as 'perseverance', 'diligence' and 'fortitude' to describe motivation is not only limiting, it is also potentially dangerous. It can encourage us to view an apparent lack of motivation as a sign of personal inadequacy and even moral inferiority, demanding derision, force and punishment as responses. Yet shame and blame, denigration and degradation do not work long term. We know that because they have been tried before. It is not so long ago that phrases such as 'moral fibre', 'stiff upper lip' and 'backbone' were common in society. Shame and degradation humiliate. Humiliation serves only to damage further that all-important self-belief which lies at the heart of motivation, and which is the undeniable starting point for self-motivation.

Motivation as Aspiration

Motivation also involves aspiration. We have to have goals, targets or objectives to aspire to. Motivation is therefore about having a sense of direction, about going somewhere, having ambition, generating momentum. It means that we have a clear idea of what we want to achieve. Role models can be very important as examples of what is desirable and possible – of who or what we might like to become or do.

If we aspire to something, we look up to it. It requires a stretch. It might be almost out of our reach, but we have to believe that it is attainable. The language of aspiration includes words such as 'hope', 'wish' and 'desire'. It is the language of optimism and expectation.

Motivation as Explanation

The psychologists who first tried to research and analyse motivation scientifically in the 1930s and 40s saw motivation in terms of inner, almost elemental, forces not easily controlled by rational thought. These forces have been called variously 'needs', 'drives' or 'urges'. It was thought people behaved in particular ways, and sought particular goals, because the goals fulfilled unconscious and fundamental human needs. More recently, researchers have preferred to view motives as rational and conscious rather than elemental. Viewed from this perspective, motives are the reason for doing something. If we understand why we want to do something, we are more likely to work at it. Adults, and certainly older children, are usually capable of giving an account of their reason for behaving in a particular way. For example, someone's motivation for getting involved in a sport can range from wanting to get fit, through wanting to do better than a sibling at something, to wanting to be best. There is a huge variety of explanations for striving behaviour. This has led those who are interested in motivation today to study the behaviour that is likely to meet each individual's personal goals.

Motivation as Self-exploration

Motivation is also about the excitement of self-exploration and self-discovery. If we did not feel pleasure in discovering new skills, talents and untapped personal resources, we would be far less inclined to make the necessary effort. Achieving, as two American psychologists, Markus and Nurius, have put it, is a process of exploring our 'possible selves'. We have to believe that things are possible for us and we have to have the courage to try. Even if we have had to do or withstand something difficult, something that might border on the intolerable such as climbing Mount Everest, we can take pleasure in discovering a new capacity to cope. Once this challenge has been met, we feel safer and stronger. Striving and exploring increases our self-knowledge, self-respect and self-confidence.

Self-exploration implies three things. The achievement is greatest when all three features are present. It involves:

- exploring our personal capacities and possibilities
- undertaking this ourselves, on our own
- having the idea in the first place, self-generated through curiosity

The more others intervene and do things for us, the less we can take the credit. Of course, sometimes we can achieve significantly more if we work on a project with others, in pairs or in a team, as partners in learning. Sometimes, we need help when we get stuck, and then we can get further than if we had been left on our own. Nevertheless, there is nothing quite so thrilling as having managed a personal project from start to finish, from the birth of the idea to its implementation and completion.

The language of motivation as self-exploration, therefore, includes words such as curiosity, initiative, competence, pride, self-management, self-reliance, self-knowledge, personal responsibility, self-determination, autonomy, mastery and courage.

The Courage to Try: Self-esteem as the Heart of Motivation

People who feel good about themselves produce good results. To be motivated, a child has to believe in himself. As well as wanting to succeed at a particular task, it is vital that he believes he can make the grade. He needs hope and faith in his capacity to achieve. On a more practical level, he also needs to have some idea of how to do it: an idea of how he can bring it about. Someone else's ideas may help, but they will only offer real support if he can make sense of them and put them into practice. He has to, in a sense, 'own' them and feel fully in control. When he is, he is better able to assess his progress. He is master of his own destiny, instead of being dependent on other people's judgements and expectations. He can view success and setback as stepping-stones in his unfolding life and not as 'proof' of his self-assessment or as unalterable omens of his future.

In summary, children need to know themselves, believe in themselves and see themselves as capable to become self-motivated. A teacher may make a particular subject interesting, but if a child does not see himself as capable of achieving, he may still not apply himself to work. Motivation is therefore tied very closely to self-esteem and self-image. 'I believe I can do it' is at least as important as 'I want to do it'.

At the beginning, self-esteem and self-image are shaped by others. The feedback we get from people whom we love, trust and admire has a profound impact on our self-belief and therefore on our motivation. Children perform best when they feel good about themselves – and they feel confident and effective when:

- someone else has let them know that they have done well
- they have been given responsibility and have carried it out effectively
- they have been understood, trusted and respected
- they feel physically and emotionally safe
- they feel accepted for who they are
- they are clearly enjoyed

If, on the other hand, children are punished and ridiculed; told off for trying new things, asking questions or making mistakes; if they are constantly criticised; if they have been ignored and made to feel insignificant; or if their parent's expectations are so high that pressure and failure become unavoidable features of their lives, they will close themselves off, leaving their potential untapped.

The importance of both the self-concept and self-motivation does not mean that parents can wash their hands of responsibility. A young child is simply not able to manage all aspects of his own learning and development on his own. Later, teachers, friends and other adults will share some of the task; but while a child remains dependent, parents have a continuing responsibility for his social, emotional and intellectual growth. Just as self-discipline grows from the experience of imposed, or negotiated, discipline, so self-motivation is unlikely to appear without an established framework of encouragement and supported application and exploration.

Parents can help children to become self-motivated by:

- creating some base-line expectations for performance and behaviour
- establishing helpful practices and routines until these are taken on by the child
- showing interest
- nurturing a child's self-esteem and self-belief

Motivation and Learning

Motivation is a subject that has been researched and investigated more in relation to adults than to children. The first push for this came from employers, wanting to increase output from their employees to increase their profits. Children, however, are not units of production; they are learners. In fact, realising that people of all ages can be enthused by the opportunity to acquire new skills and develop themselves, many companies now describe themselves as 'learning organisations'. The pace of economic and social change demands that Britain becomes a 'learning society'. We are all being urged to adapt and update in order to match skill levels and attitudes to new demands. Encouraging parents to prepare and equip their children to become life-long, self-motivated learners is part of this thrust. Perhaps, then, managers can learn from parents and teachers as much as we can learn from managers.

Given the fundamental link between motivation, self-development and learning, it is helpful to look briefly at some central features of learning. First, learning is risky as it raises the possibility of failure. To develop at anything we have to try something for the first time and risk not getting it right. If we cannot take that risk, we cannot make any advance. We have to have the courage to try. Mistakes are an essential part of learning, for all of us, and at any time in our lives. They are inevitable, especially in childhood which is a time of exploration, discovery and experiment. Mistakes provide feedback on what works and what does not work. It is vital that we grow up being comfortable with mistakes, so we are able to learn from them and adjust our behaviour. Independent learners confront and learn from their mistakes: they do not shy away from them. The stronger our sense of self, the better able we are to withstand setbacks and criticisms. Self-belief does not come from a sense that we are perfect but from the knowledge that we are good enough but have more to give.

Second, learning is potentially threatening as it requires us to change. For people who are secure, this can be exciting. For the vulnerable and uncertain, it can be uncomfortable. If we do not really know who we are, we cling on to an idea, or outer shell, of ourselves. Changing means letting go of that idea, which can be disturbing and frightening. When we do master new information and skills, we have to prove it through tests and questions and move forward yet again. For those who do not like the risk of challenge, it is easier to avoid trying and drop out of the race altogether. People with low self-esteem and low self-belief will have neither the courage to take chances nor the confidence to change.

Self-esteem is therefore important as a basis for learning as well as motivation. The earlier this is recognised, the better. The Royal Society of Arts' (RSA) special investigation into early years education in 1994 recognised this. Chaired by the educationalist, Sir Christopher Ball, his report, 'Start Right', listed the three key objectives of preschool education – more important, he argued, than the three Rs – as developing in children:

- a sense of self-worth
- the ability to care for others
- a willingness to learn

Motivated to do What? Defining Success

Important though educational achievement is, a parent's task is about far more than helping a child achieve academically. Deep down, we probably all know that neither good examination results nor excellence in any sphere automatically guarantees personal happiness or even success in chosen careers. This commonsense view is now supported by research. Increasingly, researchers and employers are finding that possessing a range of personal qualities is more important than qualifications to success and personal fulfilment. Top of the list is the ability to get along with others. For this, we need to be able to:

- understand other people's perspectives
- adapt to changing situations
- communicate effectively
- defuse potential conflict
- share decision-making
- be aware of and take into account the likely effect on others of our behaviour

We will only be successful at these if we know and understand ourselves and can think about how we come across to other people. Those with these qualities, now defined by various writers as 'emotional intelligence', 'emotional literacy', 'social competence' or a 'sound self-concept', often get on faster and further than those whose sole claim to fame is impressive paper qualifications. Daniel Goleman, author of the best-seller *Emotional Intelligence*, suggests that high IQ accounts for no more than 20 per cent of personal success stories. Exploring a similar issue, studies have also found that people who follow a range of interests in their leisure time are more likely to be successful in work and relationships than those with few interests, even if they outshine others in one or more of them.

In 1995, 50 employers were surveyed by the employers' organisation, Industry in Education. The survey confirmed that employers look for more than high academic achievement in their potential recruits. They want staff who can make an overall contribution to the workplace: people with initiative, determination and self-discipline, and communication skills that enable them to work in a team. Employers reported that they believed too many teenagers lacked these attributes.

This is an interesting list. It so happens that these attributes are also the key components of motivation. The strong message sent by the survey was that employers want schools to concentrate less on exam success and more on developing the personal qualities identified. Personal qualities, then, matter at least as much as, if not more than, exam success. If we want our child to be successful, we need to attend to his social and emotional as well as his academic development. If we do, it will pay multiple dividends. The truth is that people who can communicate well, who can reflect on events and their behaviour, who are sufficiently in touch with their own feelings that they can empathise with the feelings of others, who can develop their own views yet see the merits in those of others and work in teams, will usually be well motivated. As the book develops, we shall see that many of these attributes hinge on a positive sense of self, and that this is as crucial to motivation as it is to wider social success, however it is defined.

2

The Five Stages of Motivation

Chapter One has introduced a number of words and ideas relating to motivation. It should now be clear that it is not accurate to say that motivation is only about effort or discipline. It is a subtle and complex process which demands a range of skills and knowledge, beliefs and feelings. Collected together, these words and ideas do not offer much practical help. There are too many of them. When faced with a discouraged child, we need to have a much clearer idea of what might lie behind his difficulty, at what point on the motivation journey he might have lost his way, and which specific practical measures are likely to have the most impact given the likely problem. To be useful pointers to understanding and action, the words and ideas need sorting out. This is the purpose of this chapter.

Striving to reach a goal is like going on a five-stage journey, which can be represented in the form of a diagram. I like to think of it as a map, because maps show us how to get somewhere. The map is useful for completing small-scale projects as well as large ones with distant targets. If children are to get support which is useful, we need to be aware of each of these five stages. We can then respond sensitively and appropriately, as their needs will differ depending on the stage at which they have become stuck.

To pass through each stage, a child needs to have two things: certain understandings and certain skills. Having the understanding without the relevant skill will hamper progress just as much as having the skill without the understanding. The first situation represents the over-optimistic child who does not evaluate his abilities accurately. This is dangerous as it can lead to disappointment and dejection. The second state represents the underconfident child, who possesses the relevant skill at each stage but does not believe it. The ideal is to have the two enmeshed, for this results in a child who has sufficient self-awareness that he can make a good judgement about the effort and skills involved in the task and his ability to meet them.

The five stages are shown in Diagram 2.1. Stage one is target setting. Stage two is assessing whether we have the right competencies and skills to reach it, and topping them up where necessary. Stage three

Diagram 2.1: Five-stage motivation journey

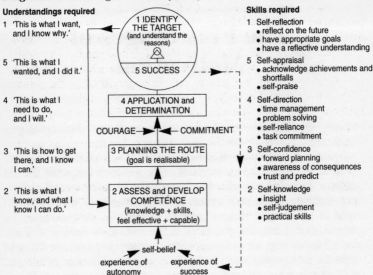

Understandings required		Skills required
1 'This is what I want, and I know why.'	1 IDENTIFY THE TARGET (and understand the reasons)	1 Self-reflection • reflect on the future • have appropriate goals • have a reflective understanding
5 'This is what I wanted, and I did it.'	5 SUCCESS	5 Self-appraisal • acknowledge achievements and shortfalls • self-praise
4 'This is what I need to do, and I will.'	4 APPLICATION and DETERMINATION	4 Self-direction • time management • problem solving • self-reliance • task commitment
	COURAGE → ← COMMITMENT	
3 'This is how to get there, and I know I can.'	3 PLANNING THE ROUTE (goal is realisable)	3 Self-confidence • forward planning • awareness of consequences • trust and predict
2 'This is what I know, and what I know I can do.'	2 ASSESS and DEVELOP COMPETENCE (knowledge + skills, feel effective + capable)	2 Self-knowledge • insight • self-judgement • practical skills
	self-belief	
	experience of autonomy experience of success	

is deciding how to reach the target. Stage four is application and determination. Stage five is success, reaching the goal identified in stage one. The diagram is primarily a model of self-motivation. The role parents or other adults can play in helping their children to help themselves – creating the right environment for self-motivation – is outlined below for each stage.

The motivation journey is almost circular because, ideally, we end up where we started – with our goal. It is also true that success breeds success: one achievement feeds our general confidence and self-belief and makes it more likely that we succeed at something else after. A circle, however, does not convey progress. Instead of going round in circles, it is more useful to think of the journey as one undertaken by one of those looping caterpillars. They firmly fix their sticky front feet on the step ahead, drawing their rear feet up behind, slowly but surely, to meet them before moving on.

Stage One: Identify the Target and Understand the Reasons

Although it sounds obvious, it still has to be said that a child has to know what it is he is trying to achieve before he can become motivated. He has to have a target, a goal. Staying with the idea of a journey, the goal is the destination. The more clearly defined the target, the easier it is to keep it in mind and stay on track. It is not very useful to tell some-one that he has to travel to, say, Yorkshire or France; he needs to know exactly where in Yorkshire or France, in order to choose a sensible route. It is not very helpful to say to a child that he can have a reward if he is 'good' for a whole day. He has to know what behaviour is considered good and, incidentally, will be approved of by the person offering the reward. Similarly, it is not very useful to a child if he says he wants to be 'best', for example at tennis in his coaching group, because 'being best' does not tell him what he has to do to achieve that status. His target should be defined more precisely.

A target can either be selected by a child, or be chosen by someone else, or be discussed and agreed jointly. Very young children will find it hard to think ahead and make sensible judgements about what is realis-tic for them, so an adult will have to be closely involved. However, to be useful as an incentive, the goal must be one that the child is happy to adopt, even if it has been presented to him. He has to 'own' it. If it is plucked out of thin air in an apparently arbitrary fashion, it will be harder for him to stay committed to it: it can be dropped again just as easily as it was accepted. The child has to be clear about the reason or reasons why that goal is important or relevant to him. Returning to our journey theme, if we know why we are travelling somewhere, we can pack the right clothes and equipment. Most of us like to know where we are going and why, and get prepared. It is also important to know when we have to arrive. We can plan a journey with greater focus if we know we are travelling to a particular event.

In summary, it is easier to stay on task during difficulties and setbacks if a goal is both given 'personal meaning', a phrase used by motivational psychologists to mean that a goal is relevant and signifi-cant, and clearly defined in terms of content and timing. Effective, or productive, goals have to be clear, relevant, wanted and appropriate.

Understanding and Skills

The understanding required to pass through stage one can be sum-marised as: 'This is what I want, and I know why'.

The skills required in identifying a target relate to self-reflection. Children need to be able to:

- look into the future safely and confidently, and see themselves there
- know themselves well enough that they can identify both what it is that they want and what their reasons might be for wanting it
- select goals that are appropriate to them, goals which are not only reachable but also sustainable

Be Confident and Optimistic About the Future

Goals usually take time to reach and are therefore part of the future. To be able to identify and accept goals, children have to be able not only to see that far ahead but also to have an optimistic attitude to the future. The extent of children's time horizons depends first on their age. The younger children are, the more they live in the here and now. Their sense of time is undeveloped and the future is confusing. The past, present and future get mixed up and statements are taken to mean what they seem to say. For example, is quite common for children starting primary school to think that they will learn to read on their first day, because they have been told this is what they will do at school.

Once children understand time, they can still have problems selecting goals or taking them seriously. This is because bad experiences in their past can make them suspicious of the future, anticipating only further unpleasantness. The more secure and trusting the child – characteristics which tend to grow from predictable, secure and trustworthy relationships – the more they will be able to look ahead and embrace the future optimistically.

Identify What is Wanted and Why

For a child to know what he wants to do, he has to have an idea of what sort of a person he is. He needs to know how to describe himself, what he likes and dislikes and what he is good at. He has to have a clear self-concept. A child with a poor self-concept and consequently low self-esteem will tend to go blank when asked about preferences, wishes, strengths and even reasons for wanting or doing something. This may be related to the point just covered – wishing to avoid failure given a general assumption that he is useless at everything – but it also stands alone: if we do not know who we are, we do not know who we can become.

The reasons for wanting to reach a particular target are very important. Reasons are our motives, and the clearer they are, the stronger will be our motivation. They can be honourable, or less honourable; positive or negative. Many people make an effort simply to get the reward which has been offered as an incentive. Others may pursue an activity simply because it is enjoyed, so pleasure is their goal. Some may take on a challenge to prove someone wrong or to shame or outshine a sibling – adversity can be a strong motivator. Another example is people who strive to succeed to avoid their own children being deprived of things denied to them. It can be dangerous to reject any reason as inappropriate, especially if it stops the child having that all-important experience of success. Too much criticism of motives may not only undermine his self-belief but also go against the guideline that children should be accepted for who they are. Having said this, research has shown that certain types of reasons are more likely to lead to anxiety than others. This is covered in more detail in the next chapter.

Select Goals that are Reachable

If goals are to deliver that crucial sense of achievement when they are reached, they must stretch and develop. If there is nothing to feel proud of, if no self-development takes place, they will not loop back to increase self-belief or the experience of being capable. Goals which are too easy, then, are not helpful. Goals which are clearly unreachable are a problem too. Self-doubting children sometimes pick impractical targets for themselves in order to jump the gun on responsibility and failure. They stay in control of their own failure, bringing about that which they fear, rather than make themselves vulnerable to someone else's hurtful judgement. By choosing an unreal target, they are absolved from responsibility for trying. Guiding children in where to place the challenge, if they do not select an appropriate one for themselves, is vital but difficult. These issues are discussed more fully in Chapter Fourteen and Chapter Twenty-one.

How Parents Can Help

At stage one, we can:

- try to make home a secure and loving place, to make the future safe
- provide a variety of experiences so our child knows what possibilities exist
- help our child to define clear goals and set clear and manageable time-frames for himself
- check our child believes the goals are achievable
- ensure that he knows why a target is relevant or important, to him or to us
- be specific about the practical consequences of his decision so he knows what to expect – the amount of time involved, for example
- encourage reflection on any problems that might lie ahead
- check if he has yet considered what he will need to do to meet his target
- encourage him to adjust a target that is over-ambitious, or warn of effort that will be involved. Don't say he won't be able to manage it.

Remember – build your child's self-belief. Motivation is about exploring our possible selves.

Stage Two: Assess and Develop Competence

Having identified the target, we then begin to assess the practical consequences – determining how we are going to get there.

First, we check to see if we have got the competence – what we need to achieve it, having already been aware of our general level of ability when selecting the target at stage one. For this we need not only to have a certain level of knowledge and skill but also insight and good self-knowledge so that our judgement about what we need to learn and can learn in the time-frame available matches the reality. There is little point in a child deciding to make, say, a toy garage from wood in one week if he has never held a saw; or to make a hand-made woollen jumper for himself if he has never knitted before.

Second, we need to believe that we are generally capable of success in such tasks. We get this from direct experience of managing something on our own to a successful conclusion, and from being in situations in which we have felt capable and in command. Even babies can be given opportunities to manage themselves, particularly feeding, to help give them this very important sense of mastery. This experience of autonomy and success contributes to self-belief and self-knowledge that help us believe that we can be effective. But again, this self-belief has to be real. For actual achievement to occur, self-belief has to bear some relation to our ability to reach the target.

Understanding and Skills

The understanding required for completing stage two can be summarised as: 'This is what I know, and what I know I can do'.

The skills required relate to self-knowledge. Children need to be able to:

- assess accurately whether they have the right knowledge and skills to achieve the target and be realistic about what they may need to develop further
- have a strong sense of self-belief and an expectation that they will be effective
- draw on as wide a range of existing practical and other skills as possible

Assess and Develop Knowledge and Skills

Most challenges that excite us and deliver the best sense of achievement are those that stretch. We cannot achieve them immediately; we have to develop and extend ourselves. Either we learn more as we work towards the target, so the learning is almost unnoticed, or we need to improve skills before we start. An example of the former is a child who starts to work for the next grade on a musical instrument. Through practising scales and pieces often enough to reach an acceptable pass grade, his technique and skill will inevitably improve. An example of the latter is a child who wants to own a pet rabbit but needs to build a cage for it himself because a new one costs too much. If he has not done more than classroom woodwork before, he will have to practise sawing and hammering on offcuts before he starts on the real thing, and he will probably have to go to the library or pet shop to get ideas for a suitable structure first so that he practises relevant techniques.

Have Strong Self-belief and Expectation of Effectiveness
Having a sense of self-efficacy helps us rise to challenges. If we feel incompetent, we will spend a great deal of time avoiding doing things that will expose our weakness. In other words, the more incompetent we feel, the less we are going to try new things and get better. It is crucial to help children feel generally capable and competent as early as possible.

Draw on a Wide Range of Skills
The more skilled we are at a range of different types of tasks, the more we can use them to help us acquire even more skills and knowledge. Just as success breeds success, so the more we know and do helps us to learn and do other things more quickly. Children who are physically fit and agile, who can read, who are clever at making or cutting things with their hands, who can reason, who can mix well with others, will have a head start when they try something new.

How Parents Can Help

At stage two, we can:

- give children plenty of opportunity to do things for themselves so they develop a strong feeling of competence
- help to make things happen when they show initiative, so they feel effective
- introduce them to a variety of hobbies and interests to broaden their skill base
- help them to be physically fit and co-ordinated, so they can feel proud of their body and feel in charge of it, not let down by it

Chapter Four looks in more detail at how we can help to build our child's self-belief, self-efficacy and self-direction.

Stage Three: Planning the Route

Having passed through stage two, knowing that you have the raw material to achieve the goal, the next stage is putting together a practical plan of action. You won't be able to build a wooden garage, even if you can saw along a straight line and use a chisel, if you do not have a plan, calculate the measurements and be clear about what has to be done in what order. Planning is crucial. It involves a sense of continuity and entails looking at the past in order to draw the relevant lessons from it and apply them to the present. It entails looking at tasks in order, stage by stage, and includes looking into the future. As already stated, children who cannot either look comfortably on their past, or have faith and trust in themselves or in the future, may find it especially difficult to devise forward-looking plans or commit to distant goals. The more unpredictable and uncomfortable a child's life and relationships, the more difficult it will be for him to integrate his experiences and approach tasks logically; the more likely he is to be 'scatter-brained'.

If children are involved in constructing their own plans, they also deepen their commitment to the task, learn more from it and take responsibility for it.

Understanding and Skills

The understandings required to complete stage three can be summarised as: 'This is how to get there, and I know I can'.

The child who passes through this stage feels capable and knows he can be effective. The skills required are those that come with self-confidence. Children need:

- planning skills, to break tasks down into logical steps and stages
- an appreciation of consequences – if they do this, then that will follow
- to be able to accept responsibility for completing a task
- the ability to trust and predict themselves, others and the future

Planning Skills

Planning skills are very useful skills to have. Whether it is writing a shopping list, thinking ahead about which decorating jobs it makes sense to do in which order to minimise upheaval, or running a jumble sale for the local school, planning skills are inevitably involved. Thinking ahead and doing any essential preparation in advance where possible are both part of planning. Without planning skills, it is very hard to see how we can get from A to B. They help to make tasks and challenges seem manageable. They usually save time and they also contribute to success. Inspiration may fire us up, but without a detailed, practical plan, our passion can end in tears. There is a useful phrase used in management training: if you are failing to plan, you are planning to fail.

Planning skills can be developed in children as they grow and mature. If they are, it will help children to be organised, approach challenges in a systematic way and develop their own routines for common tasks. Good planning skills help children to be focused and self-directed, to become, and remain, self-motivated.

Accepting Consequences

Some individuals find it very hard to accept that various things can happen as a consequence of something they have said or done. They don't think about their impact on someone's feelings, about the disruption and work involved in the aftermath of something or about the clearly stated punishment that will follow their forbidden act. They will therefore find it hard to know how to prepare for success, for the same ability to think ahead and predict outcomes is vital if motivation is to become more than a wish or a dream.

Consequences can be appreciated and understood better if they are not just regular, and therefore predictable, but also explained. For example, if someone does not tell us he gets upset when we do a particular thing, we cannot begin to appreciate this as a consequence. While very young children cannot think very far ahead, parents can nonetheless pay attention, gently and progressively, to increasing their child's awareness of consequences of both behaviour and attitudes.

Developing Personal Responsibility

Those who can see and accept the consequences of their actions are taking personal responsibility for them. They think, 'if I do this, then that will happen'. They, not anyone else, are the agents of what follows. To be able to imagine what is likely to happen when, people have to be able to acknowledge their contribution; they must realise what they have done so that they can repeat it or undo it if they discover what they did was wrong, misdirected or unhelpful. Being held accountable for actions and behaviour is the essence of responsibility.

Being Able to Trust and Predict

It follows from the above that being able to trust and predict is crucial. If there is no predictability or consistency in our experiences, we cannot be certain what the result will be of anything. We see no patterns which can give us clues. Without patterns, it is far harder for children to make any link between their behaviour and the consequence of it, and therefore to take appropriate responsibility for it. If children never know, for example, whether parents will ignore, approve of or punish them; whether someone will be in when they get home from school; or whether there will be food in the fridge, it will be hard to establish those clear patterns through which they can further interpret their world.

How Parents Can Help

At stage three, we can:

- encourage our children to think and plan ahead. Before we ask them to do jobs on their own, we can model planning skills, explaining why we are doing things in a certain order. When tidying away toys with young children, we can, for example, explain that the bricks are going in their box first because the other toys sit on top of this in the cupboard. When children are able to do things on their own, such as staying the night with a friend, we can then ask if they want help with planning what they might take, before letting them do it on their own. Encouraging older children to make plastic or wooden models from kits will help them approach tasks in an orderly way. Giving yet older children household duties which have to be planned around other commitments will also help them to think ahead. As parents, we must:

- make our children aware of the consequences of their decisions and actions

- let them know how they make you feel – happy or sad. Let them experience relevant 'consequences', when they misbehave or flout the rules

- gradually and appropriately give them experience of responsibility, first for themselves and then for others. For example, they can be responsible for putting their used clothes in the laundry basket, for putting mugs and plates back by the sink ready for washing, for packing their school bag the night before, and even preparing a family meal from time to time. Carefully selected choices can also be used to increase the experience of responsibility (see also Chapter Thirteen, 'The Motivating Power of Choice').

- chart all changes, and behave in trustworthy and predictable ways. For example, we can try to establish some household routines which lay down clear expectations about what happens when. If we are feeling low and liable to unpredictable swings of mood, we can warn our children of our state, and perhaps seek some help for it if it does not go away. We can let children know in good time of changes in our lives which might affect them, and we can certainly let them know of changes which will affect them directly.

Stage Four: Application and Determination

Having a practical plan helps to make a reality of any stated application and determination to achieve something. Those who define motivation as the energy required to reach a goal may see this fourth stage as the essence of the process. However, determination without a well-thought-through plan can result in the best of intentions fizzling out; and a clear plan without determination and application may also lead to disappointment.

What things help a child to have those essential attributes of application and determination? It is not enough to refer back to stage two and say 'self-belief'. That is part of the answer, but only part; and accepting this does not give us any extra clues as to how to help children become determined and apply themselves well. To stay the course and not give up in the face of difficulty, children – and adults too – need to be able to manage their time well, to problem solve and to think rationally so they can see their way through to the end. Application and determination can also require both courage and commitment, depending on the task at hand. Courage is needed to try when there is the chance of failure, of damaging our self-worth if not our actual physical selves as in the case of some sport-based achievements. Commitment is needed to ensure we are not deflected by setbacks or side-tracked by easier alternatives.

How can parents help a child to have courage and commitment? Courage grows from plentiful encouragement, acceptance of failure and from the experience of success. Commitment to a task or target flows from knowing that others are personally committed to you and from having been helped through previous difficulties (itself a form of commitment), so the sweet taste of achievement is familiar.

Understanding and Skills

The understanding required to complete stage four can be summarised as: 'This is what I need to do, and I will'.

The skills and attributes required are those involved in self-direction. They include:

- problem solving
- self-reliance
- resilience
- time management
- task commitment

Problem Solving

Staying on task often involves solving unforeseen problems which arise. Solving problems entails taking risks, just as learning does. It helps to plan ahead for any likely problems. This will help either to be one step ahead and avoid them, or to manage them better if they arise. Even so, there will be times when a problem was not foreseen. Good problem-solving skills generate confidence and help people to feel self-

reliant and self-directed. Being able to solve problems is extremely useful in managing challenges and setbacks and preventing dejection and
deflection.

Self-reliance
Self-reliance is the ability to manage on your own: to know how to
think independently, combined with the ability to take risks and to
solve problems. With self-reliance, there is no need for other people's
approval before moving forward or doing something new. There is no
need, either, for detailed and constant guidance on how to achieve the
end product. We can rely on ourselves. Children who are self-reliant can
also be relied upon. They are independent, flexible, creative, able to
show initiative and be self-sufficient.

Resilience
If we are resilient, we do not crumble when faced with unexpected or
difficult challenges. It means accepting personal responsibility for
errors and not blaming others, thereby shedding responsibility.
Resilience means not taking mistakes or criticisms personally but
instead reflecting back on the task. Life is full of disappointments and
difficulties. If we can give our children the self-belief to withstand the
knocks and to bounce back, we will have given them something of
great value that will last them for life.

Time Management
Life is becoming increasingly stressful for all of us. When we feel overwhelmed, we can lose sight of what's really important and fall down on
everything we try to do simply because we attempt to do everything
at once and reel from one half-done job to another. This is when time
management skills are useful. Time management involves deciding
priorities: agreeing the most important thing to achieve, allocating
enough time to that; taking care not to waste time on other diversions,
such as the telephone, the computer or television; breaking tasks down
into manageable chunks – making them bite-size; and building in some
rest and relaxation to avoid burn out. Time management helps us to
work efficiently, to stay focused and remain productive.

Task Commitment
Task commitment, or 'stickability', is very important. Those who can
see jobs through receive the positive feedback from their success and
achievement. Achievement is a fixed reality and it feeds into self-belief.
On the other hand, those who find it hard to see a job or task through to
the end, even when the task is one they have set themselves, will have
to live with disappointment, frequent failure, low achievement and
ultimately self-hate. More important, they can retreat from this discom-

fort into a protective fantasy world in which they imagine either that some outside factor is to blame for their failure or they could have succeeded if they had really tried. In other words, the sky becomes the limit and goals selected become increasingly unreal.

How Parents Can Help

At stage four, we can:

- encourage our children to believe they can solve problems on their own. We should avoid stepping in and taking over when they get stuck. Instead, we can support and encourage them and ask 'what if. . ?' and 'might it be possible. . ?' questions to help them consider new approaches or directions
- act as a model, and involve them when we are trying to solve a practical problem of our own
- have the patience to let them do things their way
- encourage self-reliance when appropriate
- help them to complete tasks and projects if they get stuck and dejected, so they do not get into the habit of leaving things half finished. This may involve offering an incentive
- give them the strength to stay committed to people and tasks by making clear our commitment to them – by showing interest in things they do at home and at school, supporting them when they are distressed, by listening and being there
- build their self-esteem and self-belief to increase their resilience
- establish routines to help children get into good habits of practising, training or working

Stage Five: Success

It may seem strange to identify 'success' as a stage, albeit the last one, in the motivation process. It is important, though, because we have completed the cycle, and success reinforces motivation. If we don't acknowledge arrival at the target, or destination, we cannot experience the pleasure of achievement which we need to give us the energy to move forward again when the time is right. Instead, the prevailing feeling will be one of dissatisfaction and failure, despite the satisfactory outcome, because the effort and achievement is not accepted as good enough. This is the predicament of the perfectionist. Where motivation is fired by the desire for self-improvement, as opposed to self-development, there is always room to take the achievement further, to prove that the new, and more acceptable, self is real. When we are not sure, we need the evidence repeated, and repeated. This is why perfectionists are often on a self-imposed treadmill.

For real achievement to have maximum reward and benefit, it is also crucial that the success is allowed to stay with the child or young person and is not taken from him, so to speak, by a parent keen to enjoy the kudos. Chapter Fifteen develops these ideas.

Understanding and Skills

The understanding required is: 'This is what I wanted to do, and I did it'.

The skills and attributes children need include:

- being able to acknowledge achievement
- being able to praise themselves

Acknowledging Achievement

Before we can praise ourselves, we have to be able to acknowledge achievement. Even small advances can be an achievement: if someone is bowed by self-doubt and did not believe he could do it; if he is learning a new skill and has not yet become accomplished; or if his mental or physical capacity inevitably limits what he can do. For example, a child with significant brain damage who learns to feed himself has made a great advance. Achievements will be easier to accept as praiseworthy if we can focus on our personal progress, and compare our performance this time with last time. Compare ourselves with other people and we can turn a real achievement into an apparent failure.

Praising Ourselves

'I did well and I am pleased with myself' is a very different statement from 'I am wonderful'. There is nothing wrong with the first thought. This is not big-headedness or self-obsession and it should not be considered socially embarrassing. We all find it easier to praise ourselves and acknowledge achievement if others around us are doing the same. If parents can celebrate their own successes, however minor, children will be able to follow suit. Praising ourselves when, and only when, the credit is due shows self-awareness. But, by the same token, we must also be prepared to be honest about any shortcomings, when we have fallen short of the target.

The capacity to praise ourselves relates to self-esteem. We have to feel that, whatever we have done, we are worthy of praise as a person. People who reject praise, who refuse to acknowledge or be lifted by it, are those who have such low self-esteem that they cannot recognise themselves as a person who deserves credit. This problem is raised again in Chapter Twenty-two.

How Parents Can Help

At stage five, we can:

- make praise a comfortable thing to receive and give in our family. If children are to be able to praise themselves, they have to hear it from others first
- 'I did well today!' Model self-praise by openly showing pleasure at our own achievements
- celebrate or mark successes, even small ones, especially if our child feels particularly proud of something he has done or achieved: for example, riding a two-wheeled bike, swimming a width of a pool, cooking his first cake or meal, passing his driving test, winning a sporting or other competition
- let our child take and keep the credit for his success, and don't undermine it with sarcasm or any comment that he could have done even better
- let him know it is fine to spend time enjoying his success before he takes on new challenges
- let him know that, pleased as we are with his success, we love him for who he is, not for what he has proved he can do

3

Theories of Motivation in Management, Sport and Education

In this chapter, we shall have a brief look at the most influential theories and approaches to motivation as practised in management, sport and schools. Each approach offers parents insights and tips about 'managing' children to ensure that they, too, explore their potential while remaining happy and enthusiastic.

Approaches to Motivation in Management

Maslow's 'Hierarchy of Needs'

Abraham Maslow, an American psychologist who wrote in the 1950s, is perhaps the most famous theorist of motivation. Maslow believed that people are motivated by common human 'needs'; that these needs, or goals, change as personal circumstances change, but conform to a set pattern; and that some needs are more essential than others and become dominant if unfulfilled. He identified seven different needs which he prioritised in line with his view of their relative importance, hence the term 'hierarchy'. He believed that only when our fundamental needs are met will we move forward to seek to fulfil the next most important need. Our prime need, he argued, is to survive. Food, sex and sleep are biological imperatives; they keep us and our species alive. Once we have enough sleep and get enough to eat and drink, we then have the time and energy to fulfil the next most important need: that of security and safety. Once we feel safe and secure, we can begin to acknowledge, and be motivated by, our need to belong and be loved; and so on. He realised that human beings also need to be esteemed, and he placed this 'need' in the middle of his hierarchy. He believed that our thirst for knowledge comes almost last. Only when all our other needs are satisfied do we become curious and seek answers.

His scheme is sometimes represented in the form of a layered triangle, showing the most important need across the wide base of the triangle and each subsequent one as a narrower layer, indicating its lesser significance, moving on up towards the apex (see Diagram 3.1).

Diagram 3.1: Maslow's hierarchy of needs

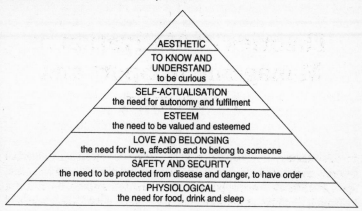

How Can This Help Parents?

Though oversimplified, Maslow's idea of a hierarchy of needs is help-ful. It helps us all – children included – to understand the importance of being in the right frame of mind, or state of emotional readiness, to undertake particular tasks; such as being sociable, learning and achieving. All too often we have a blinkered, insensitive view of children, assuming that they can, and should, meet our every wish in the precise way we want.

For example, when children start a new school, it suits us for them to make friends quickly. We see it as a sign that they have settled in, and are happy and liked. It means we can relax, maybe even meet new friends through them, and get time on our own when they go off to play. We might even try to push new friendships on them to get these benefits. Yet Maslow should warn us that before children 'need' the company of others, they need to feel safe and secure. They need to get used to their new lives, deriving security from us, before they spend time happily away with others.

The same caution applies with older children. Faced with a poorly motivated and under-performing teenager who spends hours on the telephone to, or out with, friends, we should be sensitive to his need to belong to a friendship group. It will usually be more productive to suggest studying alongside his friends, or to fit practice, training or homework around social commitments, than to expect behaviour which will isolate him or show him up as different.

Maslow's hierarchy can also help us to understand why, for exam-ple, our child might suddenly find it difficult to study or might lose interest in a previously stable passion. At any age, if a child experiences an event which undermines his sense of security, such as the death of someone close or parents getting separated or divorced, he may find it hard to focus on the less pressing need for personal development and learning. This is explored further in Part Three.

Herzberg's 'Satisfiers' and 'Dissatisfiers' (1966)

Frederick Herzberg developed a different approach. He suggested that people's satisfaction at work is influenced less by attitudes than by two types of factor: one concerning the job itself, its content, and the other its surrounding features, or context.

Features of the work environment, such as room temperature or location of the canteen, which Herzberg called 'hygiene factors', will make people dissatisfied and demotivated when wrong but will not necessarily improve performance when put right other than for a short while. They concern things workers would expect to be satisfactory. Herzberg also named these factors 'dissatisfiers'.

'Motivators' or 'satisfiers', on the other hand, which concern the nature of the job itself rather than where it is done, can positively motivate people to perform well long term.

Here is Herzberg's list of aspects of work which tend to satisfy and dissatisfy.

Satisfiers	Dissatisfiers
Achievement	Organisation, policy and administration
Recognition	Heavy-handed supervision
Job interest	Poor interpersonal relationships
Responsibility	Inadequate salary
Advancement	Uncomfortable working conditions

Herzberg also identified two types of rewards: extrinsic and intrinsic. Extrinsic rewards, things such as money, social status, career development and good friendships, are gained from the work situation. They have nothing to do with the nature of the work itself. The nature of the job, what it entails, by contrast, delivers intrinsic rewards such as fulfilment, scope for self-direction and autonomy, and achievement. We will look at the value of different kinds of rewards and incentives in more detail in Chapter Nine.

How Can This Help Parents?

Herzberg offers a useful insight to life at home because there are parallels. For example, have you ever heard someone say, 'He moaned that I was never at home, and now that I've cut my hours to be around more he doesn't even bother talking to me' or 'She said she found it hard to study at home because I was always shouting at Dean. I've calmed down a lot but she still doesn't settle to her studies'? In both cases, a parent has responded to a child's criticism or complaint but it seems to have made no difference. Anger, frustration and recrimination are likely to follow.

They are probably examples of Herzberg 'dissatisfiers'. If we realise this, we should feel less resentful and critical when we do not get the results we hoped for. Sometimes, of course, the changes we make have no impact, because a child or young person's explanation for his behaviour – saying it was because of something we said or did – is just an excuse, and the real problem lies elsewhere. Equally, sometimes we see no change because we're expecting too much too soon. We expect an immediate response whereas most children make sure the change is permanent and repeated before trusting to change themselves. Nonetheless, it is well worth while thinking, next time your child complains that you never do things together, he doesn't get enough pocket money or that he wishes you would remember to buy his favourite flavour of crisps for his packed lunches, that these complaints are about dissatisfiers and you should not expect great favours from him in return.

If we want more permanent results, we should pay attention to the 'satisfiers'. These are far more likely to generate self-motivation and longer-term improvements in behaviour. Achievement, responsibility, recognition, interesting work and advancement, the satisfiers listed above, are all things that can be given to children as easily as to working adults. For example, when our children ask to help us with a weekend job – home improvements, washing the car, gardening or even some office work – because it looks exciting, we should try to give them something real to do, not make them simply our bag carriers. We can make sure we recognise their achievements, and that they have a sense of advancement – being given more responsibilities, freedoms or privileges as they prove themselves capable. It takes planning and forethought on our part, but it will pay dividends.

Goldthorpe and Lockwood: Personal and Social Influences

Goldthorpe and Lockwood, two sociologists writing in the late 1960s, observed that the car workers they were studying had different 'prior orientations' to work, influenced mainly by who they mixed with socially and by job content. These two factors largely determined their attitudes to work and to rewards. Three different approaches to work were identified:

- 'instrumental', in which work is simply a means to an end and holds no social or emotional significance. Rewards are almost exclusively financial, and are therefore extrinsic
- 'solidaristic', in which work is valued as a group activity, often through shared skills. Work is central to their lives and is part and parcel of family and friendship networks. Rewards are both extrinsic and intrinsic
- 'bureaucratic', more typical of management jobs, in which the valued reward is not only money but also status, career prospects and security. The reward is again extrinsic

How Can This Help Parents?

The idea of a 'prior orientation' encourages us to think about how our own values and attitudes influence our children: our attitudes to study or to work; to money as a significant or insignificant reason for working; and to commitment, both to friends and to organisations. Someone who has an 'instrumental' approach to work may also have an arm's-length relationship with their child's school, encouraging a similar 'instrumental' attitude in the child towards his school or college. An 'instrumental' child is less likely to feel committed, and may not expect to enjoy the process of studying. He will probably also exhibit less stickability as a result. Parents with a more 'solidaristic' approach to their job and work are more likely to pass on this attitude to their children who will, in their turn, choose subjects that interest them, get more involved in the variety of activities offered in the school, feel more integrated and be happy to contribute to the life and community of the school. Parents with a 'bureaucratic' orientation will encourage their child to study to succeed, force the taking of subjects that lead to a good, high-status, professional job, and wish for their child to become a prefect or sports captain for their own ends.

Path-Goal Theory

Another approach to motivation, developed by House, Campbell and others, is known as the 'path-goal' or 'expectancy' theory. This states that we will do what it takes to get what we want, to meet our own personal goals. If high productivity is seen as the way to achieve personal goals, someone will produce efficiently. If low productivity is viewed as the way to meet personal goals, someone will not try very hard. Thinking about this in more concrete terms, if the personal goal of a child is to be liked and accepted by a certain group of people in the class, and that group believes that studying is definitely not cool but being good at football is, then that individual is most unlikely to put more effort into working for good marks than perfecting his football skills.

How Can This Help Parents?

The path-goal theory encourages us to realise that our child's goals may not be the same as our own. Parents may prize the goal of academic achievement and expect their child to work hard enough to make the grade. Their offspring, on the other hand, may have other ideas, especially when they reach their teens. Top of any teenager's agenda is likely to be self-discovery – through relationships, increasing independence or even through music. Some will work only the minimum necessary, though pressure to get good grades is changing attitudes. Indeed, there are times during middle and late childhood when it would be strange to find any congruence between our and our children's short-term or even longer-term life goals and values. Accepting this, especially if we want to retain any influence, the best approach is to sit down together and jointly agree performance targets and standards for our goals and each of theirs, acknowledging each one to have some validity in their terms.

This is one method of smoothing the 'path' as defined in the theory. Another is to help to remove any obstacles to reaching the target. As we shall see in Part Two, we can have a crucial role here as 'enablers' – creating the right environment for application, providing encouragement and supporting achievement without directly interfering.

As goals and values are closely related, it is worth noting that a recent study of children's own values, for a book called *Values in Education and Education in Values* by Monica Taylor, found that respect, fairness, loyalty and trust came at the top of their list. Those who seek to push their child to excellence, in whatever domain, could find themselves violating the very values their child holds dear. Through exhortation and pushing, we may demonstrate that we do not respect our child's point of view. We may make demands which come across to our child as unreasonable and unfair. We may fail to understand the strong loyalties and firm commitments our child feels towards close friends; and we will certainly be demonstrating a clear lack of trust in his ability to manage his own time and targets. The result will be conflict and a hostile atmosphere that will inevitably demotivate.

Approaches to Motivation in Sport

Interest in sports psychology is growing. Tennis and soccer stars often employ their own personal psychological coaches to help them concentrate, stay motivated or to lift their game when their performance drops. Increasingly, other disciplines are looking to sports psychology to get tips. From my own reading and from conversations with Dr Howard Hall, Principal Lecturer in Sports Psychology at De Montfort

University, Bedford, I think parents can learn a great deal from the approaches to motivation developed within sports. They make a great deal of sense.

Hall is convinced that all students can be motivated to learn provided they have the right kind of experiences and are supported by people who are respected and who say and do the right things. These experiences and strategies are:

- to start from the reasons anyone has for wanting to do well
- to concentrate on getting better at the task, not on proving worth in relation to others
- to avoid investing any self-worth in winning or losing
- to make rewards or other forms of encouragement reflect the achievement, not the person
- to increase competence and reduce anxiety by putting students in charge of their learning and progress

Understanding the Social Influences on People's Reasons

Hall's starting point is that we are all influenced and changed by things that happen to us in our daily lives. We take in other people's opinions and reactions, both positive and negative, and change how we see ourselves as a result. Our reasons for doing things are inevitably many and varied, and can change over time. If parents or coaches ignore these reasons, they will be less effective at helping a child to do well.

For example, a young child may be very good at numbers. Despite this, he sees the more advanced work of his older sister as a sign that he is no good. Being also good at sport, which she is not, he decides to get an edge over her by developing his sporting skills, and his interest in maths flags. Unless his parents understand his reasons, they will find it hard to get him to spend more time on maths and less on sport.

How to Handle Competition

It is probably natural to feel competitive but it does not always help motivation. A child who competes against himself and focuses on self-improvement is safe. One who constantly competes against others in the hope of proving himself and his self-worth can get into problems. Effective motivators help children to focus on their own improvement and avoid judging themselves against what other people can do.

There are three ways children's progress can be measured:

- against what is typical or average for all children of that age, for example SATs (standard assessment tests) which children take in school, known as 'normative'

- against others in a particular group, such as a child's swimming class or year group in a particular school, known as 'comparative'
- against his own, previous performance, known as 'self-referenced'

Think of the last time you felt especially pleased with something you had done. The pleasure may have come from:

- realising that you had done better than some other particular person
- believing that other people of your age or weight might have had problems doing what you did
- knowing that the last time you tried this, it had not worked so well

Were there any other reasons? Why do you think you selected the answer you gave?

Normative measures are the least helpful to children. They don't tell them anything about how well they are doing compared with what they could be achieving. Schools find out whether their pupils are doing better or worse than expected, given their age, but a bright seven year-old who learns he is above average will not find out he could be reading even better with more encouragement. Normative measures can therefore act as a glass ceiling. 'He's in the top third for his age group. Why are you worrying?' is a common response to concerned parents who nonetheless believe their child is underachieving and consequently unhappy.

Some children are spurred on by competition but it can be the undoing of others. 'I'll never be as good as him!' is a frequent cry from those losing heart. Even when children are able to keep up, comparisons can backfire and cause resentment. 'Stop comparing me! They are not me!' is the retort I hear on the few occasions I have said 'But so and so manages to. . . '.

Dr Hall spoke about a student who had been happily committed to her studies. All of a sudden, her attitude changed. Coming to discuss a failed essay, she admitted to feeling generally nauseous, a sign of anxiety. Then he realised why this might be. A set of marked essays had been left out for collection recently in a public place, enabling comparisons to be made. When she saw the written comments on her work and looked at others, she felt shamed, convinced that fellow students would now know her work was substandard. Her confidence was knocked to such an extent that she could no longer work effectively.

We should, therefore, be careful about holding up the star performer in any group as a standard to aim for. Especially in mixed-ability groups, average and low achievers may simply not believe that they are in the same performance league. They will not bother to try. The target will have no impact unless each child can discuss what he might need to do to reach the same standard. It would be better to present the work of an average student who has done really well because this comes across as achievable.

Another problem with the competitive approach to motivation, for example asking a child to come in the first three, is the lottery of succeeding. A child cannot control the result. He can do his best, and really improve, but if others have done even better he will fail. Comparative targets should not be used by parents as a condition for a reward or incentive.

Of the three ways of measuring improvement, the self-referenced approach is best. Focusing on the task in hand, getting satisfaction from his own progress, and not testing his self-worth against others, it protects a child from getting easily discouraged. Hall's research has shown that a task focus also helps to reduce the amount of precompetitive anxiety: there is no 'face' to save or lose. It should also help to reduce exam nerves. Where children invest their self-worth in achieving excellence, they can nose-dive if others constantly pip them at the post. A child may end up happier being sixth best at four different activities than second best in one.

How to Raise Feelings of Competence: Achieving 'Flow'

To increase the feeling of competence, reduce anxiety and achieve 'flow', we need to identify our weaknesses and work on these in ways with which we feel comfortable. Athletes who have lost confidence can get it back. They set clear, manageable targets for improvement, choose the methods to use, monitor their efforts closely, get fast feedback on their efforts and evaluate their progress themselves. They are in charge.

They have to be aware of the performance curve. How many of us have started a diet, been delighted by the early weight loss which seemed significant and easy but then become disheartened when the rate of progress trailed off? Losing the later pounds is a different ball game. If we see others who started after us in their first flush of enthusiasm, our dejection can spiral. We readily and frequently give up, justifying this by stating that the initial pounds shed are good enough.

There are similar patterns in learning. The first techniques and principles are relatively easy to master and we seem to stride ahead. Unfortunately, as we get better, our rate of progress slows. It takes more effort to make noticeable improvements so we may feel less competent and our motivation wanes.

Knowing how to get better helps to reduce anxiety and achieve flow. 'Flow' is a term used first in the field of sports and now applied more widely to describe a state in which mind and body are in sufficient harmony that we achieve our best performance. It refers to those times when everything 'clicks'; when we are totally absorbed in the activity

Diagram 3.2

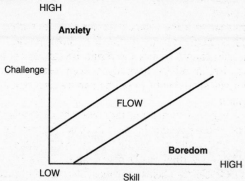

and enjoy the feeling this gives us. We seem to perform without effort – without consciously trying or understanding why. 'Flow' is also used to describe other, perhaps more spiritual, heightened and harmonious experiences.

M Csikszentmihalyi, the originator of the concept of flow, writes that it exists when the challenge matches the skill, or the skill rises to match the challenge. A simple graph illustrates this (see Diagram 3.2).

The amount of challenge is measured on one axis and the degree of skill on the other. Where the challenge demands more skill than we have or think we have (high challenge and low skill), we feel anxious. Our arousal level rises too far, stopping us thinking straight or functioning effectively. Where the challenge requires less skill than we have (low challenge and high skill), we become bored and stop concentrating. Our arousal level drops so low that we lose the necessary focus, energy and enthusiasm to succeed. Flow, therefore, represents a level of optimum arousal – not too much and not too little – and is achieved in the area on the graph between anxiety and boredom where, at any point, the degree of challenge matches the skills possessed. In this band, confidence and relaxation replace both anxiety and boredom, and concentration becomes deep but effortless.

How the Flow Approach is Useful to Parents

Children can be helped to achieve flow. This can be done either by increasing the challenge for children who are bored, which is fairly straightforward, or by increasing skills. Reducing anxiety levels is also possible but less straightforward. Certainly, simply telling a child not to worry will not have much impact. The only approach that works is to identify the precise cause of the anxiety and work to eliminate the concern.

Confidence can be raised by:

- raising competence through, for example, extra practice or training
- reducing the challenge temporarily through, for example, setting smaller, more achievable goals
- attending to the personal meaning of the activity for the individual – discovering why, or indeed whether, he actually wants to do well at this task
- increasing the sense of control over the learning process – increasing 'mastery'

Only by allowing a child to convince himself that his skills match the challenge and his progress is in his own hands will his self-belief and confidence increase.

Approaches to Motivation in Schools

Naturally, teachers and other education professionals have given a great deal of thought to how to get the best from children. Children who thrive at school will be influenced both by effective teachers, and the policies, atmosphere and ethos of an effective school, one able to sustain improvement in its pupils and staff. To find out how schools encourage good performance and produce self-starting learners, we can look at the growing evidence from studies of school effectiveness.

Effective Schools

From Professor Peter Mortimore's long-term research into school effectiveness, conducted from London University's Institute of Education, and from work undertaken for the National Commission on Education, we know that effective schools have certain common characteristics. Mortimore and his team have shown that effective schools demonstrate:

- positive leadership
- a learning culture, encouraging self-reliance, self-monitoring and reflection
- high and consistent expectations of staff and pupils
- a shared vision and one set of goals
- teamwork
- the recognition of rights and responsibilities
- a strong emphasis on students' self-esteem, developing a range of talents
- positive feedback through realistic praise, encouragement and approval
- clear, consistent and fair discipline

- collaboration with the local community and constructive parental involvement
- quality adult-child relationships that demonstrate mutual respect and trust

These characteristics create a framework for positive and creative learning. Indeed, they are almost preconditions for effective learning. Successful schools do not leave everything to the child. Neither do they leave it to individual teachers in separate classrooms. They develop school-wide policies. Effective classrooms, research tells us, are places in which there is concentrated learning, purposeful teaching, monitored progress, actively involved pupils and appropriate role modelling. The last three matters require whole school policies. In effective schools, teachers and students are involved in creating that policy so they want to, and do, sing the same tune, but there is, nonetheless, clear leadership. This is a useful lesson for families.

I have selected three of the approaches mentioned above to look at in a little more detail. The other characteristics of effective schools will be addressed in later chapters.

Actively Involved Pupils

Children can be actively involved in their own learning in several ways. They can 'learn by doing' – find things out for themselves through experiment. They can 'practise by doing' – having been taught something, they check their understanding and see how it works in practice. They can help to set their own targets – plan their work and review their progress, under responsible guidance. They can learn interactively by asking questions, offering answers and discussing approaches to problem-solving and ideas. They can have some choice in what they do and when. They can learn at their own pace, alone or in groups, and use different learning methods.

Each of these approaches can be made available to children, in the classroom or elsewhere, to different degrees and balanced with appropriate guidance from the teacher. To prepare them for the world of work, children need to be able to work with others – to understand, work independently within, and be able to extend, someone else's expectations. Research by Kathy Sylva on preschool children which compared three different preschool environments – 'free play', formal curriculum-based learning and active learning programmes – showed that children in active learning environments do best long term.

The report of the National Commission on Education, *Learning to Succeed* (1993), stated: 'The process of learning is as important as its content, since it often determines how much information and understanding is retained and the extent to which it can be applied in practice'.

All of these different ways of learning, sometimes described as 'flexible learning', were shown by the Commission to develop not only independence but also interest and commitment and, not surprisingly, in consequence, to improve children's motivation.

Appropriate Modelling: the Role of Good Relationships

In *The Heart of the Matter: Education for Personal and Social Development* (1995), a discussion paper issued by the Scottish Consultative Council on the Curriculum, it is stated: 'Supportive relationships contribute to more effective learning and teaching: they encourage the disposition for learning which enhances individual achievement and promotes self-esteem: they contribute to effective communications both within and outside the school: they are central to positive behaviour. Young people are more likely to respond well when they feel secure, in contexts where they have a sense of being valued and where they have opportunities to succeed'.

Shoreham Beach First School in West Sussex has put this approach into practice, believing that the relationships which children establish with adults and other children are, indeed, crucial to their learning and development. As reported in the *Times Educational Supplement* in February 1996, Shoreham Beach has impressed the education inspectors.

Mary Grafham, the school's headteacher, believes that bossy teachers do not build good relationships. Instead, giving even infant school children a sense of responsibility for their own behaviour and the opportunity to express their opinions in an open environment helps to establish trust. She has created two council meetings, one for Reception and Year 1, another for Years 2 and 3. In weekly meetings, the children help to solve a range of problems and issues facing the school, including conduct and behaviour. The emphasis on trust, sharing and teamwork has resulted in a school in which, school inspectors noted, 'pupils were found to have high levels of motivation and a keenness to learn'.

Creating a Learning Culture

What is 'a learning culture'? It exists anywhere where curiosity is encouraged, answers are found to questions, and where both adults and children are keen to learn new things and discover hidden potential. It exists where learning is promoted as an enjoyable end in itself instead of something done at someone else's command which must be merely tolerated. It exists when people care about the quality of their performance, are willing to improve, take pride in their work and achievements, and are happy to celebrate the achievements of others. It embodies the sort of attitude implicit in the 'solidaristic' approach outlined earlier. People who are prepared to open themselves to discovery and to other people will have a richer and more successful intellectual and emotional life. The more we put in to something, the more we get out of it. Of course, children are often rebellious and may not copy everything we do but they have the model in place. It will not seem strange to take up these practices later in life when it may matter a great deal.

Children, then, benefit enormously from being surrounded by positive attitudes to learning and personal development. If commercial companies see the value in becoming a 'learning organisation'; if policy makers see the need for Britain to become 'a learning society'; if schools believe their success depends on both teachers and children relishing a thirst for discovery and development; then families should consider the advantages of creating a learning environment within the home.

What Do Children Say Works for Them?

The National Commission on Education asked students to identify things about their school which helped them to learn. They mentioned:

- good teaching practices, such as frequent praise, high expectations and regularly marked work; in other words, speedy, accurate and positive feedback
- clear, firm discipline
- well-maintained premises
- a school with a good reputation

What Can Parents Learn from Effective Schools?

Work on effectiveness and motivation in schools teaches us that:

- clear, firm discipline provides a secure framework for trust and self-development
- high expectations and clear goals work. If we did not do well at school, we must not assume that our child will also be unsuccessful
- children enjoy learning new things more when they have some involvement and control over their learning and when they generally feel capable and effective
- presenting clear guidelines is not the same thing as being directive or bossy
- teamwork is important. Parents should try to agree on the attitudes, values and expectations they have for their child's learning and development
- children like to be praised, and to have their efforts noticed
- frequent feedback helps children to know whether they are on the right track

Self-esteem: the Heart of Motivation

This chapter explores further why and how self-esteem influences motivation, learning and achievement. It covers:

- why a positive sense of self helps us to work, play and socialise better, and it offers parents some practical suggestions for strengthening their child's self-belief, self-efficacy and self-direction
- how children with very low, or even negative, self-belief and self-esteem react and compensate for this – with clear implications for motivation and self-development amongst other things
- how the state of children's self-esteem affects their ability to listen, concentrate and remember things – three crucial aspects of learning

Exploring Our 'Self'

How we feel about ourselves has a fundamental effect on what we believe we can do and on what we actually achieve. If we believe something is possible for us, if we experience ourselves as capable and if we expect that we can influence what happens to us, then we are on track for fulfilment and self-satisfaction.

In an earlier book, *Positive Parenting*, I have written in more detail about self-esteem: what it is, why it is important to have it, what can go wrong if you don't have it and, most important, how we can help our child to develop it. I also wrote that, alongside self-esteem, parents can actively help to develop their child's self-confidence and self-reliance which flow from it. Taken together, they represent three central goals of child-rearing. Amongst other things, they help children to feel motivated. Thirteen key words were selected to act as guides to parents, to nurture their child's self-esteem, self-confidence and self-reliance. The key words were: explain, example, praise, peace, play, trust, touch, time, talk, sympathise, empathise, apologise and compromise.

In this book, concentrating as it does on motivation, I have chosen self-belief, self-efficacy and self-direction as the three beacons. There is no contradiction. In fact, they complement the earlier trio. Self-belief relates closely to self-esteem. If we have high self-esteem, we will have a strong sense of self-worth which flows into our self-belief. If we are self-confident, we feel able to take on challenges because we feel capable and have experience of being effective at what we set out to do. This feeling of competence generates a sense of self-efficacy. If we are self-reliant, we see ourselves as autonomous, independent people able to be self-directed – to be in charge of ourselves and where we are going where necessary.

We will now look at these three beacons, and at some practical strategies we can apply to nurture them in our children.

Self-belief

Children with self-belief have a clear and positive sense of who they are. They are able to view themselves in a favourable light, in many different ways. Children will believe in themselves when someone else has demonstrated a belief in them. Children who lack self-belief are filled with self-doubt.

The Building Blocks

People Understand and Trust Us
Children's self-belief takes root when they are trusted, respected and listened to, and when others show faith in their ability to manage things. Self-belief starts with plenty of positive and successful, practical and emotional experiences with people whose opinions, judgements and company they value. Without good relationship experiences, children can be left with a profound uncertainty: a feeling that there is something wrong with them.

Knowing Who We Are
Children cannot believe in themselves if they have no idea of what they think, what they like or do not like, or what their strengths and weaknesses are. They have to have a clear identity, or self-concept.

Knowing We Can Do Things Well
Children get pleasure from knowing they can do things well, but their self-belief will not be strengthened if any particular achievement is considered a fluke. They need to be able to recognise what 'well' means. With no sense of how they managed something or what made it good, they cannot repeat it. Clear targets and accurate feedback contribute to this understanding, and help children to set their own standards.

An Optimistic Attitude to the Future
The fourth building block is believing that doing well is worthwhile, because the future is viewed optimistically and can be influenced. We are able to hope. If someone says, 'There's no hope for you', 'You are

hopeless' or 'More of this and you'll end up on the scrap heap', hopes will be dashed. The future is cut off, leaving little space for self-belief.

Strengthening Your Child's Self-belief
Here are some tips for boosting your child's self belief. Try to:

- make it safe to make mistakes
- help him to know and feel good about himself
- find something he is good at, and appreciate his skill
- see things from his point of view and show respect for his interests
- give him hope, about what he might be able to learn and do
- help him to feel safe and optimistic about the future
- avoid nagging and unconstructive criticism – keep it to a minimum
- make him feel important and significant to you, through spending time with him and showing interest in his thoughts and what he does

Self-efficacy

Children have a sense of self-efficacy when they feel capable of managing a number of things effectively: when they believe in their capacity to be successful. Self-efficacy helps them to be confident when faced with a challenge, and to stick at tasks until they master them because they know persistence works for them. Children who lack this belief that they are capable feel hopeless and incompetent and give up easily.

The Building Blocks

Other People Respect Our Skills
Confidence grows through competence. If we assume our children are able to manage things, they will feel more confident.

Discovering New Skills
Everyone is good at something, is capable of doing something well and taking a personal pride in this talent. Encouraging this talent will help a child to feel competent and effective. There are many skills which are useful in our everyday lives, helping us to look after ourselves and to work with others as well as achieve high standards in a more obvious way. Families and schools are sometimes rather one-sided in the skills and talents which they consider important and worthy of praise. As well as acknowledging existing skills, we are all capable of enjoying and doing well in other, untried fields. Chances to try our hand at new hobbies and interests help to deepen our sense of self.

Experiencing Success
Nothing succeeds like success. This is common knowledge, yet we can

be remarkably inept at setting the right sort of – or, indeed, any – targets for ourselves or others which, when met, generate the pleasure of success. Different people need different targets. High flyers need targets some way ahead. Those who are less talented need targets set closer to their current skill level. What is important is not what we achieve in absolute terms, but what is a significant achievement for us.

Developing Responsibility

Giving children responsibility is important. It makes them stop and think further than the immediate moment. Only through the experience of responsibility can we discover that we are reliable. As Charles Handy said to me, 'We need responsibility in order to find out about ourselves'. Responsibility gives us the chance to uncover hidden inner resources.

Strengthening Your Child's Sense of Self-efficacy

Here are some tips for increasing your child's self-efficacy. Try to:

- encourage him to develop practical, self-help skills
- let him complete tasks at his own pace
- help him to make sense of his experiences

Self-direction

Children who are self-directed are able to manage tasks and problems independently. They experience a degree of control over themselves and feel free to influence at least some aspects of their lives which are important to them at the time. Children who lack the ability to direct themselves feel helpless and become dependent on others to take them forward. Being able to control, or at least influence, both your present and your future is vital.

The Building Blocks

Being Trusted

We must know that we can manage our body and our life, and that we are entitled to have a say in what happens to us.

A child's first experience of self-direction, making him feel capable rather than helpless, will be whether his mother or carer understands and responds to his basic needs: for food, warmth, comfort and attention. If these needs are met, they will also reinforce self-belief. Older children will develop their feelings of 'mastery' further if they are given increasing responsibility for managing themselves, are encouraged to question, explore, express negative as well as positive feelings, and learn how to negotiate.

Autonomy Through Choices

Choices are important. They say something about who we are. We express and define ourselves through choice. Used appropriately, they also reinforce personal responsibility. Asking a child 'Do you want to do this task this way or that way?' not only helps him invest something of himself in the task, but he also feels he has some control over what he has been asked to do. The very act of taking a decision encourages a child to accept a commitment to the consequences of that decision. This is important. However, it is not appropriate for children to have free choice about everything. The younger the child, the more choices have to be limited and managed. It is a parent's responsibility to remain in overall charge until children become legally independent.

Experience of Independence

Self-direction and independence feed each other. The more self-directed children are, the better they can manage independence. The more independence they are given, provided it is appropriate, the more they develop the confidence and skills to become self-directed and self-reliant, and show initiative and creativity. The more adults tell children what to do, the less competent they will feel – so they end up asking for direction. It is self-fulfilling: directive people create dependency.

Time Alone

Having the space to make decisions, take risks and make mistakes is important. Children cannot become self-directed if they do not have any discretionary time – time which is theirs to fill at their discretion. Boredom is not unhealthy. That awful whine, 'I'm bored' can give us a heavy heart, but boredom represents a pain barrier through which children have to pass to help them discover their inner selves or find new interests.

Strengthening Your Child's Self-direction

Here are some tips for increasing self-direction. Try to:

- encourage independence, within appropriate limits
- give him practice in taking decisions which directly concern him
- encourage him to take some responsibility for tasks appropriate to his age
- allow time spent on his own, without the television on. This will encourage him to have ideas of things to do
- let him do things his way, not the way you would do them
- encourage him to plan ahead and manage his time, meeting both his needs and yours
- give pocket money as soon as a child can understand money, so his spending decisions are his

Maslow's Needs Rearranged

In Chapter Three, the first theory of motivation discussed was Abraham Maslow's hierarchy of needs. It is probably the most well-known, if not the most influential, model of motivation and is still very widely used in professional training to explain human behaviour. In Maslow's hierarchy, the human need for esteem is placed fourth in order of importance, and it is described as something separate from needing to be loved and belonging, from autonomy and personal freedom, from security and safety and from needing to know and understand. I want to reassess the interrelationship proposed by Maslow.

Maslow's scheme was, of course, designed to help managers understand human motivation in organisations. In the context of parenting, the relationships and experiences are more complex and extended. To refine Maslow's model for explaining motivation to make it fit parents' and children's experiences more closely, we need to reweight the elements, and focus more directly on the importance and complexity of self-esteem.

Good self-esteem is closely associated with each of Maslow's listed needs. Our self-esteem is fundamentally affected if we are left hungry or deprived of sleep, as people who torture others well know. Self-esteem is also affected positively and negatively by whether we feel secure and safe; whether we feel loved and belong somewhere or to someone; whether we understand what is happening to us and feel understood; and whether we are given opportunities for autonomy and personal fulfilment. Good self-esteem is constructed from positive experiences in all of Maslow's dimensions. It is not a separate slice of ourselves; it is central to our view of ourselves and has a practical impact on our ability to manage our lives and relationships.

For example, children who are well fed and clothed and whose parents or carers ensure they get enough sleep will automatically feel that someone has at least some of their interests at heart. The important thing is that they will feel significant to the adult who shows thought and consideration for their basic needs. This is the first test for establishing a feeling of self-worth and positive self-esteem. A child who often feels cold, hungry, tired, vulnerable, unsafe or ignored will be inclined to feel neglected and unloved. It will be hard for him to develop a positive sense of self-worth and therefore self-belief. On the other hand, a child who feels loved, safe, secure and stimulated will have a healthy sense of self-esteem.

Some people might say that Maslow was referring to our need to be and to feel esteemed – a conscious desire to be esteemed by others – and that this is different from self-perception – whether we value

Diagram 4.1: Maslow's needs rearranged to show impact on self-esteem: when a child's needs are fulfilled

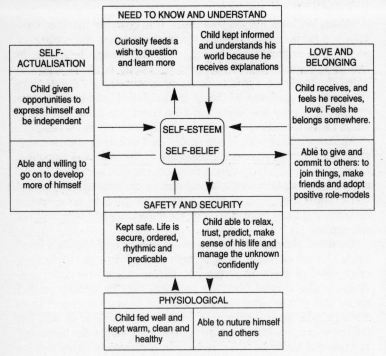

ourselves. However, the most robust pieces of our 'self' jigsaw are laid in place by others during our early childhood. It is how we observe and interpret other people's behaviour towards us, and what others tell us, that will influence both how we view ourselves and whether that picture is a positive or negative one. Once that picture is created, how we feel about ourselves will strongly influence the depth of our need or desire to be esteemed by others. If we feel confident about our self-worth, our ideas and our abilities, we will have less need for them to be confirmed and reinforced by others. The strength of our esteem needs and the state of our self-esteem are linked inversely: the higher or more positive our true self-esteem, the less we will seek approval from others.

Maslow's treatment of self-esteem does not explain adequately either how self-esteem develops or why children behave as they do in the family or at school. I have therefore rearranged Maslow's needs to illustrate these points. In this alternative format, self-esteem is represented

Diagram 4.2: Maslow's needs rearranged to show the impact on self-esteem: when a child's needs are not fulfilled

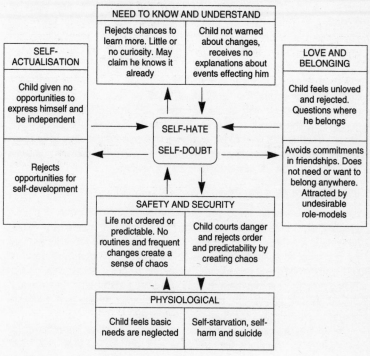

as the heart of ourselves. Not only does good self-esteem act as a life force and keep us going, as our biological heart does, but it also indicates self-contentment – not to be confused with self-complacency. Diagram 4.1 shows how a positive self-esteem is the crucial by-product when each of a child's needs is met, and how a child with strong self-belief is able to perform well. Diagram 4.2 illustrates what happens when the system goes into reverse. When children's needs are not satisfied, children not only doubt or even hate themselves but also go on to deny and then reject those things they need but do not get.

The Need for Security and Safety

When children feel safe and secure, they can trust themselves and other people. They feel someone is taking care of them and watching out for their interests, so they feel esteemed and worthy of care. The certainty of their life helps them to predict the future with confidence. They can therefore relax and open themselves to new experiences.

Safety and security are threatened when life seems disorganised and chaotic, when the adults who are responsible for children ignore their needs, perhaps threaten them physically and fail to offer any sense of direction. If this situation persists, children are likely to reject the importance of safety and security to them as the only tactic left to end their vulnerability. Instead of looking for comfort and security, they may actively court danger, doing things which directly threaten their safety and security, such as joyriding, clinging on to trains and other death-defying displays of bravado. It may be seen as fun and it may relieve boredom. It will also make them feel in control of themselves and not at the mercy of others. The greater the risk, the lower their sense of self-worth. For older children, this risk-taking may give them status within an alternative group and offer them the comfort, tenuous though it may be, of belonging at least somewhere.

The Need to Feel Loved

Everyone likes to be loved and to feel important to someone. A child's greatest need is to feel loved by the two people who made him. When he feels loved, he will feel he belongs somewhere. We are underpinned by our sense of belonging and, as children grow, the more groups they feel connected to and can identify with, the deeper is their sense of self. When they fit in somewhere, it says something about who they are and that there are others like them. Belonging also means that they are wanted, have been accepted and are acceptable.

When children feel rejected, as a result of cruelty or humiliation for example, and therefore feel unloved and unlovable, they will erect emotional barriers, withdraw from the painful relationship, and try to demonstrate that they have no need to love and be loved or to belong to that group. They will stop trying to please because it is too distressing to seek love and acceptance and not to get it.

They will also feel badly let down and deeply disappointed. Their hopes for love and attention will have been dashed on numerous occasions. Eventually, they stop hoping, because it is too dangerous and too painful. In the process of withdrawing, and as a consequence of it, children have to tell themselves or admit that they do not belong to those who hurt them or let them down. Their self-esteem and self-belief cannot flourish when they feel both insignificant and emotionally isolated.

The Need to Develop

The same negative dynamic can occur with the need for 'self-actualisation', the need to find out about and develop ourselves, and the need to know and understand. A vulnerable child can build a protective wall which may make him refuse to learn or try anything new. He may turn down invitations to test and show what he can achieve. He may state either that he does not want to, or that he does not need to, learn because he knows it all already. John Holt, in his book *How Children Fail*, writes 'The problem is not to get students to ask what they don't know; the problem is to make them aware of the difference between what they know and what they don't.'.

Far from suggesting that such a child is happy with himself as he is, this attitude belies a very poor sense of self. He has to tell himself that he is fine as he is. He has to avoid exposing himself to the unknown or to the knowledge-power of others to avoid feeling even more inadequate, inferior, uncertain and ridiculous. His fear and self-doubt make him cling tightly to himself, to define himself not by substance and content – a well-rounded view of what is inside him – but by his psychological outline, his frontier, perimeter, or 'edge'. If that line alters, is dented or is penetrated, he will be in danger of not only losing his sense of who he is but also feeling frighteningly exposed. This understanding provides a new meaning to the description 'edgy'.

To hold on to this edge, outline or shell of themselves, vulnerable children have to maintain themselves in a state of tension. Every challenge threatens penetration. Every new experience may require them to change. Every relationship, particularly a new one, requires them to watch and protect their own boundary. They have to remain on constant battle alert.

Yet learning and motivation require the opposite. We have to open ourselves up, trust, believe in ourselves, and enter and explore the private world of our inner resources. We have to relax and release our surface tension which, like the skin of water, sometimes holds us together. We have to let go.

The Role of 'Self' in Learning: Listening, Concentration and Memory

Letting go is what we have to do when we learn. Learning involves listening, concentrating and remembering things. None of these processes is as straightforward as it might seem. Children who have problems with learning often find it hard to do them, and children who do not listen or concentrate often have poor motivation and low self-esteem. How we feel about ourselves influences how well we listen, concentrate, take in and remember things.

To listen properly, or effectively, we have to concentrate. Both actions involve a consciousness of 'self' but also an ability to let it go to allow a mental and emotional focus elsewhere. We have to step outside and be at peace with ourselves. Listening and concentration involve 'self' awareness, because we have to have a sense of what it is we are letting go of and where to go to return to base, and 'self' control, knowing how to let go. We shall look at these three elements of learning in turn.

Listening

We begin life as natural listeners. Babies learn by watching, listening, copying and communicating. Babies who are only a few hours old can copy, for example, the tongue movements of an adult whose face is close to theirs. The concentration involved in watching and trying to control the muscles of the tongue is immense and clearly visible. In the development of speech, babies have to listen to sounds. Their life depends on communication. Babies have to be natural listeners. As we grow older, however, we listen less and less well. We become increasingly selective in what we want to 'hear'. Increasingly, we only 'hear' what we want to hear, which tends to be things which reinforce our views and values. In particular, we may avoid listening to things which could imply criticism, could create feelings of failure and which might require us to respond in unwelcome ways. Many people end their life at the other end of the listening spectrum. They become more and more fixed and inflexible and end up as natural 'ignorers'. But so do some children. For those who are hurt frequently or feel threatened by what they hear, the stone wall is built much earlier.

If we start as listening 'naturals', why is it so hard to sustain? What goes wrong when people tune out or fail to 'hear' what another person is saying? What is it about true listening that is so difficult? It is difficult for several reasons. First, it requires us to let go of ourselves and sometimes to confront the unexpected. Second, it involves empathy and understanding. Third, it sometimes requires action and, occasionally, demands we do something or change ourselves on hearing the message. Listening can disturb our equilibrium, or status quo, and is therefore potentially threatening. It involves releasing our surface tension. The more uncertain of ourselves we are, the less flexible we are and the more vulnerable we will feel when facing change, so we stop listening.

When Children Listen

Children have to listen to hear – things like instructions. They have to listen to learn – things like explanations. They have to listen to remember, recognise and also to understand. A child who finds it hard to listen may have a low concentration threshold because he is maturing at a slower rate and remains very self- or 'ego'-focused. He may be bored because he genuinely knows what it is he is being asked to work at. He may be switching off because he has not understood something explained earlier and the further information cannot be understood, processed or pigeon-holed. He may, however, have emotional problems which might make him withdraw or he may cause a rumpus to block them out.

Putting Theory into Practice

Listening to children helps their motivation. This is explored further in Chapter Nineteen. We can also help them by developing their ability and willingness to listen. Elsewhere, I have discussed the idea of one-way and two-way communication, applied particularly to touch and spending time with children. Whatever the activity, the one-way form does not require a child to respond or even, sometimes, to acknowledge your action. It is therefore more relaxed, less tense and less threatening. The same model can be applied to listening. Both forms are important for learning.

One-way listening is listening to sounds such as music, bird-song or traffic, not to people. The sounds can either be heard and enjoyed for their own sake, or they can be thought about and interpreted. For example, we can lie in a corner of the park on a warm day, close our eyes, hear the range of sounds and let them waft over us without separating them to decide what is what. We can listen to a piece of music and respond emotionally, without thinking about which instruments are playing or how many different melodies are used. Alternatively, we can try to identify the songs of particular birds; we can guess whether the engine sound is a car, a taxi or a lorry; and we can listen out for the tune played by the violin. We are in charge of what we take in and what we do with that information. It is a safe way to practise listening. Swiss researchers have shown that children taking daily music lessons at school, listening to music, and playing instruments together, had better language and co-operative social skills after three years than those who had fewer music lessons and more time studying their language (*The Independent*, 29 August 1996). Good listening skills benefit wider learning.

Two-way listening involves listening to people and is fundamental to communication. This kind of listening is important for academic learning but it is also an important social skill.

We can encourage our young child's listening skills simply by:

- talking with him as much as possible, providing the conversation is relatively free from criticism, blame, reprimand and other negative messages that a child will not want to hear
- reading to him, and talking about what we have read, so he is encouraged to listen in order to understand

- looking at him when we talk to him, which will encourage him to look at us in return and notice our expressions. This is the start of non-verbal communication and the ability to read body language. Looking at someone in our culture conveys confidence, though in others it can be deemed rude or impudent
- encouraging singing, especially songs which involve body actions and repeated sections that the child can join in, because he has to listen to know when to add his special bit
- listening to and concentrating on sounds in the garden, park or busy street, to musical sounds and rhythms on the radio, by closing our eyes
- playing sound guessing games of a 'what am I?' kind in which the child has to interpret the sound of the animal or object being imitated
- above all, listening to him, so he will learn to listen to us and others in return

Concentration

Listening requires concentration and to concentrate we need to be relaxed. Normally, we think of relaxation as a physical process involving muscles. Muscles are relaxed when they are floppy and not doing any work. Concentration does not need to involve this type of relaxation – lying down flat supported by the floor in a meditative state – but it should involve what Alexander, father of the Alexander Technique, called release. When muscles are in a state of release, they are not tight but they are working: holding parts of our body as we want but with only the minimum degree of tension necessary for support. The muscles are, as it were, alert and ready for action but not over-tight. Although concentration is a form of mental rather than physical release, there is a strong connection between the two. To concentrate, we usually have to stay quiet physically. Crucially, we also have to release our minds; let go of, or break through, our 'self' defences and go inside ourselves.

Sportsmen and women do have to maintain concentration while they are active. However, they usually compose themselves quietly beforehand and train themselves to focus intensively on specific things as they play – on the ball, the opponent, counting their score in a certain way or something similar. The cricketer Mark Ramprakash, writing in Darren Gough's *Book for Young Cricketers*, offers several tips on concentration. The first is to maintain physical fitness. This may seem strange, until you realise that concentration takes effort and is hard work. Fit people also breathe better so are better able to relax. The second is to practise. By repeating and working at good technique, the action can transfer to the subconscious and happen automatically. The third is visualisation. Many top players and performers visualise themselves out on the pitch or stage, performing well. They focus on the task. They try to feel the atmosphere and see themselves doing well, which helps to reduce anxiety and build confidence and therefore concentration. The final tip is to balance any necessary 'psyching up' with relaxation. Too much tension will damage performance. 'Of course', he writes, 'everyone has to be focused and pumped up to do well, but relaxation is a key factor to good concentration.'

Poor concentration in children can be caused by many things. It can be dangerous for parents to jump to conclusions about their particular child. Although it is undoubtedly true that we still do not fully understand how the human mind works, there are some patterns. As with listening, personal problems – fears and anxieties – can prevent concentration. Boredom can impair it too. But for some children, the process of letting go is akin to losing themselves and is sufficiently unfamiliar and frightening that they find it almost impossible to do. In extreme cases, this may lead to children never sitting still, never apparently controlling their thoughts and never doing anything unless it is a clearly defined, short-term task with a clear, and therefore safe, outcome.

While some children find it hard to concentrate, the majority of younger children will not understand what concentration means. They either do it or they don't. I clearly remember getting a school report when I was 10. Miss Parkins complained about my lack of concentration. I read the report and I did not have a clue what she meant. When my parents said I should try harder to do it, I had no idea of what I had to change in order to create this desirable state. So beware challenging your child with the question 'Why do you find it so hard to concentrate?'. If you do, the likelihood is that you will not get a true or a coherent answer.

Putting Theory into Practice

How can parents help a growing child develop the kind of effective concentration that will help him to think creatively and apply himself well? Of course, how and how well children concentrate is part of their personality. Each one will think and behave slightly differently. There is a natural range of behaviour that we can describe as 'normal' which allows a child to function more or less effectively in a variety of situations and ways. The following suggestions apply to this range. Children who have a special learning or behaviour problem which makes it particularly hard for them to concentrate, such as Attention Deficit and Hyperactivity Disorder (ADHD), may need more specialised help (see Useful Organisations and Addresses at the end of the book).

Practice at Mental Release

The best and most natural way to encourage a child's concentration is through:

- playing
- drawing and painting
- reading
- developing enthusiasms

Later, perhaps he can take up a musical instrument. The concentration involved in playing and reading music develops the habit of concentration and listening.

Play, and drawing and painting, take a child into his imagination. Play allows a child to express and explore ideas safely – at his own pace. By delving into fantasy, he can forget the present and lose an awareness of time. Imaginative play, especially, helps any child to 'let go', to move away from the limiting barriers of reality to discover the rich potential of extended exploration within himself. When a child becomes fascinated and self-absorbed in his own imaginative play, the concentration is not only intense, it is also entirely spontaneous.

Reading encourages concentration for similar reasons. When we read to our child, and when our child reads to himself, he can become lost in the world created by the story. 'Letting go' to enter that world is safe, either because we are sitting close by or because there is a thread back to reality when the cover closes.

Developing enthusiasms is a wonderful tool. An enthusiasm is like a magnet; it draws a child away from the here and now into another world. An enthusiasm can be about something fairly conventional, such as fishing or collecting stamps, or it can verge on the bizarre. I knew two children who were obsessed with, and extremely knowledgeable about, lawn mowers. However strange the enthusiasm is, it should not be belittled as it has important implications for concentration.

Practice at Physical Release

Some children take rests naturally and unconsciously as their mind and body need them. These children have, in Howard Gardner's terms, good intrapersonal skills. For those who are not so self-attuned or not so able to switch themselves off, we can step in to help. We can:

- encourage them to take quiet time, in a bath, on their bed or in front of the television
- massage their backs, heads and necks if they get too anxious and het up
- find out their favoured method of winding down
- consider introducing certain ritual actions to start the relaxation and

concentration process, such as tennis players use before they serve, or the All Blacks use before their games. Simply breathing deeply and slowly aids relaxation

- introduce them to martial arts classes if they are available locally. Martial arts involve training in mental and physical concentration and relaxation

- encourage good posture, which helps the lungs to expand well. Putting hands on the head with elbows pointing outwards while sitting straight automatically puts the spine in an upright position which will start good breathing spontaneously and naturally

Memory

Without memory, we cannot understand, learn, develop or make sense of our world. It is, therefore, highly relevant to motivation. If we have difficulty remembering things, or how to do things, we will lose motivation and stop trying. But what is memory? Beyond a certain level, researchers and academics are still debating what it is and how it works. It is easy to see that memory is important for learning and study when it involves knowing and recalling facts, the story line in books, the detail and explanations for scientific processes and so on, which are tested in exams. It is relatively easy to accept the existence of two separate parts to memory – short-term memory and a deeper longer-term memory which impacts on our understanding and therefore becomes part of ourselves.

Memory is most obviously active in children's learning in two ways. It is active when children receive, hold on to and process information – so it is about what goes in and what is drawn upon to help with comprehending that information. It is also active when children demonstrate their understanding and show their knowledge on demand – so it also concerns what comes out.

But we are not always able to recall things that we know. Just because something is placed in our memory, it does not mean it can come out. We will all have had the experience of knowing that we know something but, deep as we might delve, our memory fails us. The particular thought or piece of information cannot be retrieved either to tell someone else or even to remind ourselves, to 'refresh our own memory' silently. The harder we try, the more locked in it becomes. Memory – is not just about remembering facts; it also involves events that have happened to us. Think about your school days for a moment. You are far more likely to remember a person or a particular incident than something you learnt. We absorb far more than pure 'knowledge', and it is not necessarily the knowledge that we treat as significant. What we remember, when and in what circumstances, remains mysterious. When memories are painful, they can become buried deep in our unconscious. We never look for them because we do not realise they are there. Memory, then, is hard to explain and the images commonly used to understand it are not really satisfactory. It is not like a library, with different events stored in different places on different shelves just waiting to be reached for. Nor is it like a computer; it is not as efficient as that. So what is it?

In a fascinating BBC radio programme on memory, a number of 'memory experts' were asked what they thought it was. One said memory is 'the internal representation of your external world'. Another said, 'Without our memory, we cannot connect, we cannot make plans. Without memory, we have no future'. Other definitions offered included, 'It is a past event which influences the future', 'It is a bodily continuity'. A contributing professor said, 'Memory grounds the self. Memories are like your feet. They determine who you are'.

Memory, then, is not a simple mechanistic or cognitive procedure governed by logic and rationality. It is locked into, and cannot be separated from, experience, emotion and our sense of self. Like experience and emotion, it has a dynamic. Emotion is central to memory – to its storage and retrieval modes. It therefore affects learning facts and information, our 'procedural memory', as much as it affects our 'autobiographical memory', what we remember of our total experience through which we define ourselves.

Children who have difficulty learning may in fact be having difficulty remembering things. The problem will not be that they are incapable of understanding. It may, instead, be that their emotional state prevents them from receiving, holding on to, processing or recalling information. A stressed or vulnerable child will instinctively protect himself by blocking out any knowledge that will require him to change. He can fail to listen, fail to absorb the information or fail to remember.

Things are always easier to remember if we can make sense of them when we hear or read them. Completely new information with alien jargon simply goes in one ear and out the other. When we buy our first item of high-tech equipment, such as a computer or video recorder, we tend to glaze over as the sales person races through the various advantages and disadvantages of different models. It usually means nothing. We do not have the relevant mental files available to sort out the meaning of the words and understand them.

The same is true for children, only more so. Naturally, the average four-year-old cannot be expected to understand mathematical calculus if he has not yet mastered simple addition, subtraction and multiplication. This is obvious. What is less obvious is that children who are in mental and emotional turmoil will also find it hard to process, therefore remember, any new information. If their lives and relationships contain no reliable pattern, they will not be able to make sense of their world at a fundamental level, let alone of more sophisticated information. If they had the right files in their heads, these will have been thrown into disarray by uncertainty and it will take them longer to locate the right ones to understand anything. The longer the uncertainty persists, the further will they fall behind, being unable to fill their filing-cabinet drawers at the same rate as other children, with the result that they make sense of less and less.

Research has shown that, emotional factors apart, the less we use our memory, the worse it gets. French school inspectors, concerned about the loss of general memory skills, are calling for a revival of memory training. We can therefore help our child if we encourage good memory habits. There are several general approaches. Rote learning is one, but only one, approach. Committing facts and figures to memory through repetition can be a useful shortcut to instant recall, and develops a skill, but it is only really helpful if the memorised information is also useful and explained. For example, multiplication tables need to be understood as well as learnt. Understanding ensures information is transferred to long-term memory; and if we can explain and relate events and knowledge in a meaningful way and as part of a wider picture, we will be helping our child to organise and integrate his memories. Explanation is therefore another general approach. Planning and organising sharpen memory, as does talking about the past and helping children make sense of their experiences. Further specific suggestions appear below.

Putting Theory into Practice

What practical things can parents do to help their child have an active memory and be confident about using it?

Children aged 0–8

Once children can understand speech, the day's events can be remembered and talked over in a daily bedtime ritual. Use simple trigger questions like 'What did we do today?'.

Many games develop children's memory skills. For example the traditional 'pairs' game, sometimes called pelmonism, when picture or number cards are laid face down and players have to try to turn over an identical pair of cards, remembering the position of unpaired ones which are placed face down again. 'I went shopping and I bought a. . . ' is another memory game in which a shopping list of objects increases as each player adds another item to the list after he has repeated the items included so far.

Reading particular books to children over and over, or singing simple songs and nursery rhymes repeatedly, will help them to remember things gradually and naturally and through different methods.

Telling personal and family memories and stories about 'when he was a baby' helps to make recall safe and fun.

Children aged 8–12
Children of this age can be encouraged to plan, organise themselves and find their own techniques for remembering tasks.

Help with learning their multiplication tables – through singing, dancing about, marching, or any other way they feel comfortable with – can offer a useful model of how to go about memorising something. Playing a tables tape on car journeys goes down well if this is possible.

Children aged 12–16
Older children have even more need to explore their own preferred styles of learning and remembering. If they have problems remembering things, rather than nag them, we can encourage them to use sticky notes or even their friends to prompt them via the telephone.

Conflict impairs memory. The more we get drawn into arguments, the more children may stew and not concentrate and focus their memory. Further ideas for assisting memory through creating an emotionally safe environment can be found in Chapter Eighteen.

Conclusion

Good self-esteem is central to learning and motivation. Our emotions – what and how we feel about ourselves and others – affect the ability of all of us to develop and feel motivated. Our inner world is not easily separated from anything we do. To understand our children, and to create the best environment for them to get the best from themselves, we need to be sensitive to the intimate, even symbiotic, relationship between their emotions and their capacity to grow, personally and intellectually, whether it is self-directed or directed by others.

5

Motivation and Us: Styles, Histories and Personalities

This chapter looks at the factors – values, experiences, personalities and expectations – which influence our personal 'achievement agenda' and motivation style. Our children have their own learning and personal style, too, which may be quite different from ours. It is not always easy to achieve a 'best fit'; however it is our responsibility to try to make that relationship work. To be an effective motivator, we have to work with, not against, the grain of their personality, sometimes adjusting our motivational style in the process. If we try to change them, we will probably lose them.

Many schemes exist to identify different personality types. The simplest describe people in terms of how they take and implement decisions, or use power, and use terms such as 'coercive', 'calculative' and 'co-operative', or 'autocratic' and 'democratic'. Others highlight ways people think and behave, and attach labels such as 'warm', 'tough', 'numbers', 'dealer'. The well-known Myers Briggs personality test uses labels which describe how individuals interpret their world. These labels identify people as 'intuitive', 'thinking', 'feeling', 'sensing', 'judging' and 'perceiving', or combinations of the above.

It is unnecessary to cover all of these schemes. In this chapter, I have chosen to look at how we might influence our child's motivation from three different standpoints:

- the nature of our personal and family history
- the effect of our own self-esteem and the jobs we do
- the way we 'manage' our child, using approaches from management

The last section will provide readers with the opportunity to identify changes they might wish to make.

Motives and Hidden Agendas: the Influence of Family Histories

Every family has its own history, or story, which influences our motivation style, whether we want it to or not. We often have a hidden agenda, which children detect. If we can be honest about our own motives, it should make the motivational environment less charged and more effective.

Which, if any, of the following personal or family stories ring true with you?

We All Try to Please

We pleased our parents by our success. We try to please our boss. We think our child should want to please us and his teachers by doing well in the way we had in mind.

Tendency: to value conformity and take lapses personally.

Failure Doesn't Fit

Everyone in our family has done well. This is how 'we' are. For example, I knew a successful family in which one child was adopted. When this youngster began causing problems, his adoptive mother was overheard saying, 'But you are a. . . Smith. We don't do things like this.'.

Tendency: to ignore individual differences and perspectives.

'Do as I Say, Not as I Did.'

We 'threw away' or wasted the opportunities we had and we don't want our child to do the same.

Tendency: to push, monitor too closely and be mistrustful.

The Reflected Glory Syndrome

It makes us feel good, taking some personal credit, when our child does well. It is the reward for all the effort we invested in his mental and educational development.

Tendency: to steal his success and be inapproriately demanding.

Symbol of Success

We have been a 'success' in our field, and we want an achieving child as one of the symbols of our success to display to colleagues. Failures are embarrassing. They suggest flaws in ourselves.

Tendency: to push, control and be intolerant of different approaches to life or problem-solving.

'I Don't Have Time for This'

Successful children are part of the family momentum. Failing children cause discomfort and inconvenience. They require attention and demand scarce and valuable time.

Tendency: to neglect, make sudden demands for perfection and blame unpredictably.

Just a Tool for a Tough World

It's a tough world out there and they have got to survive. Qualifications and skills will help them.

Tendency: to offer challenging goals with good support and encouragement, and relevant autonomy.

'I Work to Give Them a Better Life'

Life has been hard and we never had the chances they have and we want our efforts to produce a better and easier life for them.

Tendency: to fill their life to the brim with gifts and experiences, sometimes offered too easily.

The Successful Rebel

We only got where we did by being different, by taking risks, by challenging and not conforming.

Tendency: to confuse children by discouraging conformity, poking fun at authority and offering mixed messages about expectations for performance and behaviour.

Their Failure Might Show Up Our Mistakes

Perhaps because of something that has happened, we feel guilty and personally responsible when our children don't seem to be making the grade. This is uncomfortable.

Tendency: to deny or ignore signs of motivation problems, or simply to 'demand' better performance.

Laziness Drives Us Mad

We can't stand them loafing about doing nothing – being self-indulgent and selfish when, at their age, you had to work during the day and possibly study at night. And you are struggling to support the family.

Tendency: to criticise and nag.

Wasting Our Money

We've spent 'good money' on education. We don't want to see it wasted.
Tendency: to be intolerant of mistakes or misunderstandings.

Missed Opportunities

We tend to live through our children, making up for what we did not do. We always wanted to be good at sport/music/art we we want our child to enjoy and succeed at these activities especially.
Tendency: to be pushy, involved and demanding.

'Stay Like Me'

We did not do very well at school or elsewhere, and feel our authority could be threatened if our child becomes 'smarter' than us.

Tendency: to ignore good work and offer little opportunity, support or encouragement for our child's general development.

'It Was Good Enough for Me'

We got by with no help from parents and no chance to learn all these fancy new sports, musical instruments and the like. Our child can do the same, make his own entertainment and manage on his own.

Tendency: to show little interest in and encouragement for interests and hobbies.

These examples do not cover all the possible variations in individual experience. They were selected to illustrate generally negative consequences for children and to increase awareness. Of course, many people have good motivation experiences in childhood which they repeat, or they successfully resolve to do things better for their children if their own were poor. Nevertheless, there is probably something each of us could do differently, and better. What has influenced your attitudes and expectations?

Personality and Experience: the Effect of our Self-esteem and Jobs

Our motivation style is influenced by the present as well as the past. It is affected by our current level of self-esteem and the kind of jobs we do. Parents can be grouped according to these factors. This is another way to recognise ourselves and judge whether we would be more effective if we change our approach. The three groups I have created do not represent real people but 'ideal types' who display idealised characteristics. They are:

- high achievers, sometimes described as 'fast track'
- normal achievers, who I call 'main track'
- low achievers, who I call 'no track'

Each category can be subdivided according to whether the parent has, on the whole, high self-esteem or low self-esteem.

From the survey of characteristics of effective managers which follows this section, we see that effective motivators:

- have high expectations and offer support
- tolerate mistakes
- praise and encourage
- foster independence

Having noted these characteristics, we can then see how each type of parent is likely to behave in relation to each one. Of course, none of us will fit one or other category in this scheme exactly. Our jobs change, we move in and out of work and self-esteem is not something fixed or static. We feel stronger or more vulnerable depending on events and circumstances, on the state of our relationships and how much stress and change we have to manage. Nevertheless, examining the key variables in this way will help us to understand our own input to the motivation dynamic.

High Achievers

High-achieving, fast-track parents can have stormy relationships with their children. Fathers, in particular, may assume their directive management style will work at home. They quickly find that finger clicking is less effective there, especially where a child is already resentful about frequent absences. To hear a message, children have to respect the messenger. If they feel both ignored and pushed about, they will not have that respect. In terms of expectations, high achievers expect more of the same from their offspring but they will apply different amounts of pressure depending on the state of their own self-esteem. Those who feel comfortable with themselves will tend to be more relaxed and have more realistic targets for their children than those with lower self-esteem. High-flying parents who use their personal successes to top up their feelings of self-worth, however, will be more pushy. They may also seek to demand success from their children so they can exploit this in a similar way when their personal supplies dry up.

A well-established high achiever will find it easier to accept a reasonable number of mistakes. No longer required to prove anything, to themselves or to others, he or she is able to take a more balanced view of what children can be expected to deliver. Those needing constantly to impress, on the other hand, are likely to have little tolerance. Their child's mistakes may be seen as reflecting badly on them and taken personally; their own inappropriately high standards may be applied, defining too many things as failures. A tendency to compete with the child will also highlight failures; and mistakes and failures will consume scarce time and energy and be inconvenient.

Fast-track parents may have problems praising their children. They may provide plenty of encouragement and high expectations, but when it comes to acknowledging 'good enough' success that is worthy of praise, those same expectations can get in the way. At each point of achievement, the parent's focus is more likely to be directed to where the child can go next, and to the dangers of 'resting on laurels', than to recognising and celebrating the current achievement as an end in itself. This is particularly true for insecure fast-trackers. For them, praise can be fully deserved and donated only when their child has reached the top, which will be some notional, almost wish-fulfilment 'top' as defined by the parent.

High achievers with high self-esteem will tend to offer their children plenty of scope to work and play independently. They are able to live with the idea that their child may well be different from them and are more likely to give him the freedom to achieve in his own way and in his own time. If they have low self-esteem, on the other hand, such autonomy will be too risky. Left to his own devices, the child may not make the grade they have in mind for him. They need their child to become like them as an affirmation of their uncertain selves. The child's leisure time is likely to be highly regulated and filled with stimulation, to maximise the chances of notable success that the parent can then feed off.

Normal achievers

Main-track parents will tend to have expectations ranging from appropriate to low, depending on their 'self' view. He or she will be able to accept failures and mistakes as necessary and inevitable, provided these remain within appropriate limits, and are more likely to have the time and confidence to explore and correct their child's misunderstandings. If, on the other hand, their self-esteem is drawn down, mistakes can become unwelcome and focused on, for the same reasons given above.

Secure normal achievers will be genuinely impressed with achievements that perhaps they never had the chance to experience. Praise will be given in plenty and the pride the parent feels will be overtly demonstrated by attendance at events to witness the child in action – on the football field, on the sports track, at the concert or in the class play. Work and personal commitments are likely to be fewer, freeing the parent up to share, and thereby increase, the child's pleasure. Those with low self-esteem will find it harder to be free with their praise. Not only may they have little personal childhood experience of praise, they may also tend to believe that praise makes children big-headed and should therefore be avoided at all costs.

The more average expectations held by self-contented, normally achieving parents will have leisure and pleasure time built into them. Some form of further or higher education or training will probably be assumed, but they are less likely to have set ideas about what it should be. Children will be left to find their own way to fulfilment and enjoyment.

Low achievers

Low achievers who feel no sense of self-pride may demand little or nothing from their child. They may not expect their child to do any better than themselves; or they may prefer their child not to succeed as it could show them up. Those with positive self-esteem will be likely to have some tolerance for mistakes, but if there are too many they may worry that their child could waste himself as they may think they have. Those with very poor self-esteem often have an excessive tolerance of mistakes, because very low expectations can lead to the blurring of success and failure. School is likely to have been a difficult time for them. It may be hard for them to accept the value of school because to do so will expose their own lack of education as something to be ashamed of. Any 'us' and 'them' attitude can encourage overly defensive reactions to any report of a child's shortcomings at school as this can easily be viewed as a direct challenge to themselves as well as their child.

Parents who feel they have not achieved very much can be sparing with their praise. Sometimes they don't realise children like to hear it; sometimes they don't know how to say it. Perhaps, as achievement is not part of their normal experience, they don't realise the range of daily activities that can be appreciated and praised. And perhaps, having few expectations and limited money, their children don't have so much opportunity to exploit their talents and do well at something.

They may also find it hard to manage and limit their child's desire for independence, especially when they feel low. But where children experience little control, structure or guidance they can drift, missing out on useful lessons about the fruits of application, achievement and a sense of parental commitment, all of which can have knock-on effects on their motivation.

Motivational Styles: The Lessons from Management

Having reflected upon what we think and feel, what we do and don't do and what we do well or could do differently or better, we can now look at how people in business and industry assess management styles to identify further scope for adjusting our parenting style.

Parents are, in effect, leaders and managers. Like business managers, we use different methods and tactics to get results. Some are more effective than others. Typically, we enthuse, encourage, cajole, offer various incentives, shame, threaten, punish, insult, insist or merely cross our fingers. Only some of these work long term.

Organisation researchers have spent the last 50 years or so trying to identify different styles and decide which approaches work best. The results have been remarkably consistent, showing two broad patterns, or styles, of leadership which can be seen as opposites. Some people have called the two styles 'Task-focused–People-focused', while others have preferred the term 'Autocrat–Democrat'.

Managers who are people-focused will take account of their workers' interests and views and involve them in making decisions, hence the term 'democratic'. Managers who are task-focused want to get a job done in the way they see as manageable and desirable and tend to dictate to others how they want it done, hence the term 'autocratic'.

Leader or Manager, Democrat or Autocrat?

So far, I have used the terms 'leader' and 'manager' to mean the same thing. People commonly use them interchangeably. Some, though, see an important difference. For them, 'leaders' are people who inspire as well as merely administer, and give other people room to do things their way, and co-ordinate this. Leaders also practise what they preach. Interestingly, the word education is linked to the Latin verb *ducere*, which means to lead. Autocrats are directive, structuring and tight; democrats are considerate, participative and flexible. Thus we can say that autocrats behave as managers while democrats function more as leaders.

Another way of understanding leadership styles is to look at how power, or decision-making, is shared. From this perspective, autocratic leaders will take all the significant decisions; democratic leaders involve others. Note, however, that the democratic-style leader retains ultimate responsibility for decisions. Someone who hands all the decisions and power to others, taking little responsibility, will be neither leading nor managing, and the same is true for parents. We remain authoritative not through being authoritarian but by continuing to guide, influence, set out boundaries for the decisions and, sometimes, direct where necessary.

How Can This Help Parents?

This autocratic–democratic understanding of leadership needs to be refined for parents, just as it has been for managers, because real life is never that simple. As children grow and become more mature, responsible and independent, parents need to change their style. Those with young children will need to be more autocratic, taking most of the decisions and offering fewer openings for freedom and choice, though there should always be some. As children become older, more decisions should be delegated to them so they can decide things for themselves. The process is gradual, although account needs to be taken of the importance of each issue and decision. The more important the decision, the more parents should be at least involved in, if not taking, it. If they take it, they should remember to explain or, at the very least, announce it. Good managers keep their teams informed and parents should do the same for their children. The continuum of decision making moves from 'tells' to 'sells', 'consults', 'shares' and 'delegates'.

This framework might be useful to parents who have to take decisions jointly with another adult – either parent or partner. By looking at how much say the child or young person should have in any instance and the nature of any limits, it should be easier to reach an agreement and offer clear and consistent direction.

The People Versus Task Approach

Blake identified five main management styles, determined by whether a manager has a high or low concern for 'people' and 'task'. Someone who has a high concern for the job at hand and ignores the wishes and interests of the people involved is described as a 'task manager'. Someone who ensures his workers feel happy but lets deadlines and work quality slip has a 'country club' style. The 'team leader' is the most successful style. This person has a high concern for both people and task. In other words, concern for people is combined with a determination to be effective and produce the desired results.

How Can This Help Parents?

Parents face very similar issues. We should not let a concern with achievement allow us to ignore the interests, feelings and rhythms of children. Such a parent could be called a 'task master'. Equally, parents should beware of letting standards slide in favour of either short-term happiness for a child or an easy life for themselves. This parenting style could be called the 'party parent'. Like managers, effective parents also need to strive to have a high concern for the quality of their children's work at the same time as being sensitive to their children as individuals with hopes, fears and feelings and strengths and weaknesses. These are the qualities of an effective motivator.

Parents can combine the task- and people-focused approaches in a practical way if we separate clearly the target, or end, from the means of getting there. A high concern for the task can be shown in the nature of the target set. Even then, this target should be relevant to each individual child, focusing on self-improvement more than beating others. Once we have agreed the target with our child, the process of reaching it must be people-focused, or child-sensitive. It is the child, after all, who has to put in the effort needed. At this point, the child should have the greater say. We may think we are putting a child's interests centre stage when in fact we are still trying to get what we want in the way that we want it. The result is manipulation, a tool frequently used by articulate parents. 'Why don't you. . ?' is the telltale phrase typical of the manipulative tendency.

Case Study

A mother whose children have now left home was reflecting on the terrible teenage years. One of her daughters had been a real worry, causing dreadful rows by going out every night during her GCSE exams. When questioned if the daughter really had done no work, she replied that her daughter had worked during the day but wanted time off in the evenings. Asked about the outcome, she said her daughter had got the grades she needed for the course she wanted and was now happily following her chosen career. Yet this mother still saw her daughter's behaviour as problematic.

Handy's Doughnut Principle

In his book, *The Empty Raincoat: Making Sense of the Future*, Charles Handy uses the image of an inside-out ring doughnut to explore similar issues of balancing central direction with defined space for choice and self-determination. Handy explains that the centre of his doughnut contains the rules, duties and expectations with which we live. The ring of space surrounding this core is our opportunity to 'go beyond the bounds of duty, to live up to our full potential'.

How Can This Help Parents?

Children can often feel their world is taken over by rules and expectations, though we, as parents, will almost certainly think otherwise. Nonetheless, we should be prepared to review the balance between expectations and freedoms. To develop Handy's imagery further, if the lump of dough in the centre is too large, not only does it take up more of the free space available but also children can become exhausted having to squelch through the doughy bit on their way to freedom. Too much control from the centre saps energy and initiative. A smaller core of duties and requirements, on the other hand, can create a motivation momentum. Having a sense of structure and direction, a sense of tasks fulfilled and fulfilled well, can give children the edge of personal confidence, experience of application and sufficient self-knowledge to help explore their potential in a purposeful, constructive and energetic way. On the other hand, too few obligations at the core do not establish a direction and can result in inactivity and aimlessness. We have returned to the challenge of balance which, frustratingly, cannot be predetermined.

In terms of how much energy children have left when they reach the 'flexible space', it is what they think and feel that matters. It may therefore help to sit down together with your child and actually draw the two circles, one inside the other, discussing which issues fall, or should fall, where and writing them in accordingly. The visible territory left for personal decisions should put any complaints in perspective. Older children could draw their own circles, and the sizes of these would show how they see things. They could draw more than one set. One set might cover their life in school; another could represent their view of family arrangements. If your child feels school offers little space for choice and personal development, he may need a larger 'flexible space' at home. Similarly, if he feels little sense of obligation at school, he might benefit from a range of clearer expectations at home.

Theory X and Theory Y

In *The Human Side of Enterprise*, Douglas McGregor suggested that managers typically have two very different sets of assumptions about how people behave at work, regardless of their actual performance and motivation levels. He argued that these assumptions have a profound effect on the attitude of workers. He called these two sets of assumptions Theory X and Theory Y.

Theory X managers tend to control and manipulate. They think:

- people dislike work and will avoid it if they can
- people must be either bribed or forced to make an effort
- people don't like responsibility, so need to be directed and controlled
- people can be controlled through money and fear of insecurity
- most people have no creativity – except when it comes to getting round management rules

Theory Y managers tend to lead through attending to people's need for self-esteem and self-discovery. They think:

- work is necessary to our psychological health and growth. People want to be interested in their work and to enjoy it
- people will themselves put in the effort if they accept the goal or target
- people want responsibility. Self-discipline is more effective than imposed discipline
- under the right conditions, people are motivated by the desire to realise their potential
- many people have creativity and ingenuity which are largely underused

How Can This Help Parents?

McGregor's approach to motivation introduces us to the important idea that we see the behaviour that we want to see. Whatever a child may achieve, or whatever his attitude towards striving, a Theory X parent will view the child and his performance negatively and critically, be untrusting and think the worst. A Theory Y parent will be much more positive and trusting, giving a child hope and leading him onward.

Think about how you tend to see your child's personality and achievements. Are you a Theory X or a Theory Y type parent? Of course, we would probably all like to think of ourselves as Theory Y parents, but that might be wishful thinking. Many people will combine elements of both types while being essentially one or the other.

Management Style and Quality of Work

Renis Likert tried to find out the link between different management styles and performance and satisfaction among subordinates. Instead of talking to the managers, he interviewed the people who worked for them. Those who worked for the most successful managers found them:

- firm but fair, being supportive, friendly and helpful
- trusting, showing confidence in the ability, integrity and motivation of subordinates
- appropriately demanding, having high expectations of performance
- encouraging, coaching and helping those not performing well
- extending, training employees for promotion and to widen their experience

These managers used both the democratic and people-focused approaches. This is beginning to sound very familiar. The same messages emerge time and time again.

Management Style and Motivation

Looking more closely at motivation in particular, Scott Myers interviewed over 800 middle managers to find out how their personal motivation was affected by the style and behaviour of their immediate bosses. He found clear differences between the highly and poorly motivated middle managers in the way they saw their bosses. Nine out of 10 people who felt motivated by their boss mentioned three things they appreciated. Their manager:

- tries to see the merit in ideas even when he or she thinks differently
- accepts mistakes if the lessons are learnt
- goes on to discuss how mistakes can be avoided

Eight out of 10 also mentioned the boss:

- is easy to talk to even when under pressure
- has consistent high expectations
- encourages people to reach out in new directions
- expects high performance and gives credit when due

Of those who were not motivated by their boss, more than half of them mentioned that their boss:

- gives only the information considered necessary
- has limited expectations; and only responds when something goes wrong
- does not tolerate mistakes, especially personally embarrassing ones
- tries to protect people from making mistakes
- is difficult to talk to

How Can This Help Parents?

Parents certainly have a very similar role to managers in creating a positive motivational climate. The Myers questionnaire can be adapted to make it relevant for parents. Assume for a moment that you are your child's manager. How do you think your child would rate you in the questionnaire below? For each pair of statements, tick the one you think would come closest to your child's picture of how you behave.

If you are feeling brave and your child is old enough, you might give this exercise to him and then compare notes. The results will almost certainly be revealing. But before you get defensive, remember that good motivators see the merit in other people's ideas even if they are different from their own.

Your attitudes and behaviour create a good motivational environment	Your attitudes and behaviour create a poor motivational environment
You are easy to talk to even when under pressure	He has to select his moment to catch you
You try to see the merit in his ideas, even if they conflict with yours	As the adult, you tend to assume that your ideas are best
You try to help him understand the family rules or objectives	You let him work out for himself how the family rules apply to him
You try to give him all the information he wants	You give him as much information as you feel he needs or occurs to you at the time
You have consistently high expectations	Your expectations change from day to day
You try to introduce him to new ideas of things to do; certain risks are acceptable	You try to protect him from taking big risks
You tolerate mistakes, as long as the lessons are learnt	You don't like him to make mistakes, especially those that embarrass you
You try to figure out why the mistake happened and how it could be prevented	When something goes wrong, you like to know who or what caused it
You expect high performance and you give credit when he meets your standards	You expect an adequate job and don't say much unless something goes wrong

Conclusion

Part One has explored what motivation is, reviewed theories and successful approaches used in other fields, and discussed how parents can affect their children's motivation. Certain clear principles of good practice have emerged.

Part Two concentrates on these principles, explores each one in turn in more depth and considers how they can be applied in practice – how we help our children stay on track for success.

PART TWO

ENCOURAGING MOTIVATION: PRINCIPLES AND PRACTICE

Part Two presents 14 principles of motivation and suggests ways to implement them. However, as children grow, parents have to adapt. What works at one stage of a child's development will not be suitable or effective at another. In order to remain effective as motivators, parents need to understand their growing child's changing, as well as constant, needs. First, then, is a brief overview of child development.

Children world-wide go through similar phases and stages in a similar order and at similar times. Of course, within this general pattern each child is unique, affected by things like natural talents, opportunities, cultural traditions and family expectations and variations. However, all children need to develop in a well-rounded way: socially, physically, intellectually, creatively and emotionally. They need to be able to make sense of events that touch them, be comfortable with their private thoughts and feelings and manage all forms of learning. Without self-understanding and emotional tranquillity, academic progress will be stunted. 'Development takes place most naturally', writes Annie Davy in *Playwork*, 'when children are accepted, respected and loved – then their sense of identity, confidence and self-worth can blossom.'

Children's development can be described in terms of their growing and changing sense of self. Though born with distinct personalities, very young babies have little sense of self. They feel most comfortable when they are intimately engaged as one with their key carer who meets their immediate physical and emotional need for food, warmth, love and physical closeness. During this first, attachment phase, the significant adults prepare the ground and place the seed of their infant's self. Around the age of two, children produce the first shoot of a self-conscious and separate identity as they begin to establish and assert themselves. The better prepared the soil, through quality attachments, the stronger the first roots and shoot. Toddlers typically yearn for independence and have an unstoppable urge to explore themselves and their world. This is vitally important but they also need to be contained by sensitively drawn boundaries, the beginnings of discipline. Discipline is like pruning. That new energy has to be directed, to produce a single, secure, strong shoot of self.

The period between three and eight is the Growth of Self. The shoot becomes a full plant. During this time, the main focus is 'mastery of learning, with the right amount of stimulation but without too much anxiety. It is the peak time for parents to influence attitudes and behaviour', as Howell, Montuschi and Kahn explain in *Parenting Perspectives*, the time when children have the chance to flesh out their growing sense of self with knowledge and skills. Parental presence, guidance and involvement act as a stake to support the child as he grows. Too many negative messages about capability, self-worth or personal traits and looks will stunt the all-important growth of self-belief and produce a weakened stem that will need and seek alternative sources of support.

The period between years eight to twelve is the Flowering of Self. All the time, attention and care given by parents hitherto pays off, enabling a healthy, strong, independent plant to hold itself straight as the stake is first loosened, then removed. Parents still need to feed the soil and nip unhelpful side shoots, but radical pruning now will distort the plant's natural form. The flowers represent self-image. When the remaining buds swell and open, the full flowers declare, 'Look at me, this is who I am.' From this public display of self, through clothes, hair styles, hobbies, styles of behaviour and bedroom decorations, to give some examples, a child is able to express himself and where he thinks he belongs. The earliest forays into self-expression may well be via the safe conformity of fashion. The earlier this happens, and the less strong the inner sense of self, the more this is likely to occur. Gradually, peer groups become important to children's identity. Different friends and personal styles may be tried out in the process of testing social acceptability and exploring potential sexual attractiveness.

The teenage years, a time of transition and transformation, see the Redefinition of Self. The plant's energy is focused on the new cycle as the youthful flowers fade, leaving the fruit of the new self to develop and mature. The plant seems less attractive for a time, and uncertain of its identity. The parent's role as guide and support becomes important again. As in the toddler years, parents help to strengthen the new self by removing the dead flowers, which teenagers will resent, to prevent premature and multiple fruiting which may weaken the new self. The flowering child is sustained for a time as educational and family obligations are met, but this can only go on for so long. Eventually, nature, through the constraints of the seasons, takes its course and a full, independent and separate identity is established.

This transformation is most successful and complete when children feel secure and are encouraged to explore and develop themselves safely. Those pressured to fulfil parents' expectations will often reach adulthood empty, confused, dissatisfied and either demotivated or propelled to search continuously for their true worth and identity. The importance of starting from where children are, not where you want them to be, is addressed in the first chapter of Part Two.

6

Start From Who They Are, Not Who You Want Them To Be

As adults, we are all different. We like different things and have different talents. We think, feel and behave differently. We learn and take in information in different ways. This, what interests us, excites and motivates us, and how we tend to think and respond, makes us who we are, forming our unique personalities. The human brain is astonishing for the great variety it produces.

Children too are individuals. The first principle of motivation is to start with your child: to recognise who he is and his stage of development. Every child is interested in different things and possesses unique qualities. Yet, despite knowing this, even teachers can be surprised to discover that children also have clear learning and working styles, often linked to their personality type. Some children are perfectionist; others are slap-dash. Some question everything; others love to be told. Some thrive on routine; others like to wait for the right mood and moment.

Some children are able to remember things instantly having merely been told them; others need pictures to help them understand and hold on to information. Some learn best by reading, having words on paper to digest at their own pace; others are happiest to learn through exploration and trial and error, in a hands-on manner, moving about or 'learning by doing'.

Children will learn more easily, perform better and be more self-motivated if they can do things in a way that suits them – whether by using sight, sound or touch – and through activities that interest them. Both of my children learnt to read at the same age. One launched straight into devouring books and avoided writing for some time, while the other wrote almost compulsively and wasn't interested in reading until later. Children's all-important sense of mastery, their effectiveness and competence, will develop best where they are allowed to start from who, and where, they are.

sonalities and Learning Styles

t who are they? It can be hard to know when we are so close. Either we cannot see the wood for the trees, and we lose sight of who they are, or we see too many things negatively. Human characteristics are like vinyl records, not CDs. They usually have a flip side. Features of our child's personality that drive us mad may be seen as plus points by other people. For example, your friends might see your child as strong-minded, while you see him as argumentative and stubborn. They might see another child as having a strong sense of fairness and great sensitivity to the feelings of others, while you see him as whinging and a cry-baby.

Having a check list of characteristics often helps to focus thinking. Here is a sample list to help you build a full picture of your child. Look at the two statements at each end of the scales below and tick where you think your child fits.

On the go all the time	☐	☐	☐	☐	☐	Likes quiet time
Loves to be with others	☐	☐	☐	☐	☐	Likes time alone
Sleep/hunger erratic	☐	☐	☐	☐	☐	Sleep/hunger predictable
Easily distracted	☐	☐	☐	☐	☐	Hates to be interrupted
Vivid imagination	☐	☐	☐	☐	☐	Down to earth, literal
Acts/speaks without thinking	☐	☐	☐	☐	☐	Thinks before acts/speaks
Short concentration span	☐	☐	☐	☐	☐	Can stick at things for ages
Loves all jokes	☐	☐	☐	☐	☐	Does not quite trust humour
Likes clear expectations	☐	☐	☐	☐	☐	Likes to act spontaneously
Likes precise instructions	☐	☐	☐	☐	☐	Likes to be original
Works at a steady pace	☐	☐	☐	☐	☐	Prefers to work in spurts
Loves facts and detail	☐	☐	☐	☐	☐	Finds detail and facts tedious
Unsettled by changes	☐	☐	☐	☐	☐	Flexible and adaptable
Recoils from new things	☐	☐	☐	☐	☐	Rushes into new things
Likes to be organised	☐	☐	☐	☐	☐	Carefree and disorganised
Puts work before play	☐	☐	☐	☐	☐	Mixes work and play

Add any other important aspects of your child's personality not covered by this list. Instead of seeing any of these features as irritating 'faults' that you wish were not there, identify a positive side to each one. Consider if your child displays this characteristic in every field. For example, a child may have a short concentration span for doing things he is asked to do but can spend longer playing with the family pet or eating food that he enjoys. This will help you both to understand the reason for the tendency and to avoid labelling your child unhelpfully. Try, also, to accept these features as the necessary starting points for getting the best out of your child.

Another way to identify a good starting point for a particular child is to ask yourself what he likes to do and what fires him up. Does he find it easy to sit down and concentrate on games and, if so, does he prefer games involving words, numbers or colours, or games which require moving pieces to get tactical advantage, like chess and many of the fantasy-based board games? How much risk, skill or imagination is involved? Are action games the favourite, 'mucking about' with others, or informal ball games? Is he sports mad or animal mad? One teacher, writing in the *Times Educational Supplement*, explained that she got a very disruptive child to make progress academically by acknowledging his passion for gardening and encouraging a class-wide respect for his unusual expertise. The answers to these various questions will often be influenced by a child's age and gender. Nonetheless, thinking in this way is useful. It can suggest ways to capture a child's interest, identify strengths and weaknesses to be encouraged or worked on, and sharpen our understanding and strengthen our acceptance of the unique qualities of our child.

Multiple Skills or 'Intelligence'

A third way to become more aware of our child's qualities, or preferred style or starting point, is to consider these qualities as skills. An American educationist, Howard Gardner, has identified seven different skills which he calls 'intelligences'. They have equal value in human terms, though schools have traditionally concentrated on the two placed first in this list because they are needed for academic learning. These seven 'intelligences' are:

- verbal: being comfortable and good with words, liking reading, writing and talking
- mathematical, logical: being comfortable and good with numbers, likely to get absorbed in counting, ordering, sorting and listing things, problem-solving and thinking logically

- visual, spatial: enjoying colour, pictures and images, liking drawing and art as well as plans and maps
- musical: sensitive to music, enjoying singing, tapping and moving to music, playing instruments and listening
- interpersonal: being good with other people, being sensitive to their needs and thoughts, able to share and offer support
- intrapersonal: being very self-aware, in touch with their own feelings, being clear about their ideas
- kinesthetic: being physical, includes sporting types – people who like to be on the go, to dance, to climb and clamber, and practical types – those who like to touch and feel, to make or build things with their hands

Our natural strengths will influence how we best learn. Visual children will learn best through sight and images. Musical children learn best through sound. Physically active children may learn best on the move, or through touch, and so on. Perhaps some children would find it easier to learn their multiplication tables if they recited them marching up and down the school playground or football pitch instead of sitting in the classroom.

These natural strengths are also the starting point for boosting confidence and creating a 'motivation momentum'. Success in one sphere will flow through to better performance and working and learning habits in another. We can all improve our skills in each sphere through application and well-directed effort if we believe we can do it. Children, especially, need to develop and fulfil their academic potential. But if we are to change, and those new attitudes and skills are to become part of a new 'us', we have to start from a place which allows us to understand and identify with the new development. A learning programme known as 'accelerated learning' uses this approach. It starts from something that a child is good at and interested in. The programme has an impressive track record. It has been shown to pay dividends, academically and socially, for children from a wide range of backgrounds.

It is easy but dangerous to try to move children forward by starting with what we like now or liked as a child, not with what they like. You know the sort of thing: 'I loved doing such and such as a lad. Why don't you try it?', 'I used to spend hours on my own, playing games against an imaginary friend. Why do you need to have someone round all the time?'. Or we can be tempted to say the opposite: 'I was quite happy as a kid mucking about with your aunt at home. We were good friends. How come you can't bear to stay in?'. The adult's frustration is as clear as the implied criticism of the child. If the suggestion is very wide of the mark, a child can feel insulted that he has been so misread as well as criticised. It will be akin to not remembering the one thing that a child refuses to eat and piling it on the plate.

If this sounds clumsy, it is even worse to start from who you want them to be. Comments such as, 'Why don't you go and find yourself a Saturday job instead of hanging around the house all day?', 'It would be nice if you could play in the school orchestra. Why don't you try the violin again?' and 'Why don't you take up ice skating? I saw a great programme about the glamorous life the young stars have' all belie a dream and can undermine a child, again suggesting there is something wrong with the child as he is.

Case Study

Neha complained she was bored. Aged 11, she had just finished playing with her mother's make-up and styling her hair. Her mum looked at the pile of forgotten toys. Weaving? Boring. Computer chess? No. Doing the plastic motorbike kit? Sad. Writing a story on the computer? Even sadder. Drawing? Come on! Realising the pitch was wrong, her mother changed tack. What about trying your hand at fashion design? Yeah, I could do that! You·could write some pop lyrics at the computer. Great! Get out your old dolls and do their hair? You're really good at this, mum, Neha said and busied herself immediately.

Unconditional Acceptance

Starting from who and where our child is validates him. It is also a way of demonstrating in practical terms that all-important unconditional acceptance which frees a child up to learn and develop in his own way, true to himself. Once we accept him as he is he, in turn, recognises who he is. The more we want him to be someone else, assume he can be different and ignore his preferred starting points, the more he is likely to lose touch with himself. As we shall see later on in Part Two, we have to accept our children unconditionally if success and failure are to be managed in a way that benefits them long term.

Starting with who they are and accepting them unconditionally does not, however, mean there is no possibility of change. It does not mean we lock them into roles and forever see them as strong on this and weak at that. Children often need to change and develop new skills as they mature to do themselves justice. For example, a child who is so disorganised that he either gets behind or told off so much as to lose heart clearly needs to change his ways. It does mean that if we want to help him to move forward, it is best done from a point he recognises, in a way he can manage and for a reason he can accept. In the words of Gerard Nierenberg, an American writer on management: 'People do not resist change. They resist being changed'.

Start From Where They Are

The very day I passed my driving test, my jubilant boyfriend took me out in his car to celebrate my newly acquired freedom of the road. It was a specialist mini – a demon-fast job. He was very proud of his driving skills – and was a typical boy racer. He wanted to teach me how to take the 'correct' line through bends to maximise speed and road holding. We left the city and he encouraged me to accelerate. I did not feel comfortable, but I was impressionable. So I tried, took the 'correct', i.e. straight, line through the bend and only just missed a head-on collision with an oncoming car. It taught me a lesson I shall never forget. Moving children forward too far and too fast can cause them to crash because they are not usually in control. Chapter Fourteen discusses the part children can play in moving themselves forward to ensure they feel comfortable with their rate of progress.

Brothers and Sisters: Don't Compare

For some children, living in the shadow of a sibling affects them for the whole of their life. Insensitive comments from teachers as well as parents, such as 'Your sister would not have produced work like this' or 'You don't have the same sporting talent as your brother', can ruin pride and kill ambition. Far from acting as a spur, I have heard people say that they spent the whole of their childhood thinking they were no good because they were told such things. Someone who has since won international praise for her work in medical research, still harbours a grudge against her mother who used to describe her sister as 'the academic one' while she was merely 'practical'. She felt not only damned with faint praise but also stupid in comparison when, clearly, she was not.

With the boot on the other foot, I heard someone complain that her parents always gave her books at Christmas and birthdays while her brothers were given fun toys because she was considered the brainy one of the family. She resented this labelling so much that she opted out of academic work for many years, going back to it as a teacher only later in life.

Brothers and sisters of budding sporting or musical stars often feel very left out when parents focus not only attention but also considerable sums of money to foster the special talent of one particular child. The twin brothers of Sharron Davies, the Olympic swimmer, said they felt they grew up without a father. For a few years he lived away in America with Sharron while she trained. Even when he was at home, they felt ignored because he concentrated on Sharron. The parents of a rising ice-skating star sold their house and moved the family to a caravan to finance coaching and competition expenses, and then the starlet decided to give up. It must have been quite a sacrifice for her siblings.

Even apportioning equal praise can be limiting. Saying, 'He's the artist in the family while she's the musical one', may give each child something to be proud of, but will make it less likely that either will explore their potential to enjoy the other's field of interest. If someone feels defined by, and loved and accepted for, a particular skill rather than for himself, it will become something he has to reinforce and defend against intrusion by a sibling. When skills become territories, children can become tribal. If, instead, we make it clear there is scope for more than one artist, poet, pianist or tennis player in the family, and that each child has his own unique ideas, feelings and experiences to contribute which enrich this activity and make it personal, each one will feel free to explore and develop in every possible way.

The better we feel about ourselves, the more we will explore and discover, and feel enriched and fulfilled. How to help children to feel good about themselves, deep down, is the subject of the next chapter.

7

Help Them to Feel Good about Themselves

Children with good self-esteem feel good about themselves, and 'People who feel good about themselves', as the *One Minute Manager* tells us, 'produce good results'. They are better at making and keeping friends, because they are less defensive, less aggressive, feel likeable and are happy to compromise and give time and attention to others. They are better at playing, because they know what they like to do and feel safe about exploring ideas and places. They are better at working, because they are curious, can concentrate better, are able to take risks and are happy to try their hand at new things. It feels great to do well. Being confident in each of these ways helps to reinforce self-esteem still further. Success breeds success. The more confident we feel, the harder we can try and the more we can risk, so we can get even better, and the benefits spread. It is important to work at it.

If our child is feeling strong and doing well, then we have obviously got something right. We can feel pleased and we should step back, letting him get on with his life, watching from a distance. For children going through a bad patch, when confidence is thin and discouragement close at hand, what can we do to replenish those inner reserves and help them to restart? We can:

- make them feel loved and wanted
- give them experience of success
- avoid blame and unhelpful criticism
- offer a framework of positive discipline

Make Them Feel Loved and Wanted

All children start off adoring their parents. They need to believe in the people who brought them into the world and on whom they rely so totally. In return, they need to feel loved, respected, trusted and wanted. If they do not experience this, they will feel very separate at a time they need to feel part of something so important to them. Children who feel unimportant and insignificant to their parents become socially and emotionally isolated and certainly are not able to develop themselves to the full.

We can help children to feel loved and wanted by:

- keeping them safe and being sensitive to their anxieties
- enjoying their company
- valuing their ideas, skills and opinions
- spending time with them, talking, walking, playing and having fun together
- showing interest in the things which are important to them
- noticing when they do something well
- keeping them informed about things which affect them
- trusting them, their way of doing things and their ability to achieve things
- respecting their needs and rights
- giving them appropriate choices, so they can learn more about their preferences, find out what is important to them and have some say over what happens to them

. . . And the most important of these is time. Survey after survey is showing that children like to have their parents around, even if they are not actively doing anything with them. They like to see fathers as much as mothers. In Britain, men work longer hours than in any other country in the European Union. This means that they spend less time at home with their families. Although young children obviously need more direct, physical care from parents or other carers, older children need their parents' time, love and attention too. In research presented at a recent Council of Europe ministerial conference on adolescents and their families, even teenagers reported a desire to see more of their parents. When parents do not, or are not able to, spend much time at home, it seems to have a consequence. Headteachers have reported a fall in children's resilience in the face of learning blocks or other difficulties. In separate research, by Michael Rutter, children's resilience has been shown to hinge on three factors: a positive disposition (self-esteem, sociability and autonomy), a supportive family, and on other social support systems. Communities and families – and fathers – matter. Children feel good about themselves if they feel significant to the important people in their life. If we are not there, sometimes regardless of the reason, it can be hard to persuade a child that he is significant and thought about. Both his self-esteem and sense of direction will suffer.

Cheering Them Up with Presents

Giving children everything they ask for does not automatically make them feel good deep down. What children ask for is not the same as what they really want. Children need and want security, love, attention, to be listened to and understood and to feel that someone is committed to them. If they believe they have this, they feel accepted and acceptable, valued and valuable, significant and safe and worth caring for. They will have the confidence to present themselves as they are to others in their world. If they do not feel they have this essential love and support, they can learn to ask for toys and presents which seem to represent love and attention. If we are not careful, these gifts can become pay-offs to end the nagging or fleeting tokens of esteem rather than the real thing. As I have written elsewhere, presents are no substitute for presence.

Give Them Experience of Success

Find something they are good at. We should not ask if there is something our child is good at. Instead, we should ask what he is good at. Every child has something he does well which he can feel proud about. It may be dancing, football, drawing, constructing models and machines, climbing trees, knowledge of insects or animals, skateboarding, rollerblading, swimming or bicycle tricks. It may not be an activity-based skill. He may be good at thinking problems through, planning ahead or getting himself organised. He may understand quickly how people feel and have friends turn to him, be generous or good at choosing presents for people because he senses what others like. He may be a natural leader or able to sort out disputes. He may be good at languages, maths, sciences, history, English, environmental studies, computers, electronics or technology. All these subjects count. He may be dependable, reliable, kind, imaginative or have a strong sense of humour. It would be wonderful to have creativity, wit and humour more valued in schools because they are a life-line to us later.

The list of different personality features and 'intelligences' in the previous chapter will help to identify other strengths if you need further ideas. And if you are finding it hard to identify any redeeming features in your child, try and involve somebody else who knows him well because they will almost certainly see things differently.

Help Them Work Out What's Going Wrong

We can interpret successful progress in many ways. Success should not be measured simply by outcomes or results, comparing ourselves with others. It should also include our ability to manage the process of getting better. We can get a sense of achievement from having mastered a new way of doing something. The first time it 'clicks', we may not do brilliantly. Nevertheless, knowing that our progress is in our hands through our own effort and feeling confident and in control is highly motivating. Mastering the skill, or being able to respond constructively to our mistakes, is a milestone to be celebrated. A child needs to be able to work out what needs to go right. 'I didn't do brilliantly but at least I now know what I was doing wrong' is as worth applauding as a good result.

Focus on the Positive

One top golfer was talking about his route to the top. He was launched by his father, an accomplished golfer himself. His father's method was to put the ball right next to the hole and invite his son to hit it in. Of course, the son managed it because it was so close. Gradually, his father moved the ball further and further away. If he missed a shot, the ball was moved closer again. The father's technique was to build confidence through the experience of success, focusing on the positive achievements, not on failures. In this case, it certainly worked.

Self-development Versus Self-improvement

Children who have the chance to discover new skills and talents as they grow are very lucky. They learn more about themselves and the experience sets a pattern of self-discovery that will enrich the rest of their life. But it can be dangerous. It can go wrong when parents and children see the activity as 'improving', making the child better and cleverer, not only than others but also compared to how he was before. This again implies that how he was before was not 'right'. He then has to go on getting better, improving himself, making himself acceptable, trying one new thing after another. Learning should be seen as a process of self-development and self-discovery, rather than self-improvement to make someone more acceptable.

Avoid Blame and Unhelpful Criticism

If we are to encourage children's self-belief and help them feel good about themselves, we have to learn to cut back on destructive criticism as well as focusing on the positive.

In a survey undertaken for the NSPCC and published in 1997, 1,000 children aged between eight and 15 were asked about how they were treated at home. Just over one in four said they were 'often' criticised or told off but the numbers were higher in larger families, where parents had remarried or found new live-in partners and where parents had lower-paid jobs. Clearly, therefore, the situation worsens for children the more their parents struggle with stress. What is not so obvious or understood is the deep impact of criticism on children. The survey asked them about this. Those who said they were criticised a lot (and about half the children were interviewed with their parents present, so we should assume underreporting), reported being cuddled, hugged or kissed and praised less, and smacked, slapped or shouted at far more than the other children in the survey. More than one in three in the high criticism group said they would be less strict with their own children, compared with under one in four among the others.

How deep the hurt goes is shown in other answers, too. The 'got at' children were far more likely to be anxious – about things like bullying, falling ill or even having their home burgled – and far more likely to describe themselves in negative terms. Criticism, together with insult, shouting and other forms of punishment, clearly sends harmful messages to children about how likeable and competent they are, with predictable and damaging consequences for their wider emotional stability as well as their self-esteem and motivation. For too long, we have lived with the idea that only sticks and stones hurt. Words, we were told, are harmless. It is time to nail this lie.

We can appreciate that hurtful things said to our children in the playground will wound, and the damage done by verbal bullying is now better understood. It is far harder to imagine and accept the impact of our own harsh words. We can bully with words, too. It is emotional bullying. Constant carping and criticism will make a child feel he can never please and leave him believing there must be something wrong with him. Endless doing down and nagging will also make him lose confidence in his ability to think independently, do things his way and develop his own judgements. Constant criticism therefore saps independence, initiative and morale. Whenever he does something, he will be looking over his shoulder, hearing our voice in his mind, wondering what we will say next, and when, and which of his actions or comments will be next in line for our disapproval. Shouting, unwarranted blame and harsh, erratic punishment have a similar effect. They tell a child he is wrong and we are right. They challenge, and in extreme cases deny, love and acceptance. They generate uncertainty; there is neither pattern nor predictability associated with the wounding, which explains the more general anxiety felt by high-criticism children recorded in the NSPCC findings. Power lies with the perpetrator. All children thrive on the approval and acceptance of the two people who brought them into the world. If they fail to please, they feel they disappoint. A child who lives with criticism, sarcasm, insults, blame and punishment cannot avoid feeling guilty for the disappointment he obviously causes his parents. In such an environment, it is hard for any child to have and to hold on to self-belief, self-efficacy and self-direction, and to remain a self-starter.

If we have any inkling that this is what we do, we will want to brush it off with excuses. First, at the time, we will think our child has deserved the comment, which excuses our negative reactions. Second, we consider we love him underneath, feel certain he knows this and that this is what counts in the end. Third, we might notice his churlish and defensive reactions and think, therefore, the barbs did not penetrate – not realising the shield he has put up is a protective fiction. Fourth, the more we do it, the more we believe our child is used to it, accepts that we're like that, so is tolerant of our ways. Fifth, we might interpret any anger and hostility he shows to us as a personal attack and a sign that we are rejected, so why should we go out of our way to be pleasant to him? Sixth, if we sense he is hurt, men, especially, are inclined to believe it's time a child was toughened up with more of the same. But children who 'cannot take' even constructive criticism have, in fact, taken a bucketful of it. They are saturated with it, and can take no more if they are to have any energy left to protect their self-respect.

If, or more likely when, we get into these critical phases – for I suspect it happens, at least temporarily, to many of us – it says far more about what is going on inside us than about what our child is doing. If we are of a mind to, there are always things we can complain about in anyone's behaviour. To do so means that we are watching and judging, which means we are also controlling and untrusting. Either we expect mistakes, so we make sure we are ready to police the errors, or we somehow need to be judgemental – to feel 'in charge' when, deep down, we feel uncertain and directionless. Blame, anger, criticism and punishment help us to point the finger elsewhere, away from us, when we feel under pressure. But all of them undermine a child and will damage his motivation either to do well for himself or to please anyone else.

Positive Discipline and Self-motivation

Research shows that criticism and conflicts feature less in families which practise positive discipline. Some children need discipline to feel good about themselves. This may seem an unlikely statement but, by discipline, I do not mean unquestioning obedience and harsh punishment. I mean having clear guidelines and expectations for behaviour, defined limits to what is acceptable, a structure to the day and week, and learning to compromise with others. Children gain from the structure and security that it provides, the approving comments when they get it right, and the care and attention that supervision implies.

In its original sense, discipline has little to do with punishment. Its roots lie in the word 'disciple'. Teaching, learning, training and education are all included in many dictionary definitions. In this sense, discipline is wholly positive. It is also a social skill. It is about making sure children have the right skills to thrive and survive in today's world; helping children to manage and control their behaviour; restricting and prohibiting certain things, not to deprive children but to keep them safe and to teach them to think of others; creating a sense of pattern and rhythm that helps children to feel secure.

It is also practical and useful, and necessary for healthy social and emotional development. Positive discipline helps children to fit in. It creates consistency, predictability, trust and respect. It uses positive demands – telling children what to do instead of concentrating on the don'ts. It is one way in which parents can show their care and commitment. Discipline is not about wielding absolute power or commanding obedience like a dictator. The target should be discipline without dictatorship – based, instead, on fairness and mutual respect.

Positive discipline means:

- accepting discipline as a positive process necessary for social and emotional growth
- giving positive demands – and making our expectations clear
- focusing on children's positive behaviour – noticing and rewarding children when they have done something right, instead of criticising and punishing them for their mistakes
- behaving positively as the adult, modelling appropriate behaviour and offering praise, support and encouragement

Positive Discipline and Self-esteem

If children are to develop self-esteem, they need to be respected and to feel secure. Firm but flexible boundaries help us to acknowledge and respect our child's needs and feelings while asking for the same respect in return. Positive discipline therefore promotes mutual understanding and empathy, a key strand of emotional intelligence. It also promotes learning. Children who feel secure in their relationships learn to trust themselves and others enough to open up and develop themselves. Harsh and erratic punishment makes them cower, and a permissive approach only confuses, especially when it is interrupted by shafts of cruelty. If we give in, say yes, let children take the lead and offer a different answer each time, we do not give children a clear view of themselves or a predictable environment. More important, it gives no experience of learning to fit in and work with others – another vital part of emotional intelligence.

Positive Discipline and Self-discipline: the Links

We bring our children up knowing that one day we must step back. We don't have influence for ever. At some point, children become wholly responsible for themselves and their behaviour. We like to think they will manage their lives happily, co-operatively and productively. For that, they need a measure of self-discipline and self-restraint. Looking at what is happening in society, we are beginning to realise that self-discipline is far harder to establish if we have not had good relationships and helpful support and guidance early on. Positive discipline is the best foundation for self-discipline. Why?

For self-discipline, we need to be able to see a job through, aided by helpful habits and routines. We need to be able to put off short-term pleasure to reach longer-term goals: to put the waiting back into wanting. We need a personal code of behaviour, to be able to accept responsibility for the consequences of decisions that affect people beyond ourselves.

If early discipline is going to help, it will contain a child but not confine him. There has to be room for creativity and self-discovery and decision-making. There will be routines, but they won't dominate. There will be freedom, but within clearly stated limits. There will be clear consequences for unacceptable behaviour, to reinforce responsibility and to encourage forward thinking about how other people are affected, but not harsh punishment. Through support and encouragement, a child will learn how to stick at difficult things and how to survive short-term disappointment.

The Link Between Self-discipline and Self-motivation

Self-discipline sounds very like self-motivation. They both involve planning and thinking about why things might, or did, go wrong. Both involve willpower. But self-discipline is only part of self-motivation. It is like the filling in a sandwich, with self-motivation being the two slices of bread. One slice is the goal, because motivation involves purpose. The other slice is our courage, our decision to have a try.

To achieve anything, even learning to live within rules and limits, children need support and encouragement along the way.

8

Support and Encourage, Don't Control or Push

Children need our support and encouragement, but it can be hard to know when it spills over into creating false hopes or pushiness. Offer no support and encouragement and a child may have no incentive to try hard. Start to control and push, however, and our efforts may well backfire, with a resentful and exhausted child deciding to snub parents exactly where it hurts – by opting out of success.

Giving Them Heart

How can we know whether we are showing interest or being intrusive, whether we are being pushy or a push-over? We will judge this better if we think first about the meaning of the terms 'support' and 'encourage'.

'Support' means to take the weight of something, or take the weight off someone. In other words, like a supporting column of a building or a walking stick, it means sharing the strain, or burden.

'Encourage' means to give someone courage – the courage to try new things which, because they are new, lead into uncharted territory and may expose shortcomings. To learn, children need to feel brave. I was reminded by an educational therapist, Gerda Hanko, that 'courage' itself comes from the French word for heart, *coeur*. To encourage, therefore, means to give someone heart, to reinforce his self-belief.

'Support' and 'encourage' are both enabling terms. This is their essence. Parents who support and encourage help their children to help themselves.

Parents who control and push are doing something very different. Both control and pressure imply more direct involvement – even the exercise of power. They convey to a child:

- that he cannot be trusted to do something himself
- that he is not really acceptable as he is
- that in some way or other he falls short
- that he should be different, and in the way his parent would like him to be

The expectations and targets set, often designed to flatter and benefit the parent, will add burdens to the child, not relieve him of them. They will tend to sow the seeds of self-doubt, undermine his self-belief, and sap his courage, not top it up. They are more likely to discourage and dishearten, making it harder for a child to motivate himself.

Parents who support well:

show interest	• watch their child doing his favourite activity
	• try to provide necessary equipment – pencils, sports items
	• attend school meetings and events
	• ask about the results of particular things that the child has put effort into
offer help	• take their child where he needs to go
	• are available to discuss a problem
	• suggest planning and time-management solutions
	• try to answer questions
	• clarify, in discussion with them, goals and guidelines
listen	• to accounts of problems or successes
	• when a child feels discouraged
	• to anything he wants to tell them about his life
understand	• the child's own learning style and concentration patterns
take decisions	• when the child is unwilling, unable or too young to take them himself

Parents who encourage well:

show enthusiasm	• celebrate with the child when there's a success to share
	• share his excitement about his goals and dreams
	• don't knock what it is a child enjoys doing
show trust	• help a child to set his own, realistic targets – in a time frame he can manage
show faith	• believe in a child's capabilities and potential to achieve
	• offer him chances to manage things on his own
	• give a child hope, and the courage to try
mark achievements	• offer praise and rewards
value many skills	• to ensure each child has experience of success

When Push Comes to Shove

Controlling and pushy parents will tend to:

- finish tasks for their child because they are too slow
- manage their child's time very closely with busy, inflexible routines, making lists for them of things they have to do
- hover over children while they do things, implying they'll need help or correction
- get physically involved in homework; in effect, taking it over – rubbing out mistakes, colouring in, redrawing lines with a ruler, unpacking school bags in preparation
- give corrective advice very promptly, without either asking first if it is wanted, or troubling to find out the precise nature of the difficulty, so it is often misplaced
- be judgemental and critical, sometimes excessively so, even where there is a teacher or trainer monitoring progress
- point out mistakes immediately, without letting a child notice his error in his own time
- sometimes be competitive
- set a new goal as soon as the current one has been reached
- see any carelessness as a sign of future failure: 'You'll never become a doctor if you don't. . .'
- demand high performance, and punish – sometimes with emotional withdrawal – if a child falls short
- find a child acceptable when he does well, but not on any other basis
- talk frequently to other people about their child's latest successes
- tend to want the child to succeed to feed their own pleasure, not for the child's benefit

We can help children through a sticky patch when their interest or commitment wears thin, to get them 'over the hump'. We can make sure they are in a position to do themselves justice when they are competing against others and it matters. But then we should back off and put our child back in control. There are two rules of power which apply in relation to children. First, 'The more you use it, the more you lose it' and second, 'You bring about that which you fear'.

The more parents get involved because they fear their children may not make the grade – get in the first team, get top marks in their tests, or pass music exams with distinction – the more their offspring are likely to choose precisely that area in which to demonstrate their rebellion and independence. A prime example of this is someone who was threatened with punishments for anything short of an A and for failure to get into Oxford or Cambridge University. He complied all the way until he graduated, when he chose to work on an assembly line in a factory just to spite them.

If we shove someone too hard, he falls over. We should again take note of the best-selling management book, *The One Minute Manager,* which urges managers to, 'Help people reach their full potential: catch them doing something right'.

Interest, Not Intrusion or Inquisition

We often show interest through asking questions. How was it? Did you enjoy it? Was so and so there too? How hard was it? If we question the wrong things in the wrong way and for the wrong reasons, instead of appearing interested, we can come across either as spies from an enemy camp or as red-robed representatives of the Spanish Inquisition. Not surprisingly, children will then clam up.

Of course, how our questions are received depends in large part on a child's mood at that moment. Even with the best of intentions, we can end up with our heads bitten off. Teenagers are the most fearsome and protective of their long-awaited and often hard-fought freedoms, but younger children have their pride too. These realities apart, the fault can also lie with us. Where we have a hidden agenda for our questions, even young children usually detect it. We have to tread carefully.

Before you fire away, it is sensible to ask yourself a few questions first.

Why are you asking it?	Is your question straightforward, or are you collecting information to discover something else? Even worse, do you already know the answer, and the question is a tactic to trip them up or raise an issue? For example, asking 'When is your first exam?' when you know it is next week, is a way to suggest they do more studying. Better to be honest: 'Your exams start next week. Do you think you are ready for them?'.
How should you ask it?	The more questions you ask in a row, the more it sounds like a courtroom interrogation with your child in the dock.
Where should you ask it?	Wherever it seems natural, but personal questions are best asked when others will not overhear, and challenging questions in neutral space, not in the children's bedrooms.

When should you ask it?   When there is time for a considered
                           answer and discussion. Not when they are
                           just going out of the house or have just
                           come in and want to flop. After an exam,
                           for example, children like to be given time
                           to tell you when they are ready. We can
                           say, 'How was it, or do you want to tell me
                           later?'.

Leisure is for Pleasure

More and more children are going to classes, clubs and lessons after
school and at weekends. French, extra maths, ballet or dance; martial
arts, and various sports such as swimming, football, tennis and gym;
musical instrument lessons, religious classes and youth clubs are just
some of the activities which fill children's 'free' time. Some children are
so committed that they have no 'free' time left. They do something
almost every day.

Many parents fear empty time. In our increasingly pressured
society, it is easy to see 'down' time as empty time. We worry our child
will 'waste' time, watching television, mooching about, not 'developing'
himself. We also worry we may be badgered for companionship if
he has nothing specific to do. We tend to make sure our child is fully
occupied, when many children would prefer to do nothing very much at
all after a tiring day or week at school.

How can we get the balance right between giving our children the
opportunity to try themselves out, discover new skills and get really
good at something, without pushing them to become something they
might not want to be? A little shove can be in the best interests of a
child. One success story is a mother who let her two boys say no to a
range of activities offered until she saw that television was taking over
Saturdays. She felt neither had a specific skill he could feel proud of.
She enrolled them both in swimming classes, and dragged them along,
protesting. As they improved, their protests weakened. When each one
started at a new school with swimming available on site, the Saturday
lessons stopped. Each child was then selected for the school swimming
team, which delighted them both. Similarly, there are many professional musicians who credit their parents for making them stick at it during
the difficult times. However, it does not always work out like this.
One mother of two young girls under seven who took them to various
after-school activities against their will was becoming depressed by the
constant arguments. After attending a parents' discussion group on the
importance of play, she changed her mind and stopped every activity.

She reported home life was now significantly more peaceful and everyone was happier.

Leisure is normally understood as free time, time at our own disposal to do what we like with. It involves choices. What we choose to do expresses something about what we enjoy and who we are. Leisure is for pleasure, not pain. Play, which is also crucial for children's learning and development as we see in Chapter Twelve, is defined as 'moving about in a lively manner', 'amusing yourself', 'pretending for fun', and 'being involved in a game'. Pushing young children to attend after-school activities before they are ready or when they have had enough, and crowding out time for quality play (not television), will do little to strengthen a child's confidence, self-knowledge or experience of self-direction. They do not have to discover everything about themselves by the end of primary school. They have a lifetime ahead of them for this. A huge number of sporting, practical, craft and artistic opportunities is available to us as adults. Not every professional musician or sports person started young.

So how do we know when our children's leisure is giving them pleasure, when it might be in their longer-term 'best interest' even if they are complaining, or whether they are doing too much? It is not easy; but we can start by asking them, or taking account of their pleas when they say they are doing too much or want to stop something. We can also inspect our motives, honestly.

The Dynamics of Encouragement and Discouragement

Diagram 8.1 shows how a truly encouraging parent can be the agent of an encouraged and self-motivated child. An encouraging parent

Diagram 8.1: The dynamics of encouragement

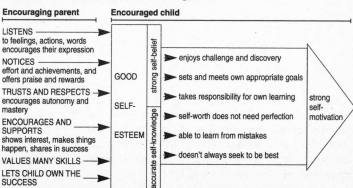

Diagram 8.2: The dynamics of discouragement

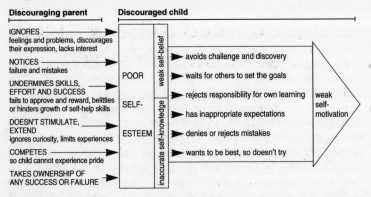

listens, notices good work and effort, trusts and respects his or her child's autonomy and need for rest, supports and encourages, values many skills and talents, and lets his or her child 'own' his own work and take the credit. These approaches nurture good self-esteem which feeds strong self-belief and accurate self-knowledge, two vital components of self-motivation.

The approaches and behaviours which children find discouraging, and which damage their self-esteem, are detailed in Diagram 8.2 which illustrates the dynamics of discouragement. Discouraging parents ignore feelings and problems and show no interest; notice failure and mistakes, and criticise frequently; undermine skills, effort and success by belittling them; fail to stimulate or extend their child; compete, increasing a sense of inadequacy and outlawing pride; take personal responsibility for their child's successes and failures; and punish acts which show initiative.

Praise is one form of encouragement. It is so important that the next chapter has been devoted to the subject.

9

Children Need to Be Noticed: Praise and Rewards

We all thrive on praise. It makes us feel good. I remember attending an aerobics class. There were at least 20 ageing mums in the hall, huffing and puffing. I was trying to bend as best I could when I heard our teacher say, 'Good! Well done!'. She was speaking to the whole group, but I couldn't stop myself feeling ridiculously pleased, taking her encouragement as personalised, positive feedback for my own efforts. Roy Hattersley, the author and former Labour Party Member of Parliament wrote something similar in the *Times Education Supplement* recently, recalling his best teacher and his awful first year at secondary school. It was a significant moment and he remembers it even now. 'But I had one big moment in that first year. Standing on the hideous windswept football field where we played games, Derek Walker asked the class "What is the answer to quick passing?" and I said, "Close marking". And he said, "Very good! That's right!" and even now as I tell the story and know I am boasting, I still feel the glow of pride that went through me.'

Why Praise and Encouragement are Important

Children love praise. It is one of the joys of living and working with children to see the pride and pleasure spread spontaneously and freely across their face, lighting it up, when they do something well and we show we have noticed. For almost every child, praise, incentives and encouragement are far more likely to produce the behaviour adults want to see than punishment and criticism. There are various common phrases which express this: 'the carrot works better than the stick', 'bouquets not brickbats' and 'a bike or a bollocking' for example. Yet despite this, it seems much easier and more natural to find fault and to criticise.

Children need to be praised for more than just the pleasure it brings or its incentive effect. It is not simply a bit of frippery, an extra, the icing on the cake. It actually meets some fundamental needs. As well as being properly fed and clothed, children need:

- to feel important and significant to someone; to believe that someone is committed to them and cares enough about them to cherish them. They need to be noticed and to feel likeable
- to receive clear, positive guidance about how they should lead their lives. They need to know what it is they should do, not what they shouldn't do
- to be enjoyed and to give pleasure – particularly to their parents. They need to hear and be told that they have pleased them and that their efforts to try hard have been noticed

Praise and encouragement, rewards, hugs, smiles and touches can fulfil these needs. Other responses from adults that achieve the same results are support, attention, appreciation and acknowledgement. We can show our appreciation and acknowledgement, and reinforce the behaviour we want to encourage, in more than one way. We can show it:

- in words
- physically
- with our time and attention
- with presents

Children who are ignored and neglected are, by definition, not noticed. They cannot feel any sense of being liked or cherished. Children who are only noticed when they are criticised and told off will not feel that they give anyone pleasure. They will only hear negative messages about their behaviour. They will learn what they are not supposed to do, not what they should do, or the reasons why. Indeed, if they are regularly ignored, children will have little reason to be good because it will very likely go unnoticed.

Many people find it very hard to give praise. Some simply do not know what to praise. Some feel uncomfortable with the words and the general activity itself. Some are also reluctant to praise their child because they think:

- praise will make their child big-headed
- praise should only be given for outstanding performance and effort beyond expectation
- 'normal' behaviour and work should not deserve special comment
- if something could be better, it should not be praised
- a child should be doing well in every sphere before praise is given for any one task, otherwise a child may think that everything is satisfactory and fail to improve where 'needed'
- they were largely responsible for the success by providing opportunity, enforcing a disciplined routine and so on
- it has not worked: their child does not accept or respond to it, so they give up

These reactions are very common. If we broaden our understanding of both what can or should be praised, and why 'praise' benefits children, we shall find it easier to use it more often.

Understanding Praise

Praise is about showing attention and appreciation, not judgement and conditional approval. Many people believe that praise is about telling children they are 'good', which involves making a judgement. Work, or behaviour, is judged to be either 'good' and praiseworthy, or 'bad' and open to criticism. But children don't want to be watched, judged and assessed the whole time. They want more freedom than that allows. Children flourish with praise not because they are thought to be 'good', but because it means their efforts have been noticed and someone has thought them important enough to pay attention. The words we use for praise and the times we give it should reflect our attention and appreciation, not judgement and occasional approval.

Praise is also about giving encouragement and accurate feedback. Many people think that praise is always good, or positive, while criticism is negative and unhelpful. Successes are celebrated, and often exaggerated, and mistakes ignored. This is not helpful. What children need is not phoney feedback but accurate information about the strengths and weaknesses of their work that signposts the room for improvement, encourages them to be responsible for making their work better and helps them to assess themselves. Praise and criticism should not be seen as positive or negative but constructive or unconstructive. Criticism can be constructive – when it shows the way forward – and praise can be unconstructive, for example when it is too general, is false or hollow, or when it sets standards of performance that are very hard to keep. We shall look at this in more detail in the chapters on managing success and failure.

What Can We Praise?

As well as academic skills, we can praise:

- the effort that goes into something (the process) rather than just the quality of the end product (the outcome)
- thinking skills, such as making choices, having ideas, using imagination, solving problems, thinking ahead and clearing up
- social skills, such as helpfulness, independence, understanding, kindness, sharing and resolving conflicts
- physical skills, such as being good with scissors, having sporting skills and successfully building and making things

The Language of Praise

Praise can mean both 'approve' and 'appreciate'. The difference is important. 'Approve', according to the dictionary, means to accept, confirm and commend. 'Appreciate' means to estimate the worth, quality, or amount of something; be sensitive to; esteem highly.

In other words, 'approval' implies the whole-hearted acceptance – of somebody, or something which that person has done, without gauging or measuring why we find them acceptable. 'Appreciation' follows an assessment, weighing something up, attaching value to different qualities, especially effort. Children need to feel approved of for who they are and appreciated for their skills, efforts and achievements.

We can show approval by saying such things as: 'That's lovely!', 'That's great!', 'Magic!', 'Brilliant!', 'Well done!' and 'You're a star!'. These are most effective when spoken face to face, with smiling mouth and eyes, and with an added gesture – a touch, or a thumbs-up.

We can show appreciation for something a child has done by saying such things as: 'Thanks for doing. . .', 'That was really helpful to me. . .' and 'You took a lot of time and care over that'.

It helps a child if the praise is specific. Describing something in detail

- proves you have noticed
- gives relevant feedback
- helps to avoid being unnecessarily and inappropriately judgemental

The essence of constructive praise is information and encouragement. It is neither hollow nor false. It is filled with detail. It points the way ahead. And it should leave as much room as possible for the child to judge himself. This does not mean we should never judge. We can say 'I think that is good, because. . . What do you think?', which is very different from a blanket judgement, 'That is good' or 'You are clever'. If children are to accept the idea of good enough success, they must hear it from someone else first.

Comments Avoiding Judgement

'Practising five nights a week showed real commitment.'

'That's an interesting painting. I like the colours you chose.'

'Thanks for tidying your room. It was a great help.'

'Well done for being selected. You deserved it because you trained really hard.'

'I am pleased for you that you got a merit. I know that's what you hoped for.'

'That model must have taken you a long time. Are you pleased with it?'

'That was a good idea of something to play. Thanks for letting Jo join in too.'

Comments Avoiding False Praise

Here are some examples of things we can say which are encouraging but straightforward. They do not pretend that things are perfect, or even good enough, when they are not. They make the scope for improvement very clear and encourage the child to understand any errors.

'What a lovely story. I like your ideas and the ending makes me laugh. I find that stories are always more interesting to read if they include how the characters are thinking and feeling as well as speaking; so next time, perhaps you can tell us something about your people's feelings and reactions. I know you can do that. Do you think you can? Good. I look forward to reading it.'

'There's lots in this report that you should be pleased with. For example, it's good that you're listening better in lessons and that your homework's not late any more. Well done. I'm very happy with it. I'm surprised, though, that you didn't do better in maths and science. I thought you were more comfortable with them now. If you know what you find difficult, we can try to find a friend or neighbour who can explain it again before term starts. Do you think the report's fair? Are you pleased with it?'

'I don't call this a tidied room. You've done well to put all your clothes and toys away but you're going to have to sort out that pile of paper and comics in the corner too before we invite a friend round. You can show it off to me when it's done and I'll bring you a cold drink to celebrate.'

'I am happy to take you shopping with me but to be honest I wasn't happy with how you behaved this time. It's not on for you to badger me constantly about having something to eat and then to nag about missing a television programme. I usually enjoy your company but I won't take you again if there's going to be a repeat performance.'

'This is much better. Well done! You got twelve sums right this time, which is much better than eight last time. Have a look at the four I've marked as wrong. See if you're making the same kind of mistake each time.'

Self-praise: Avoiding Conceit

Children are more likely to become independent learners when they feel comfortable with themselves and are able to assess their work, honestly, praising themselves when it is due. Praising yourself is often considered arrogant, big-headed or conceited, so we are reluctant to do it. Many people have the same reservation about praising their child. They believe it might make him cocky. It is part of the British reserve to be happier fading into the background than to have a fuss made of us. However, children deserve to be praised if they do well or have tried hard, and they have to hear it from others if they are to be able to do it for themselves.

To avoid making our child conceited, we can separate clearly the person from what the person has done, the deed. His achievements may be impressive, but they should not make us value him as an individual any more or less. As soon as the two become confused we enter danger-ous territory, especially if our own self-esteem comes to depend on his activities and achievements. If any child begins to brag unduly about his achievements, it may be because this is the only way he can value himself and feel accepted by others.

Bribes, Rewards and Incentives

Discussions between parents about the benefits of praise and its limita-tions usually come round to the subject of rewards, and the difference between incentives, rewards and bribes. It is helpful to look at the differences. We can then understand better how they can be misused and become a bone of contention, with children trying to negotiate bigger and better rewards before they agree to something.

Bribes

'Bribe' is defined in the dictionary as 'pervert (lead astray) by gifts or other inducements the action or judgement of'. Literally, then, a bribe is used to make someone do something illegal or wrong. When parents use the word, they usually mean an inducement to get their child to do something, legal and desirable, that otherwise they would not do. 'Bribe', in this context, is not really correct. The appropriate term is incentive, and is therefore quite legitimate.

Rewards

A reward, according to the dictionary, is a 'return or recompense for service or merit'. When we offer someone a reward, we might say, 'This will be hard for you. When you've had a go, I'll show you that I appreciate your effort'.

Rewards come in three forms:

- social rewards, such as verbal praise and time and attention, which may involve a special outing
- material rewards, based on money and what it buys, such as pre-sents and sweets, or even money itself
- non-material treats, such as staying up later, having a friend to stay or play, doing favoured and responsible errands for the teacher, being let off a chore, going to the park or swimming pool or, if the child is older, having a lift somewhere

Praise, therefore, is the adult saying something. It shows we have given our child our attention. But we can also give something else of ourselves – our time, which is an increasingly precious commodity, to talk, play, generally be around or go out together.

A reward can be agreed in advance, as an incentive, or it can be a surprise, given afterwards. A renowned 'father' of parenting, the American Haim Ginott, wrote 30 years ago: 'Rewards are most helpful and enjoyable when they are not announced in advance, when they come as a surprise, when they represent recognition and appreciation'.

Incentives

The dictionary defines incentive as, 'tending to incite, incitement, provocation, motive'. It can be the motive, or reason, for striving to achieve something, and it may provoke us into doing it when we otherwise would not. In other words, an incentive is usually conditional on some agreed target(s) being met, and is designed to act as a spur to effort.

Incentives come in different forms, too. There is the:

- 'sweeten the pill' incentive: 'What you have to do is hard and I can see you are running out of steam. When you have done it, I'll give you something to show I appreciate what you have done'
- 'kick up the backside' incentive: 'If you get all As, I'll buy you a new bike'. What this parent is actually saying is, 'I'm not sure you'll do it unless I tempt you with something'
- negative incentive or threat: 'If you don't pass all your exams, I won't pay for your driving lessons' or 'If you don't run this lap in under two minutes, you won't be selected for the team'

The first two forms are positive incentives, because the child will get something if he succeeds, even though the 'kick up the backside' will almost certainly have negative consequences because it implies lack of trust. The phrase 'a bike or a bollocking' suggests a prize if a child succeeds and a punishment if he doesn't. In this case, failure would result in a double punishment.

Threats sometimes work, but only sometimes. It is important to understand when they have constructive force and when they are likely to cause resentment and backfire. They are more likely to work where:

- the target is achievable, and one the child would choose for himself and has not had foisted on him
- the child has complete control over his performance and outcome
- the threat, or consequence, is relevant to the task under discussion

When Rewards and Incentives Backfire

Rewards and incentives can backfire, or distort motivation, for five reasons.

1 People can become controlled by rewards and incentives. Dr Howard Hall, Principle Lecturer in sports psychology at De Montfort University, explained:

> 'You can get people to do things through public recognition and incentives – giving them certificates, writing their names up on public boards if they are slower than a certain speed, and so on. But their behaviour will not reflect what is going on in their minds or their emotional responses. In one study, operating just such a technique, a group of swimmers increased their standards by 27 per cent. Incentives and threats seemed to work. However, nobody asked them why they stayed in the studied group. The reality was that they didn't want to face public humiliation and public identification, not because they wanted to improve. People can become controlled by the rewards, and end up continuing their sport for the wrong reasons. Some footballers, now, won't get out of bed unless they get paid a certain amount. This is not what sport is about.'

Children can become reward and praise hungry, too. It can happen either if they receive too much of the wrong sort of praise, or if they get none. If they develop an appetite for praise, they will not develop their own personal goals; they will lead their lives according to other people's values and not their own; they will always be looking over their shoulder at what others think, and try to please and appease; they will constantly think there is something wrong with their performance and feel inadequate if praise is not forthcoming; and they will become unable to motivate themselves when the attention or rewards are withdrawn.

Healthy praise and acknowledgement are therefore necessary for the full development of moral awareness. We are far more likely to become inappropriately dependent on praise and rewards if the approval of the key people in our lives is conditional, when we are accepted only for what we can do – when we succeed in some field or other – not for who we are.

2 When children are offered rewards and incentives, it prevents them from achieving something for themselves. In effect, the success is stolen from them because they are never able to prove they did it on their own, for their own benefit and for them only. Somebody I know expressed her fury at her father, years after 'A' levels, who not only promised her £50 for every A grade achieved but also required her to pay him an amount for each grade she fell below an A. She got her three As, but she has still not forgiven him for interfering and staining her success.

3 Incentives can reinforce bad or lazy behaviour. Children have to continue to be bad, to justify and ensure the continued supply of incentives. As Haim Ginott wrote, a child will be seduced into thinking 'I get what I want by keeping my mother thinking I'll be bad. Of course, I have to be bad often enough to convince her that she is not paying me for nothing'.

4 Children can start to negotiate their reward, and up the ante. This can easily happen with star-charts or sticker-based incentives. We can begin the process as a helpful gesture, with a warm heart. We want to give them something, to make it easier and even fun. But then it turns nasty, for example 'that deserves two stars, not one' or 'I'll do it for £5.00, not £2.00', and we end up feeling exploited. Why? Probably for three reasons. First, we can all get greedy. Second, where things become measured by money and expensive gifts, children will feel the bigger the present, the more they are loved. Third, it gives a child power. To argue and negotiate is an obvious way for a child to take control of a situation in which he feels manipulated by the parent's power to control him through money or other goodies.

5 When threats or incentives break basic rules of fairness, where the target is either unwanted or unreasonable, where the threatened punishment is irrelevant to the task or overpunitive, or where a child does not see how he can be certain of reaching the target, regardless of his effort, he is quite likely to weigh these factors up, feel insulted and resentful, and decide not to cooperate. Children of parents who habitually issue threats will have their standard responses. Many will simply ignore the threat, and their own potential in the process. Any additional stick waved over work and achievement will probably produce the same outcome, failing totally as a spur to effort.

Keep Praise Constructive

Praising children does not always have the desired effect. Most of us will have had, at some time or other, our kind words thrown back at us. 'What do you mean? It's awful!', 'No I don't. I look terrible!' or 'It's a horrid picture' are some familiar responses. The problem can lie:

• with the messenger: he is not trusted, not respected, or he is feared
• within the message: it is false, unqualified, given too readily, is manipulative, or it is double-edged
• within the child: he has low self-esteem, feels defensive, or has clear views which differ

When children have a very low opinion of themselves, they find it hard to accept anything positive said about them. They don't believe the compliments, and their defences are so strong that they will not allow themselves to be 'taken in' by what they see as undeserved flattery. Every comment will be inspected for the slightest sign of either insincerity or qualification to allow them to reject it. For further comments on this difficulty, see Chapter Twenty-two.

The Ten Principles of Constructive Praise

1 Praise the deed rather than the person

Children need to be approved of for who they are regardless of what they can do, and appreciated for their ability to manage any particular thing. If parents only accept and approve of their child when he shows talent and succeeds, they can create a treadmill of perfection for their child.

2 Praise the process rather than the product

When children are young, the process of trying is crucial. They cannot write, draw or manage all maths perfectly. At the beginning, what they produce matters less than the learning process. Later, however, it does matter. If something is wrong, or not good enough it is just that. Constructive criticism signposts the way forward and acknowledges and appreciates the efforts made by the child to that point.

3 Make it mean something – be specific

Describe in some detail what it is a child has done that is pleasing, so the child knows exactly what it is he has done right and what he should do again.

4 Don't qualify it, say it straight – and no sarcastic jokes

For best effect, praise should be given straight, with no ifs and buts, sarcasm, reminders of past failures or other put-downs to dilute its effect. 'You did well – surprising for an idiot!' or 'This homework is good. Why haven't you done such good work before?' would negate any positive effect the praise might have.

5 Keep it honest and real

False praise is as offensive to a child as it is to an adult. False praise blurs a child's self-awareness, undermines his trust in the adult and can increase fear of failure.

6 Keep it spontaneous: say it like you mean it

Say it straight away and not as an afterthought. Say it to the child's face, not as you turn away or from another room, so he can see your expression.

7 Don't forget physical ways to praise

Touch and facial expressions can talk too. Hugs, smiles and kisses are important. They communicate love, appreciation and wonder, and can seem less judgemental and more spontaneous than words.

8 Don't constantly move the goal posts

Let the child's achievement, at some point, be 'good enough' to deserve praise and the parent's pleasure and appreciation. The child can then relax.

9 Let the child 'own' the success

Don't say 'Great, you passed! I told you that if you revised using my method you'd do well', 'If I hadn't pushed you to go to the swimming lessons, you wouldn't have got this badge' or 'She's a great reader, but I read to her every night for five years'. Let the child take the credit for his achievement.

10 It takes four 'praises' to undo the hurt of one destructive criticism

American research has shown that it takes four 'praises' to repair the damage of hurtful criticism and unjustified blame. This is true for all of us, regardless of our age. Heavy criticism makes children feel bad, stupid and unloved. To preserve their self-belief, we must preserve that important 4:1 praise to criticism ratio.

10

Make it Safe to Make Mistakes

Mistakes are an essential part of learning, for all of us, and at any time in our lives. They are inevitable and are even important. It is vital that we grow up being comfortable with mistakes, so we are able not only to take risks and be creative but also to face and process what it was we did wrong in order to work out what it is we need to do differently. This is particularly true for children, who have so much to learn about both their own capabilities and the social expectations of the world they live in. I asked a primary school teacher in London's most deprived borough how he motivated the children in his class. Without hesitation, he said he first makes sure they realise it is okay to make mistakes. But adults, too, benefit from losing their fear of getting things wrong. A manager in the training department of a well-known company, when told about a few of the things to be covered in this book said, 'It's our biggest problem'. 'What is?' I asked, as I'd covered quite a few points. 'Making mistakes', she replied. 'We find it really hard to get our managers to move things on, be creative and use their own initiative, because so many are too afraid of making mistakes and getting told off.'

When a child makes a mistake it is proof that he is having a go and is at the frontier of his understanding and is extending himself. Mistakes provide useful feedback and can be used 'to illuminate the task', in Gerda Hanko's phrase. They tell a child whether he has understood something, worked hard enough or is using sensible methods or techniques. They tell a teacher whether his or her chosen teaching method has got the point across to that child, or whether the child is in the right frame of mind for learning. They can tell a parent whether their child is fully committed to developing himself in any particular area of skill, whether homework is being done in the best place or manner to maximise concentration, or whether something more serious could be distracting him. In other words, mistakes are outcomes – neutral pieces of information – which tell a story about why something has gone wrong. It is the story we need to understand.

Once the reason for the mistake is understood, it provides information for action. Nothing can be put right without knowing what was wrong in the first place. Most people do not realise they are making a mistake when they make it, otherwise it would not happen. For learning to occur, then, the error has to be pointed out, if it is not eventually spotted by the person himself. However, a balance does have to be struck. Too much unconstructive feedback on mistakes will destroy children's hope and belief that they are capable – the belief that they can do things well and make a difference. The trick is to let children know, in an encouraging, supportive and non-judgemental way, what they can do to prevent the mistake from happening again.

Zero Tolerance of Zero Tolerance

'Zero tolerance' is an idea which has its origins in industry. It was developed to improve the quality of manufactured goods which regularly left the factory gates full of faults. More recently, in both the United States and Britain, the term has been applied more widely, first to business, and now to crime and education. In education, it is no longer to be tolerated that so many children leave primary schools with reading and maths skills below what is normally expected. Of course, as many children as possible should be able to read and write, so they can carry on learning and fulfil their potential. But it is troubling that, even in places of learning, mistakes or misunderstandings are to be seen as shameful and not to be tolerated.

Childhood is a time of exploration, discovery and experiment. Children are bound to make mistakes in the general business of finding out about life, themselves and others. If failure is not only tolerated but also accepted, it will encourage growth. The experience of failure is very useful; it teaches us what works and what does not work. It helps us to build up a large dossier, or filing cabinet, of experiences which all combine to develop our common sense – that essential resource which helps us to adapt, survive and be practical when confronted with the unknown or unexpected. Learning to accept failure as a constructive experience helps children to realise they can survive setbacks, and that these need not be crushing.

Children's mistakes will involve their:

- behaviour – when they do not realise something is not allowed
- judgement – when they will not appreciate when to stop
- physical competence – when they will try to achieve too much and drop, spill and trip over things

It is important for children's development that they keep experimenting, exploring and taking appropriate risks. Learning requires resilience. If a child is punished, ridiculed or derided for mistakes and failure, and if an adult's expectations are too high – so that failure is a common feature of a child's life – that child will ultimately create for himself a zone of safety. This is a safe area within which he can operate comfortably, where he deals only with the familiar, with what he knows is acceptable or what he finds manageable. Once closed off within his safety zone, he may then become suspicious, or worse, of the unknown, and either numbed into inaction or impelled to behave disruptively by the challenge of the unexpected. If, on the other hand, he knows that mistakes are understood and even welcomed as part of the process of pushing back the frontiers, he will be freed from guilt, and released to be open, honest, and happy about trying out new skills and experiences.

We need to be tolerant of our own mistakes, too. Parents make mistakes – through ignorance of children's needs, through overconcern, through stress or marital and relationship problems, through having to meet other family needs which often conflict. If we can accept that we can get things wrong, and show that life goes on when it happens, we can teach our children by example that it is also safe for them to get things wrong too. The more demanding and perfectionist we are for ourselves, and the more we are crushed by a sense of failure for relatively trivial shortcomings, the more we send the message that mistakes are shameful – regardless of how positive we try to be in the face of our child's errors.

Of course it is right that children should work to achieve higher standards when they are underachieving. Naturally, it is appropriate for parents and teachers to say that certain behaviour is unacceptable and will not be tolerated. But unplanned mistakes are different from conscious acts of misbehaviour. What is important is not that mistakes of learning are never made, but that they are acknowledged and lessons are learnt from them when they happen. Within schools and families, there should be zero tolerance of zero tolerance for genuine mistakes.

Clones, Clowns and Clams: the Three Zones of Safety

Children who find mistakes uncomfortable, for whatever reason, have to find alternative ways of behaving and being that are easier to live with. They create safe retreats, or zones of safety. They become clones, clowns, or clams.

Clones become someone else. They model themselves on a key person in their life, someone who sets themselves up as right, good and successful. This person will often be very critical, intolerant and judge-mental, measuring everybody and everything against themselves – their likes, dislikes, talents and achievements. They find it hard to accept alternative approaches. Faced with criticism and uncertainty, a safe course of action for the child is to become that adult – or, eventually, any other adult who is currently in authority over them. This is the route not just to acceptance and a quiet life but also to becoming something defined as desirable. Unsure of themselves to start with, in the process they lose themselves completely.

Clowns become jokers. Some joke only through words; others use ridiculous and challenging behaviour to get the laughs. Children who are clowns are sometimes described as attention seekers as they seem to crave the spotlight. However, they are far more likely to be avoiding situations in which they have to risk being wrong. Ask them a serious question to test their knowledge or understanding and they will respond, often instantly, with a diversion. Any spoken answer will be silly. Instead of risking being wrong, they will cancel out the risk by creating a certainty – a ridiculous answer. Or to avoid saying anything, they may behave badly, drawing the questioner away from the question.

Clams close up. They decide not to risk themselves at all. Clams will be very reluctant to get into conversations and discussions, and won't volunteer answers. If they begin to close off their ears as well as their minds so they stop listening, they will then stop learning.

Clones, clowns and clams can also be clueless, when they cultivate an attitude of helplessness. They avoid risking mistakes by claiming they need help and guidance at every possible moment. They seek constant confirmation of their efforts. They seek help with choices. They feel safe only when someone is physically or metaphorically holding their hand. This 'learned helplessness', as it is generally called, is the opposite of the self-direction needed for self-motivation. If a child tends to behave in any of these ways, the best response is to build their self-belief and help them to realise that it is okay to chance themselves and to make mistakes.

Lying and Cheating

Anyone who is loath to make mistakes will also be reluctant to admit to having made any. He is far more inclined to lie and to cheat. Clones, clowns and clams are especially open to this temptation. Clones and clams will sit on their secret for some time, keeping things to themselves. Clowns may soon declare them, but in a flaunting manner as if to challenge, rather than as an act of contrition, because that is their style.

Lying, cheating, being secretive and stealing are related activities which often have complicated explanations. In simple terms, children lie:

- to get themselves out of trouble
- to present a different image of themselves (pretending they are something when they are not)
- to maintain a fantasy they have developed about themselves or their life

- to avoid facing up to an unpleasant truth
- to 'play' with others: to manipulate and confuse – and thereby control – them

  Cheating is a form of lying. Children cheat because:

- their self-esteem depends on success – they cannot accept any failure
- they cannot accept the consequences of their behaviour (no revision or practice)
- they are only acceptable to others if they succeed in those people's terms
- they want the reward that will be due very badly

  Cheating gives children no relevant feedback. Lying denies the mistake. They are both forms of pretence which prevent progress.

How Should Parents React?

If we discover our child is cheating, lying or keeping important issues secret, it is, of course, distressing. We will feel angry and ashamed. But it will not help to raise the roof. This will only make matters worse and prove to a child he was right at least to try to keep things quiet. I heard the mother of a 'problem' child say in a radio interview, 'You can't get them to tell the truth by roaring at them or smacking them. They'll tell the truth if you sit down and talk to them. That's the only way'. So we have to be calm, and we have to get to the root of the problem to stop it from happening again. In purely practical terms, lying and cheating prevent children from understanding and learning from their mistakes and from taking responsibility for them.

  The most helpful ways forward if we find our child is lying about marks or cheating is:

- let him know, clearly but calmly, that what he did was wrong
- talk openly about why he was so afraid to let us know or to do less well than he wanted to, remembering to ask if it had anything to do with our expectations
- encourage him to think about what it was he did which led to the errors (e.g. not enough effort, lack of understanding), so it can be put right, making further pretence unnecessary
- begin to rebuild our child's self-esteem and self-belief through the variety of measures discussed earlier
- consider the changes we can make to our expectations and reactions

  Make it safe for children to make mistakes and to take their time to master things. Let them tell the truth about their mistakes. Children need to be allowed to seek consolation for their mistakes, without the fear of being judged. Finally, always reward honesty about mistakes with understanding and practical suggestions.

11

Build Confidence Through Competence

Competence means the ability to manage something. When we feel competent and capable, our confidence increases. The dictionary definition of confidence is 'firm trust, an assured expectation, or boldness'. It also means having faith. When we are confident, we trust ourselves and firmly expect that we can cope. Our faith is based largely on past experience. So the bottom line is: children have to be given the chance to manage things for themselves and try themselves out if they are to become competent and feel confident.

Children's self-belief is also rooted in our confidence that they are capable. The more we do for our children, the more they get the opposite message and the less chance they get to manage themselves, practise tasks and get better at them. Of course there is a balance to be struck. If we expect, for example, a seven-year-old to get his own tea, he will probably think we do not care because we are asking too much of him. Children therefore need appropriate independence and responsibility to find out what they can do.

We have already looked at a wide variety of things children can try their hand at to develop new skills and competencies. Those who live in urban areas often have a vast array of after-school, weekend and holiday activities available locally, if they can be afforded. Schools are increasingly offering after-school clubs on site, and find that these have a positive, knock-on effect on their students' motivation. This is no doubt partly because students are feeling more positive towards school, and partly because the discovery of new talents is boosting their confidence. This chapter looks at how competence and self-direction can be encouraged day by day, from early childhood onwards, in a range of ways. 'Self-help' skills not only increase autonomy and personal confidence; they also encourage a self-respect and independence which is vital for self-directed learning.

Encouraging Self-direction

Children can be helped to manage certain things for themselves from an early age. When they are very young, they have an unstoppable drive to become independent, to gain some control over their life. They can be ferocious when they reject adult help. If we stop them from trying, or show frustration or disapproval at their clumsy efforts, we may damage their growing sense of autonomy and undermine their belief in themselves.

In Charge of Themselves

Self-direction can be encouraged in stages. The process can be represented by five circles, each one inside the other. The smallest circle is the child himself. Gradually, his responsibility will extend outwards to other spheres.

First, then, children can be given the chance to manage their bodies – feeding, toileting and washing themselves, brushing their teeth and hair and getting dressed.

Second, as they become more independent, their responsibilities can extend to directing their own thoughts and play.

Third, they can be expected to manage themselves more generally within the home, taking on some simple domestic responsibilities, organising their leisure time with friends within guidelines, having their own pocket money, managing their own homework, getting their school clothes and bags ready.

Fourth, they should direct and take responsibility for themselves outside the home – get themselves to school or friends and begin to shape their social life.

Fifth, they should begin to take on some responsibility for other people, at home and outside, for example baby-sitting, helping to run any clubs they are involved in, undertaking more important household chores such as cooking meals or managing the rubbish. This will develop important planning and time-management skills.

Some years ago, a friend was faced with a dilemma. Her daughter was six and asked to join her older brother on a week's residential activity holiday. When the friend telephoned to book, she found his fishing-based centre had no remaining places for six-year-olds. If she was to have such a holiday, it was to be elsewhere. She found out that there were places available in an alternative centre two hours' drive away from their home. When told about the new situation, her daughter still wanted to go, on her own, knowing no one. Should the friend use her 'better judgement' and tell her six-year-old she would not be able to cope; or trust her and book it? She let her go. On the fifth evening of daily telephoning, the youngster was tearful and wanted to come home. When she was collected the next day, she was busy with her activities, not morose. In no sense had she failed. She had had a good time but had had enough. She learnt new things about her abilities – and her limits. She asked to return the following year.

A boy was obsessed with electrical knobs, wires and plugs from the time he could walk. He was always turning televisions, vacuum cleaners, music systems and video recorders on and off, breaking some along the way. Friends and family were sometimes exasperated but he would not be stopped. Realising she had been defeated, his mother stopped telling him never to touch plugs and taught him how to handle them safely, and why and when electricity was dangerous. Before very long, he had graduated from plugs and knobs to extension leads, which even went on holiday with them, and not long after to building simple circuits, making light bulbs flash and so on. Aged seven, his family's new house was stripped down and rewired, replumbed and replastered, and he followed the electrician everywhere, in seventh heaven. Aged 11, he is now immensely practical and competent, mending neighbours' equipment and building complicated anti-burglar devices. His skill in electronics keeps him going when he struggles elsewhere. It gives him status and earns him respect. If his natural curiosity had been thwarted, and his yearning for competence ignored, he would have missed out on an important part of himself which has certainly increased his confidence.

In Charge of Their Learning

When children can manage themselves, they are much more likely to become independent learners and workers in and outside school. They don't need to be told what to do all the time which helps them to think for themselves and progress faster. They feel effective, responsible and in charge, which also increases their motivation. We have already seen that 'mastery' and self-efficacy are crucial to helping a child to be self-motivated, to be willing to learn.

Coping with Risk

The story above raises a stark and common problem for parents. How much danger, and at what age, do we let our children risk in the process of becoming more competent and independent? There are dangers inside the home as much as outside, though it is the dangers of traffic and strangers outside which tend to grab our attention.

Managing Dangers

There are many danger threats to child safety in the home, not only electrical equipment, but also knives, scissors, stairs, high cupboards, hot water, matches, cookers and maybe garden ponds – to name just a few. Older children will want to light candles, fires and barbecues. Should parents never let children near danger or risk hurting themselves, or is it better to teach children to handle potentially dangerous objects and situations safely? Children who learn to manage knives can help to cook. Children who help to cook learn to cook.

Keeping potentially dangerous experiences at bay may close down possibilities and limit the growth of competence. For example, many families with young children concrete over the garden pond, if they have one, to avoid the danger of a child falling in and drowning. Yet monitoring the pond and its animal and insect life safely can start an interest in nature which can be life-long. Someone I know who built her own wooden kitchen developed her interest in carpentry from collecting strange-shaped pieces of wood while walking in local woods in her teens. Perhaps times were different 30 years ago, but it is not unreasonable to suggest that the freedom to wander and explore helped to build the confidence necessary to undertake the project. If we obsess too much about the threat of danger, children may become overly fearful of new places and new situations and will not trust themselves to manage. They will be less able to take care of themselves and less willing to 'go' even when parents are ready to 'let go'. This has an effect on motivation. How can children have the confidence to meet educational and personal challenges if they receive constant messages about their inability to cope – even to walk – alone in the street outside their home? It is better to empower our children and give them the skills to survive, rather than cocoon them in the security of our homes. Confronting dangers and fears helps to keep them in proportion; hiding from them makes them grow and does nothing to help us deal with them if we ever have to.

Of course, some places are much less child-friendly than others. Living in crime-torn areas will change anyone's assessment of risk. In these cases, perhaps there is more need to encourage independence and self-direction within the home to compensate for restrictions elsewhere.

Reducing Risks

There are a number of ways in which we can help our children to grow up safely, competently and confidently. We can encourage independence and responsibility from the start and allow our children to develop common sense through experience. Travelling in cars or staying indoors is no way to develop life skills. We should walk and go on public transport more with our children so they can develop road sense and begin to detect the difference between normal or strange behaviour.

We must teach children coping and survival skills, such as always staying in public view and in populated areas. They must be allowed to learn to avoid back stairways, underpasses or subways; go out in a group and stay with people they and we know; keep their risk-taking in line with their physical strength and co-ordination; carry money safely – a small amount in a purse and the rest elsewhere; and plan ahead and think through alternative strategies.

Children must have the confidence to say 'No!'. In potentially dangerous situations, children may need to question and challenge. Those who are always expected to be 'good' and who always feel they need to please, will find it much harder to get themselves out of danger, either with friends or with other adults. They need to be able to size up situations and trust their judgement; have the confidence to be in a minority – sometimes of one; be prepared to be unpopular; and stand up to an adult whom they may have trusted previously.

12

Make it Fun, Relevant and Bite-size

We all enjoy doing things far more if they are fun, if they mean something to us and if we can see ahead to the end of the task. Commitments that seem endless or pointless are much harder to stick to. This chapter looks at some tactics we can use, including the use of computers, to spice up our children's learning to make it more palatable when they are finding it hard work or, dare it be said, boring. It also looks at the need to balance work with play so children develop in a well-rounded way.

Some people say that, hard as adults try to make things interesting and relevant, it is inevitable that some children will find some tasks or subjects dull and boring. Children, therefore, just have to get used to it. Doing well often involves slog. Life is not a non-stop party, and children are let down if we lead them to think that it is. Especially as they get older, they should be able to apply themselves when they feel disenchanted and not wait for someone else to make it easier by jazzing up the process.

Task commitment is, indeed, a crucial element in successful motivation. We have seen that children are at an advantage if they are able to persevere. The trouble with this argument is that it is fine for children who have a clear goal or watchful and supportive parents to help them through the tough bits. Those who don't are, by contrast, dangerously vulnerable. First, they switch off. As a result, they then fall behind. Finally, faced with an apparently impossible challenge, they opt out. It is not just primary school-aged children who need tasks to be fun, relevant and bite-size. Young adolescents need this too, to protect their futures. Learning, though, involves a clear contract. If work is made pleasurable and more accessible, children have to do their bit and deliver. Clear and consistent expectations about finishing school and homework and handing it in, and close monitoring and self-monitoring, will also be important to ensure all children have the chance to make the most of themselves.

Play as Work and Work as Play

Work can be fun, and for most young children, it is. This is not just because schools and sports teachers have taken on the message that children learn through play and so present tasks in a lively and relevant way. It is also because most young children want to learn. More than that, those who are ready are desperate to learn; they are like sponges. They soak up anything that is going. They get such a thrill from finding out what they can do and mastering tasks and techniques that they ask for work, even if it is not as sugar-coated as play, because they enjoy it. For them, work is play just as much as play is work. It is adults who think there is a clear difference between the two activities and hold children back from too much 'hard work'. But if children's thirst for knowledge and self-knowledge is left unquenched at this critical stage, they will be left apparently directionless which will undermine their motivation.

At the other end of the spectrum, there are some young children who are not so ready to develop. They need to be encouraged to concentrate and apply themselves. Making tasks enjoyable helps. People who think that play has less value than work deny some young children the chance to make progress in a way that suits them. In warm weather, children may like to read and work outside. Older children often prefer to work alongside a friend. Special cosy corners full of cushions can be created to entice children to read. Coloured sweets can make multiplication problems much more real. Odd and even numbers can be studied out in the street, with a child having to say what the next house or shop number will be. If you are stuck for ideas, teachers will be able to help.

Many children like to work in front of the television, though schools do not recommend this. It is almost impossible to think and write well while following a story line the other side of the room, looking up and down constantly. If there is no other suitable, quieter place in your home, you might ask if the school or the local library has provision for after-hours homework. If you show that you value quality work, your child is more likely to see it as important too. Think about how you could make work learning more fun for your child if he has lost heart.

Make it Relevant

A few decades ago, rote learning was the norm. Children used to learn maths, spelling, poetry, foreign languages, history and other subjects largely through drilled repetition. Modern educationists have questioned the value of this style of learning because, although some things stuck for some people, so much else was either forgotten sooner or later, or too abstract and never really understood, and therefore of little practical use. Information that has no personal or wider relevance is both harder to learn and easier to forget. Rote learning has its uses, but it is most valuable when it is used to reinforce teaching that seeks to explain things and make them relevant.

People who are born with a natural flair for a subject or skill are better able to cope with the subject matter 'in the raw'. Those without that natural talent need to make sense of the subject in their own and often very different way. It has to be made relevant to them. For example, how did you feel reading the chapter which reviewed management theories of motivation? Did you need to read the section that related each theory to parenting in order to appreciate the relevance of each one to you, or were you able to make the connections yourself immediately before the practical implications for parents were spelt out?

Most educators, and probably most parents, know the importance of making things relevant, but it can still be intensely frustrating when something that is blindingly obvious to us is so difficult for our child to understand and pick up. And when we do realise this, how do we know what to make it relevant to? What will make sense? A good guide is to start with what interests the child. For example, most young children like to eat. Anything to do with food, sweets and biscuits will whet their appetite for learning. To start an interest in words and reading, the names of the food a child is eating can be spelt out in magnetic letters stuck to a fridge or similar item where he eats. You can then play a game changing one of the letters to turn it into another word, thereby showing something about the sounds of letters and rhymes at the same time.

As children get older, they like to know why they are learning or doing something. They ask why something is going to be useful to them. Foreign languages are now taught not through grammar and recitation but through likely holiday experiences. History is often introduced to children through a short study of local or family history. GCSE and 'A' level projects often give young people the chance to follow an angle that interests them. For children who enjoy computers, 'relevant' might mean finding some software on the subject, as discussed below. At the very least, we should take the trouble to explain to our children why procedures or knowledge need to be mastered.

Making it Bite-size

Any task is more likely to be completed, and completed well, if it is planned in such a way as to appear manageable. Children are easily put off by tasks that seem easy to adults but daunting to them. Breaking projects down into bite-size chunks can remotivate them. And most children will find it even easier to apply themselves and show determination if the stages of the project are recorded on a wall chart and can actually be ticked off as they are completed, so progress is visual.

Case Study

An 'A' level student had let work slip, badly. She was 26 essays behind by the end of her first year, having written only two from her three subjects during the whole year. Her school was threatening her with exclusion from the second year of the course if she did not present 16 of the missed essays by the start of the autumn term. She had six weeks to do them in. She broke down, thinking the task was impossible as she had a two-week holiday booked, but bite-size chunks came to her rescue. Her father sat down with her and together they wrote a study schedule. For each essay, time was allocated to reading, planning and then writing. It was tight, but do-able if, and only if, she stuck to the schedule. She made it, and went on successfully to university. She knows that without her father's help, the story could have been very different.

Case Study

It was six o'clock in the evening, the day before the start of a new school term. Ruth, aged 10, had not yet got her things ready. She was expected to do this and she knew it involved such things as checking through her pencil case, sharpening pencils where necessary, getting her sports kit and uniform together. When reminded of the time, she wailed that there was too much to do and she could not cope. To help her see the task as manageable and not to get frazzled, she was given a small pad of sticky-backed notes so she could write a list of the jobs involved. She chose to write each one on a separate sheet. She fixed them to the wall and got going, peeling the sheets off one by one as each task was completed. Her mum could so easily have taken over, done most of it for her, or even made sure she did it earlier. This way, she had to face up to the consequences of her delay and it was a practical lesson in responsibility and self-management.

Remember, bite-size chunks:

- help with personal planning
- help with time management
- help with organisation
- are an important tool of motivation

The idea of using lists, schedules and plans can be introduced to children when they are quite young. We can:

- show their usefulness by example – with holiday packing and shopping lists, and personal reminder notes
- introduce them when they have to put toys away – inviting them to choose which ones they will do in which order and ticking them off as they are done
- encourage children, as soon as they are old enough, to write or compile their own lists

However, there is a balance to be struck, as there is in so many things. First, people can become list-dependent. We need to be able to cope in emergencies when we don't have time to write lists. Second, to be most effective, plans need to be 'owned' by the person carrying them out. Lists written by parents for children can undermine their sense of being competent and trusted. Third, there is a danger that parents will go too far in mapping out things for their children, at the expense of children learning through their own experience.

Making it Byte-size: Using Computers

Computers can be great fun, and not just for the games that can be played on them. It is exciting simply exploring what they can do and feeling in charge. Children are naturals at computers. Once they get over the first hurdle of how to start, they are in tune with the technology, which can be part of the appeal. It's one of the few areas where they often know more than adults and it makes them feel good. Computers may be fun, but what effect can they have on children's motivation?

The answer almost certainly is, it depends how they are used. There are many good educational software packages which develop children's logical thought, decision-making and reasoning skills, as well as others which focus on reading, spelling and maths. For children with learning problems, there are particular advantages. As a special guide on support for learning difficulties produced by the Parents Information Network (PIN) explains, computers give children the chance to: change, correct and develop work, so mistakes can be managed and don't require complete rewrites; experiment in freedom; be tutored by something non-judgemental and with infinite patience; and present work in an exciting way, using sound and pictures as well as words. In other words, the combination of gaining knowledge, developing skills, seeing their work look 'official' in print, receiving instant feedback on performance, overcoming obstacles and being in control can help children grow in confidence. Any child who is computer literate will certainly feel more competent and able to use a range of machines and accessories. Computer buffs have a status of their own when they know enough to help straighten out their friends', parents' and even teachers' computing problems.

There are two possible downsides to pushing computers. The first is that their use needs to be kept bite-size, because children can get hooked. A primary school teacher told me she was surprised at the number of eight-year-olds in her class who listed cutting back on their daily computer game playing to half an hour as their new year's resolution. I wonder if they saw the television as a similar 'problem'?

Children who get caught up in computers and spend too long in front of screens of any description can fail to learn vital relationship and emotional skills, through friendships and time with parents, and fail to develop a healthy range of interests. As well as this, any dependence on the instant feedback and excitement of computer games can make the classroom and the teacher seem boring, and their work skills weak compared to their games skills, thereby lessening, not increasing, motivation to learn in school or elsewhere.

The second downside is that using computers for non-educational games, either excessively or moderately, will not teach children the IT skills the National Curriculum states they should acquire. Some games are very sophisticated, and are sometimes referred to as 'edutainment', but others have little to do with presenting information, storing it, communicating, handling and searching information, or measuring and controlling external events. Used well and wisely, however, computers at home can support learning, help iron out problems, encourage independent working and new ways of thinking, be the starting point for getting a demoralised child back on track and offer hours of family fun if they are kept where everyone has access.

Independent advice for parents on how to get the best from computers is available from two organisations. Parents Information Network (PIN), already mentioned, has two free easy-to-read guides, *Buying a Home Computer* and *Buying and Using Software*. Membership will give access to regular mailings and more in-depth information about the range of software available, from those designed to match the National Curriculum – and which can support homework, to packages for home learning which offer more depth and breadth than schools can provide. PIN has developed its own Quality Symbol to guide parents in making relevant, quality purchases. The National Council for Educational Technology (NCET) has published two books, *IT Works* and *Learning Together with Computers*. Contact addresses for both organisations are listed at the back of the book.

Work, Rest and Play

No one can work all the time without becoming slightly unstable and a huge bore. In our long hours culture, in which lunch hours and even evenings are disappearing let alone regular refreshment breaks, we are pushing ourselves to the point of collapse. Stress levels are reported to be higher than ever. At work now, people are monitored and measured; made responsible and accountable; evaluated and assessed. There is no let up and it cannot go on. We seem to be in danger of doing the same to our children. To guard against Far Eastern suicide rates taking hold here, we must ensure that quality work is balanced with quality rest and play.

The Importance of Play

Children with lots of experience of play have a head start in life. It certainly helps with learning, at many levels, and with motivation. Through play children try themselves out and find out who they are and what they can do, so it develops self-understanding. Physical play helps children to become fit and healthy and feel proud of their bodies, so it develops self-belief and competence. Having fun gives us energy for the more demanding parts of our lives; and how we choose to spend our leisure time is an expression of who we are.

Children of all ages need to play, including teenagers. It encourages a 'can do' and 'want to do' attitude to life because it protects, cherishes and develops each individual's natural:

- curiosity, and the excitement and wonder of discovery
- creativity and flexibility, through exploring fantasy and solving problems
- confidence, through self-direction and initiative, and because trial and error is safe
- concentration, through the tendency to become 'lost' in play
- co-operation, through playing with others, learning to take turns and compromise

Play also develops the skills children need to do well. Games and play encourage children to:

- talk, making it easier to express themselves in words and on paper
- read, where the games involve shapes, sounds, matching and reading words
- use numbers, where children count, use dice, or keep scores
- write, through scribbling, drawing, handling objects and gaining manual control
- socialise and reflect, and understand the needs and feelings of others
- apply themselves, where games encourage memory, listening and concentration
- plan ahead and organise, as they decide what they need to do to make something happen
- problem solve and compromise, as difficulties arise
- accept consequences, through clearing up afterwards

Play and Children's Development

As children grow, their play develops and changes. They begin by playing alone. They then progress to playing independently but alongside one another, moving on from that stage to playing co-operatively in pairs or threes, at about the age of three. Co-operative play involves increasingly sophisticated social skills which very young children do not have. Learning to wait, share and take turns, coping with rules and winning and losing, is also hard. Children start to do this from about the age of four, though it can take a few years for them to become completely comfortable with losing in competitive games of skill and to relish rule-governed challenge. Some people reach adulthood without getting this far.

Adolescence: Motivated to Party

It is one of life's unfortunate mistimings that adolescence coincides with critical school examinations. Just when 'the system' demands that young people get their heads down and prove their academic worth, they are wandering about, wondering whether they are worth anything – sometimes going to enormous lengths to try themselves out and piece together a notion of themselves. They do this through friends and through play. They also use play to experiment with risk and prepare for their future roles. They will often gather in larger groups, which demands even more advanced planning and social skills such as negotiation, compromise and team work. Younger teenagers will often have an intense relationship with someone of the same sex before getting used to having the opposite sex as friends and finally moving on to the traditional couple relationship. Work and other hobbies may slip in their order of priority and their only apparent motivation is to party, but at least they are developing some useful organisation and relationship skills in the process. Provided they get enough sleep and do not appear to be losing their direction through irresponsible use of alcohol or drugs, it is important that they have a social life. They cannot be expected to work all the time, just because we are worried they might not make the grade.

The 80:20 Rule

There is a familiar saying that if something is worth doing, it is worth doing well; but that depends. It depends on how long it is going to take and what else could be done with the time commitment involved. There is another saying, or rule, used in management called the 80:20 rule. I prefer it to the traditional saying. It comes from an understanding about trade-offs between the effort and the result: in management-speak, input and output. The first 20 per cent of our effort in any project is usually the most effective and can get us 80 per cent of the way there. The more effort we apply thereafter, the less effective that effort will be. If we arrive at a situation where we have to put in 80 per cent more effort to improve it by 20 per cent, the effort is not worthwhile, especially if it is at the expense of starting some other task or activity, or even leisure. Teachers sometimes express concern about the amount of time certain GCSE students devote to their course assignments. The marks are allocated in such a way that the 80:20 rule often applies. They wish their students would let up and, instead, have some fun to help them through this testing time.

Regardless of age, 'quality play' is any activity which:

- uncovers, or builds on, an individual's inner resources for coping
- develops powers of understanding, and therefore intuition
- deepens and enhances the sense of self
- offers scope for experimentation and personal development
- enriches imagination
- develops social skills
- explores and expresses feelings, thereby developing empathic skills

The Importance of Rest and Relaxation

Children need rest time as much as adults do. Rest is not necessarily the same thing as sleep or leisure; it means stopping, having quiet time in which to think, reflect, relax and let go. Sleep is time when, by definition, we do not consciously reflect, though we almost certainly do in dreams. Relaxing through leisure is usually interpreted today as rushing about, blocking out thoughts of work with an alternative activity. There is merit in that as it can refresh mind and body. But winding down normally means slowing down, mentally and physically, to a point from which we can explore our inner selves and learn to feel at ease with who we are. This gives us a second wind, partly because we use this time to sort out all manner of issues, whether we are aware of it or not. We all need, in the poet T S Elliot's words, 'a still centre in a turning world'.

I have seen children struggle with problems – in particular arithmetic problems and with playing a piece of music – and, without further practice in between, return after a day or two to perform each task perfectly. Rest made perfect, not practice. The difficulty must have been mulled over, consciously or unconsiously, while the mind was resting.

Children who are on the go all the time and who are not encouraged to take time out are likely to have a poorer sense of themselves and less opportunity to process problems subconsciously. Rest regenerates. Perhaps this is why all the major religions incorporate a weekly day of rest in their rituals.

Encouraging Rest

All children need times when they do absolutely nothing. They need to be allowed to rest, so try to:

- identify their preferred way of winding down, and give them some time on their own
- encourage them to do this, especially after school or other times of demanding mental, emotional or physical activity
- respect their need for their own quiet space, even if they choose somewhere other than the family home if this is too busy and bustling for them
- encourage times of quiet togetherness, as a family or between you and each of them
- help them to know how to relax themselves, and not simply rely on other vehicles such as sport or television

13

The Motivating Power of Choice: Encouraging Responsibility

Choice is a significant feature of life today. Most of us have much more choice about how we lead our lives than our parents did; and the choices before us continue to grow. Provided we have the money to make them a reality, we have a vast array of clothes, food, shampoos, beer, colours to paint our homes, holidays and television channels to choose from, to mention just a few areas. Our sense of fairness tells us that if we enjoy variety and opportunity, children should have choices too. Most of us want it that way. We like to please our children, to give them what they want. Having choice is a symbol of freedom and personal expression, and allowing choice is a symbol of caring.

Choice, though, is about much more than freedom, self-expression and caring. The very act of choosing makes us feel more personally committed to whatever it is we have chosen. We feel more involved. Having made something happen, we also become responsible for the results of that choice. Most people find this feeling of involvement and control highly motivating. Any child is going to be more inclined to strive for a goal that he has chosen for himself than one given him by someone else, and happier about getting there his way rather than someone else's way. Choice is a powerful motivator; but it must be used wisely.

In this chapter, we shall look at ways to use choice to increase motivation; use choice to encourage children to behave more responsibly; manage choices, because too much choice can undermine its value; and balance personal freedom to choose with the advantages of providing structure, obligations and routines.

Using Choice to Increase Motivation

A friend of mine fell out with her father when she was a child over how to do a jigsaw puzzle. It would be a trivial story if this occasion was not the moment that she separated herself from him psychologically and emotionally. He insisted that she start the jigsaw by picking out the edge pieces and complete the outer frame first. She wanted to work on sections that took her fancy and join these blocks together as they were finished. He refused to let her do it her way, insisting that his way was best. It was an empty victory. Was the argument over the method really worth the outcome? It certainly turned her off jigsaws.

Howard Hall, sports psychologist, considers it essential to put people in charge of their own improvement, and let them decide how to proceed. 'Improving skills is the target', he explained. 'There is more than one way to get there and it's up to each person how he does it. People then realise they can enhance their self-esteem through their own, controllable, efforts.' The England cricketer Darren Gough, talking about 'professionalism' in his book, reinforces this point: 'Professionalism is not about everyone following the same rigid routine. Individual players require individual training routines, to suit both their character and their role in the side'.

Joan Freeman, an educational psychologist, makes a similar point in a book on gifted children, her speciality. 'So much research has shown that motivation and achievement levels go up when children are encouraged to take more control over their classroom activities.'

Provided the expected results are achieved, it does not matter which route is chosen. This proviso is important; it is where responsibility comes in. If the chosen method is not working well, it should be adapted or another method tried. What works for one person might not work for another, so it is not usually helpful to dictate any method as 'the best'. For example, is a one-handed or a two-handed backhand tennis stroke best? Different players think differently. However, a child should not be allowed to stay with his chosen method if it is clearly not working, just because it is his choice. He has to learn to assess his progress and consider whether his approach is effective. Learning to evaluate in this way is a more valuable lesson for the future than reaching a target in the fastest possible time, on a route set by someone else. In any case, in the long run, the fastest method will be one a child understands, feels in charge of and takes responsibility for.

Using Choices to Encourage Responsible Behaviour

Choices can be given to children at home to increase their motivation to behave responsibly. 'You can watch television for one hour tonight – you choose the programmes' is far more likely to get co-operation than saying, after one hour's watching, 'That's enough. Switch it off right now'. The same tactic can be used with homework and other evening commitments. 'Tonight's a piano practice night. You can do it before tea or after. Which would you prefer?' Similarly, if television seems to expand to fill apparently infinite time available, a useful tactic is to suggest your child writes down a timed plan for the evening, to include his favourite television programmes and tea. Deciding what he is going to do and when not only makes him feel in charge, less burdened by commitments and more responsible for delivering, it also teaches important time management and planning skills.

Case Study

One year, Sarah devised a cunning plan to involve her teenage children in the Christmas Day cooking preparations. Instead of allocating tasks, which from past experience would have got her nowhere, she wrote out a timed plan of all the jobs which needed to be done. She filled in her share, and what visiting relatives had agreed to bring and do, and simple tasks for the younger children. She then invited the older ones to select their jobs. They could see that the allocation was fairly distributed. They saw the times when each thing needed doing and they made their choice. The list was pinned up a few days before where it would be seen easily. On the day, everyone was out of bed in time and Christmas passed without a nag, hitch or sulk.

Choices and Consequences

Behaving responsibly means more than being 'good'. It means thinking through the consequences of behaviour – what happens if and when – and accepting that we have a choice, play a part in and contribute to what happens. This is something children develop over time. They cannot think ahead when they are young. Gradually they learn the difference between acceptable and unacceptable behaviour, and after that they are able to think further ahead to longer-term consequences. This is why the age of criminal responsibility is set at 10.

We can encourage children to become aware of consequences through making it clear they have a choice about how to behave and spelling out the implications. For example, 'You have a choice. You can either do you homework now and be free to play with Darren after tea, or you can watch television now, leaving your homework 'til later and miss playing with Darren. Which is it to be? I'll give you three minutes to think about it'. Alternatively, we can say, 'When you have done your homework, then you can play'. This is matter of fact. Choices must not be presented as a threat. 'If you don't do your homework, then you will have to stay in' may come across as a challenge and might be ignored. Staying in will be seen as a punishment rather than a consequence of a child's own choice for which he must take responsibility.

Learning to Wait

The suggestions so far have involved giving children a choice about how something is achieved; in other words, about the means. Children can also be involved in choosing what they want to have or achieve, which is about ends. Here we have to be a little more careful. It does not always benefit their motivation if they get things too easily.

If we choose something, it usually means we want it. The more we want it, the harder we are going to work to try and get it. Choice, then, is about wanting. But it is often hard to decide how badly children want something. Young children, especially, are renowned for wanting almost everything very, very badly, now. They have neither patience nor judgement. You buy them what it is they can't bear to be without and then, after two days, they have forgotten they own it. When they get a bit older, there is nothing more frustrating than to respond to their pleadings, sign them up for this activity or that and buy the required outfit or equipment, to find after one term they have lost the bug. It is part of all children's development that they must learn first to wait, and then to judge – whether it is a wise purchase, good value for money, something that is worth doing, that they will enjoy and so on. Learning to wait is important. Impulsive behaviour often gets us into trouble even though, in moderation, it can be fun and exciting. For most of us, it is only after we have wanted something for a while that we realise how badly we want it.

As we saw in Chapters Two and Seven, self-motivation and achievement involve thinking ahead, and being able to plan and wait for the prize of success: putting up with short-term pain for long-term gain. If we want something very badly, it does not necessarily mean we should get it quicker. It might mean we should be content to wait for it, and then we really know. In my childhood this was called 'delayed gratification'. It was thrown out in the 1960s by children who felt stifled by it, a rejection reinforced by a well-known credit card company whose slogan was 'take the waiting out of wanting'. We may be helping children's self-motivation and self-discipline if we start to put the waiting back into wanting for choices about certain wants or goals.

Keeping Choices Manageable

Children need choices to become responsible and to discover themselves, but they still need limits. The choices offered should be appropriate and managed, because too many choices can be worse than not enough.

The great thing about choice is that it helps children to:

- develop their self-image and identity, because choice clarifies what they do and do not like
- accept restrictions elsewhere, because they do not feel put upon all the time

- become responsible for their behaviour, because if they choose to behave inappropriately, knowing it to be wrong, then they must face and accept the consequences of that decision

Too much choice, though, can undermine each of these advantages. Too many choices can make children:

- feel insecure, through having too much control
- develop little sense of personal priority or judgement, because they can have everything
- become intolerant of any restrictions, anywhere
- become insensitive to other people's needs, and unwilling ever to take a back seat
- lose sight of the boundaries and limits to acceptable behaviour, because the boundaries become fudged
- take less responsibility for choices and actions, because unpleasant consequences can be side-stepped with another choice – 'Whoops! Sorry, wrong choice; I meant this one.'

Choices can be managed by offering a few, suitable, ones. For example, 'Would you like to come out with us or go round to Jamie's?' is better than 'What would you like to do about us going out?' because it closes the option of staying at home alone if that is not suitable. 'Would you like me to read a story to you, do a jigsaw or play cards together now?' is safer than, 'What would you like to do now?'.

Where choices cannot be closely managed, which happens particularly as children get older, children may choose friends, activities or buy things we would rather they had avoided. What can be done then? Much of the time we can and should do nothing for this is part of letting go, especially if they have spent their own money. As long as they fulfil their responsibilities to the family and school, and accept the consequences of any decision, the choice is theirs.

The Freedom to Be Creative Versus Structure and Routines

The more choice children have, the less room there is for regulated and ordered living, and vice versa. Self-motivation requires both, so a balance needs to be struck. Creativity and self-direction cannot thrive where routines rule, where everyone is expected to do something in exactly the same way at the same time. But too much freedom about how and when things are done can mean they never get done at all. Children can be given so much rope that they hang themselves, as the saying goes.

It is this dilemma which has troubled our politicians. They despair of our schools which, they say, encourage too much choice and diversity, and look instead to schools in the Far East which get much better results through discipline and routines, despite large class sizes. The interesting thing is that Singapore, one of these Pacific Rim countries, considers its students lack initiative, flexibility and the skills necessary to adapt in a changing world. The Japanese, also in the Pacific Rim, used to be famous for exploiting ideas born elsewhere because their schools did not create innovators. The Singapore government recently hosted a conference for other countries in the region to discuss how they can equip their students to become more creative and independent in their learning so they can self-start as adults, and it invited university professors from North America and the UK to offer advice. There are no easy answers. However, managed choices, which achieve freedom within boundaries, achieve a good balance. It is hard to get it right, and most of us are never sure that we do.

The Motivating Power of Necessity

Powerful though choice can be as a motivator, we should not forget that necessity has its virtues too. If we have to do something, we tend to get on with it. This is not quite the same thing as being told to do something, though even this can work in the short term. If we see for ourselves that something has to be done, we are likely to do it more willingly than if someone else directs us to act. For example 'You're off to camp first thing tomorrow and you haven't packed yet. You'll need an early night and time to do any washing. When do you think you'd better start?', to which the reply is likely to be, 'I'd better start now'.

14

Greater Expectations: the Importance of Challenge

People tend to live up to – or down to – their reputations. They perform according to expectation. The truth is well documented: high expectations produce good results; and low expectations produce poor results. It is also true that people tend to produce their best when they are working with – or, if it is a sport, playing with – others who are slightly better than themselves. Quality 'players', in the workroom, boardroom or on the sports field, lift our game. The research mentioned in Part One was clear: high expectations motivate. Adults and children like to work with others who expect well of them, because that is when they give of their best and experience pride in their progress.

Underachievement in school is thought to be largely the result of teachers who have lowered their sights too far. Worried that they might place the goal posts too far away and 'cause' too much failure, many teachers have been setting targets that are over-easy. Yet children need to be stretched. Doing well when the challenge is easy is neither exciting nor rewarding. Indeed, it can be demoralising and even turn children off learning altogether.

Case Study
Gemma, aged 6, brought home her school report on the last day of term. She sat down on the sofa next to her mother so they could look at it together. It was complimentary about every aspect of her work and social development, so when her mother had finished reading it she said how well Gemma had done and how she particularly valued her obvious caring for others. Gemma turned away, buried her face in the cushion and, on the verge of tears, declared it was 'a stupid report'. When she was asked what she meant, she choked, 'What's the point of telling me I'm good when it's so easy?'.

Placing the Goal Posts

Challenges must tempt children to develop themselves, not threaten them and put them off. Children clearly need to be challenged, but these challenges must be realistic and manageable. A target set too high is as unhelpful as one set too low. Challenges need to be pitched carefully, at a level that will motivate someone to perform at or near his current best: his 'achievement frontier'. Goal posts placed beyond reach become daunting and off-putting, sapping self-belief and resolve. Placed too near and the task will seem boring and pointless. A challenge which excites and energises because a child feels he is making significant progress and discovering new things about himself can be called an 'optimal challenge'.

Identifying precisely where to place the goal posts for optimal challenge is difficult enough; yet this is only one part of the problem. Achievement also depends on one other vital, and sometimes problematic, factor – the child himself. He will have his own view of what he can achieve, which may be very different from someone else's. Despite any confidence expressed by others, if his own sense of what he can manage is significantly less, he may reject the target and refuse to try.

For parents, struggling to lift their child's 'game', feelings of impotence, frustration and wishful thinking inevitably add to the difficulties. We are, unavoidably, emotionally involved with our child. We identify too closely with both past and future successes and failures. So where should we start? The best place is with our child. As self-belief significantly affects performance, it seems only sensible to give him a say. With his involvement and agreement, he is more likely not only to see the challenge as manageable but also to take on the responsibility for meeting it. Children should be involved in setting their own targets. This approach works with younger and older children. The successful HighScope early learning and development programme, with its 'plan, do, then review' scheme for under-fives, proves that young children can be actively involved in, and take responsibility for, their own learning, and that it produces enduring results when they do.

The structure of computer games illustrates this approach well. They all offer different degrees of challenge and the player plays at the level that matches his expected ability. At every moment, the player remains in control of the degree of challenge he confronts. He can try competing at a higher level but there is no public loss of face or wasted effort if he cannot manage the greater speed or complexity. He can return immediately to a lower level and a more realistic challenge. All computer games increase their level of difficulty very gradually. Progress takes place step by step, and the player receives instant and detailed feedback on his skill level, through scores, happy music or smiling computer faces. Equally important, he is allowed to enjoy his new achievement before moving on to a higher level: he is in total charge of deciding when the glow of success fades to boredom, and when he needs further challenge. The player experiences complete mastery and autonomy over his learning and skill development.

Achievement Frontiers and 'Circles of Competence'

This process of development through optimal challenge, and the role of the child's own self-belief, can be presented in diagrams.

In the each diagram, each circle represents the child and his current sense of self at different moments in time. The process of learning moves the child forward from left to right, creating a series of circles, some of which overlap while others do not, hence the arrows pointing rightwards in the Diagram 14.1. Our sense of self, or self-knowledge, as we have seen, is built from feelings of competence and self-belief. If a child sees a challenge as falling within the scope of his current competence, something he feels he can achieve, then it will seem manageable and he is likely to strive to achieve it. The optimal challenge at each stage is located at the right-hand edge of each circle. Having met the challenge, a child will feel different. The achievement creates a new sense, or circle, of competence and moves him on. Actual achievement will therefore represent progress from the left-hand edge of the circle to the right-hand edge. In Diagram 14.1, the circles overlap, but they could just touch each other, as in Diagram 14.2. In each case the child will feel connected to the next challenge or stage of progress. But if the circles overlap, this area offers the child some unpressured time to enjoy his

Diagram 14.1

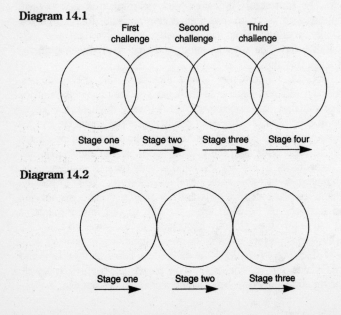

Diagram 14.2

Diagram 14.3

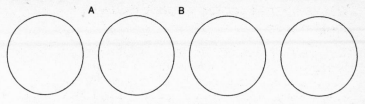

newly acquired skills and knowledge. The shift from the end of stage one to the beginning of stage two, the new launch point for the next leap forward, also gives the child more chance to accept the connection between his old and his new self. Savouring his achievement, and experiencing new control, understanding and competence – mastery – also help to increase his belief in his own ability to be successful. He will accept and feel at home with his new self and therefore be more comfortable about meeting the next challenge.

In Diagram 14.3, the circles neither overlap nor touch. They have gaps between them. Here, the child believes that the challenges placed at A and B are too far away for him to achieve. He can see no connection between the target and who he is. They may be achievable for someone else, but not for him. He will not know how to get there. Instead, he will be likely to make wild, ill-considered and inappropriate attempts to deliver the goods. Random, hit-and-miss gestures are unhelpful. If he hits, he will not be clear about what he did to enable him to repeat the success. If he misses, his failure will not teach him what to do differently next time. It will serve only to undermine his confidence and pride still further. An insensitively placed challenge for an insecure child can certainly do more harm than good.

The idea that each child has his own personal view of what he can achieve has been described by a psychologist called Bandura as 'perceived self-efficacy'. This need not be fixed; the perception can change. We know that 'success breeds success', so this self-belief can change over time for any one child. With this in mind, the circle model used for the first three diagrams can be further refined to explain further features of motivation and its impact on learning. The size of the circle representing each child can be made bigger or smaller to match each one's view of how capable he thinks he is. In other words, a child with low self-esteem and poor self-confidence can be represented by a small circle, while a more confident and more able child with a stronger and broader sense of self will have a larger circle. The effect on learning is illustrated in Diagram 14.4.

Offered the same target at point B, the first, self-doubting, child will

Diagram 14.4

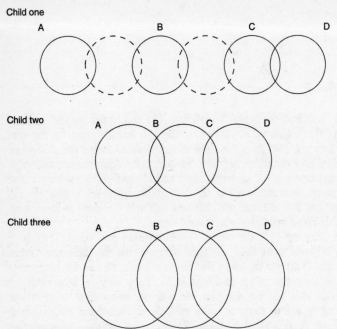

Child one

A   B   C   D

Child two

A   B   C   D

Child three

A   B   C   D

feel threatened by it rather then tempted because it falls too far away, in a distant circle. It can only be managed in smaller steps, through intermediate targets, which will take more time. The second, more confident and competent, child, on the other hand, will see it as something he can reach with effort and will stride forward to reach it. For example, a child who is naturally athletic, and knows it, is eager to try to jump the distance set as a challenge by a sports teacher. He does not make it first time, but makes it on the third try having tried a different run-up. A less athletic child thinks there is no chance he will be able to jump that far. He did not want to try because of the shame of falling so far short. The teacher then shortens the distance for him and a few others. He succeeds on his second attempt, repeats the jump a couple of times, and is then ready to try a longer one. This child takes two full lessons to improve his technique and confidence to make the distance the first child achieved quickly, but he made it, jump by jump.

Now consider child three, a very able and confident child who is represented by an even larger circle. He will consider this same challenge B well within his capability. Meeting it will be easy, too easy,

Diagram 14.5

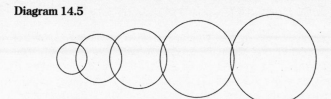

and therefore give him no feeling of self-development or progress. He will not discover any more about his abilities or himself. Being capable of more, he will feel not only bored through lack of challenge but also humiliated that the person who set the target has underestimated him. He will feel increasingly disconnected from his true self. Though able, he will be lucky if his circle of competence stays the same size. It is more likely to shrink as he begins not only to question his own judgement but also to make himself appear as others apparently see him.

Moving even closer to the subtleties of real life, over time a child's circle of competence will get larger as success feeds confidence and self-knowledge. Progressively, then, each successive target will become easier to accept and achieve, assuming that the targets present the same degree of challenge. This is because the larger the 'self' circle, the closer its circumference will be to the next target. Also, the more successful the child, the less time will be needed for regeneration, redefinition and confidence boosting in the area of overlap between circles. Provided there are no setbacks to damage self-esteem, confidence will increase making learning easier, speedier and, presumably, more enjoyable. This progress is represented in Diagram 14.5.

The Importance of Literacy and Numeracy

Having the basic skills of reading, writing and working with numbers is crucial to keeping children moving forward. Those who have not acquired these essential passports to learning by the age of seven or eight will find it hard to keep their circle of competence – representing what they think they can manage – growing. First, their circle will shrink in actual size at this stage, because they will feel a failure when they see others doing better. Second, the gap between them and the achieving children will grow ever wider as the successful children grow in confidence and progress at a faster and faster rate, making them feel even more inadequate. No wonder children without basic literacy and numeracy skills fall further and further behind and eventually turn away from education altogether.

Implications for Very Young and Preschool Children

This model shows clearly why children do better when they experience warm, supportive and stimulating relationships from the start, with people who respond to their needs and nurture their self-esteem. It sets them on the right road for learning, and all children deserve such chances. In the current climate of 'achievement' some parents are tempted to registering the very young with professionals prepared to instil the three Rs as early as possible, but they should resist. The size of the competence circle early on is not linked solely, or even primarily, to skills but instead to our three beacons: self-belief, self-efficacy and self-direction, all encompassed in the term self-esteem. In the early years, the most important aim is to nurture the child's sense of well-being and general competence in order to provide the right psychological and emotional base for effective learning. Indeed, it is counterproductive to focus on academic skills too early. The time spent away from the significant carer can introduce insecurity and a mistrust of adults. The process of asking children for more than they can deliver comfortably may introduce ideas of success and failure too soon. Less opportunity to play can deny the all-important experience of mastery. All of these may undermine a child's developing sense of self.

This understanding of the process of learning suggests five things. First, experiences which help to lay down strong foundations of self-belief and mastery are crucial to effective learning and self-motivation in later childhood and beyond. Second, in order to identify the point of optimal challenge, children have to be consulted and actively involved. Third, to feel successful and be willing to meet challenges in middle childhood, children need relevant skills, such as reading and writing, as well as strong self-belief. Fourth, schools must accept clear responsibility to ensure that children are sufficiently literate and numerate to benefit from the wider curriculum by the age of eight. Fifth, increasing a child's self-belief and sense of competence is the best way to reduce underachievement through:

- developing confidence in his ideas, preferences, and feelings
- developing a variety of skills
- providing and applauding the experience of success in any dimension and in any manner available

15

Keeping it Sweet: Managing Success

Any discussion of challenge inevitably raises the spectre of success and failure. On the face of it, these two terms seem straightforward and different. They are usually seen as opposites. Success is when we do something right and is always good, desirable and something to feel pleased about. Failure is when we don't come up to scratch and is always bad, undesirable and something to feel ashamed of. They are certainly loaded with moral significance. However, the truth is not that clear cut. This chapter and the next one look at the positive and negative sides of both success and failure – at how each one contains within it the seeds of the other.

Earlier chapters have looked at how children thrive when they feel successful, at how we can adjust our thinking to ensure children have plenty of experience of success to build their confidence, and at how to praise and encourage. This chapter unpeels a few more layers. It addresses:

- the need to see success in relative terms
- the importance of getting children to judge their own efforts themselves
- when success can lead to failure, through parents' thoughtless reactions
- the idea of 'good enough' success

We know the phrase, 'the sweet taste of success'; we need to make sure we keep it sweet, and avoid responding in ways which may cause our child to lose heart, opening up the route to future failure.

Success is Relative

It may sound obvious but it has to be said at the start that success is relative as well as absolute. A successful result for one child may be a disappointing one for another who is capable of better. When results are compared between children, there will always be losers. It can be very limiting and dispiriting. A child who does not come first – in a race or in a test – or is not 'best' at something, is always able to view

himself as a failure if he is so inclined. However, if a child's performance is measured over time, and viewed in terms of personal progress
and development, 'success' and 'failure' are self-referenced and become
neutral. They provide feedback on whether teaching and learning has
been effective. For example, a child who is a budding athlete who runs
faster then he has before but does not win a particular race is not 'a
failure'. He has merely not run as well as the fastest, and he must look
to his tactics, breathing or starting techniques to see where there is
room for further improvement.

It is hard for children not to compare themselves with others, and all
too easy for parents to join in this often destructive sport. However,
long term, comparisons demotivate and undermine more than they
encourage. First, there will always be someone who is better than them
at something, so any personal success will be marred. Second, if we
show our children that the only way to judge themselves is against
other people, we are telling them their own judgement is not reliable.
Third, and most important, this kind of comparison can be made
irrespective of how hard a child tries. He will get no detailed or
constructive feedback on his own performance, which even the 'successful' high achiever needs if he wants to progress and grow.

Of course, seeing others doing better can be a spur to greater effort.
The significant factor will be the size of the gap to be jumped. Thinking
back to the circle of competence learning model, the larger the gap, the
more it will tend to reduce the underachiever's motivation. So often,
parents and teachers hold up the example of the best for other children
to follow. It would be far more effective if the especially pleasing
performance of an average child were noted, making such standards
appear relevant and achievable to the majority. Do we, in any case,
think it is good to make every child want to be 'best'? There is far more
to life than coming top. As Martina Navratilova, the tennis star, said,
'The moment of victory is far too short to live for that alone'.

Encouraging Self-appraisal

As success is relative as well as absolute, there are many situations in
which success has to be judged. We have to ask, was it a successful
outcome for that person at this point in time? There are often factors to
take into account. Has he taken up the activity only recently? Was he
away or ill for a time? Did he have long to prepare for the event? How
does it compare with his previous efforts? Did he manage it all on his
own? However, instead of always doing the judging ourselves, we
should encourage our child to have the confidence and self-knowledge
to judge the quality of his performance himself. Ultimately, children

have to do things for their own satisfaction and apply their own standards, not rely on the demands and views of others.

We can help them to make well-rounded judgements. We can suggest they pay attention to factors such as those listed above, and offer alternative views if they judge themselves too harshly. Although it gives us enormous pleasure when our children do well, we should always be on the lookout for signs of undue perfectionism which can be very unhealthy, as we shall see.

When Success Can Lead to Failure

Both success and failure contain a contradiction. Success can lead to failure and failure to success. It is easy to understand the latter. Failure shows us what we need to know and gives us the chance to get it right. What is less obvious is that success, managed badly, contains within it the seeds of future failure. What can sour success? We have all heard of the 'busted flush' syndrome, or burn out: people who were destined for a golden future who fizzle, opt out or even commit suicide. What might have gone wrong, and how can we prevent it from happening to anyone in our family? Three useful guidelines are:

- don't make your approval conditional on the child's success – keep the achievement separate
- make sure he does it for himself, not for you or for anyone else
- let the child take, and keep, ownership of the success

Keep Approval Unconditional

Being a clever and successful musician, sportsperson, mathematician or budding actress does not turn any child into a better or more loveable person. Children can and should feel proud of their skills or talents, but their sense of self-worth should not rely exclusively or substantially on how good they are at these things. They need to be loved, unconditionally and at all times, for who they are, not only when they do well. We must separate the achievement from the person.

In Chapter Nine, on praise, the approach recommended was to approve of our child for who he is and appreciate him for his talents and efforts. No child should suffer the burden of believing that his successes are the only way to maintain his parents' love and approval. Some time when this child is angry, he might decide to punish his parents by hitting them where it hurts most and opting out.

Who Are They Doing it For?

There was a television programme not very long ago about the Covent Garden Opera House. In one episode, young hopeful ballet dancers were being auditioned to join a performance of Tchaikowsky's 'Nutcracker Suite' with the Royal Ballet. After the final decision, the successful ones were interviewed. One young lad of about 10 years old was asked if he was pleased. He answered, 'My mother will be thrilled'.

This is not unusual among exceptional, or even merely talented, young performers. To reach that standard, the level of dedication is such that parents are inevitably closely involved, ensuring practice, driving them – in cars as well as psychologically – watching them and constantly encouraging them. Often a lot of money is invested, in equipment and instruments, in lessons and coaching, in travel and even in lost earnings. It is, perhaps, not surprising that children lose touch with their own motivation and see themselves as the vehicle for their parents' dreams. When the young champion golfer, Tiger Woods, won the US Open, his father is said to have shouted, jubilantly, 'We made it!'. In a television programme about musical prodigies, a child psychologist warned parents against getting too involved and taking over their child's soul. The child must be doing it for himself and not for us.

If a child gets a great deal of approval and personal satisfaction from success, it can be unhealthy and even dangerous. It can lead:

- to the treadmill of perfectionism, having to stay at the top through constant effort, living on the edge of disappointment where success is not kept up
- to a reluctance to take risks and try new things in case he loses his position of supremacy or finds out there is something he is not so good at
- to a tendency to look down on others who do not have the same desire for success
- to a need to look to others for approval, confirmation and validation instead of deciding for himself what he wants to do and be

Who Owns It?

Which of the following might you say?: 'I am really proud of you for doing that!', 'I hope you feel proud of yourself for doing that. You deserved to do well' or 'I feel proud to have you as my child'.

Of course, our child owns his success, but it is very easy to take it over and away from him. It happens in two ways, usually without us realising it. First, we 'own' the success when we use it to make us feel successful – to feed our own sense of self-worth. We become so thrilled by the achievement that we cannot resist running off with it and telling everyone else. Instead of seeing the success as our child's private affair, something designed to let him know how he is doing, we use it for our own benefit.

The second way we take 'ownership' of our child's success is when we invest so much of ourselves and our time in the hoped-for outcome that we believe it could not have been done without us. Earlier, we saw that rewards and incentives can have a similar effect.

Which of the following have you heard yourself or someone else say?

- 'He's a great reader, but I think it's because I read to him all the time.'
- 'You would not have got that distinction if I hadn't made you practise so hard.'
- 'I told you you were a natural sprinter. That's why I signed you up for the course.'
- 'He's a great artist. He gets his talent from me.'
- 'Congratulations on being in the team. Aren't you pleased, now, that I dragged you to all those training sessions?'
- 'I'm not sure you would have made it to Oxford University if I had not promised you £500 if you did.'

These are just a few examples of typical responses from parents who take some of responsibility for their child's achievements and who, in effect, therefore steal the credit. Here is another little test of your 'ownership tendency'. If your friend's child does something notable, for example, gets into a favoured school, wins a prize, comes top in something or is selected for the County team, do you congratulate your friend, or simply say, 'I heard Sammy did very well. He must be delighted'?

What Happens Next?

How might a child feel if his success is taken by a parent? He will feel not 'ful-filled' but 'ful-empty', not to mention puzzled and resentful. His first reaction will be to fill up his emptiness with another success, and hope that he is allowed to keep this one. Later, though, if he is always left empty, he will direct his resentment against his tormentor and opt out of success as a way of punishing that person.

Personal success should be seen as a child's, not a parent's, property. Friends and neighbours should not be told about it without first checking with our child whether he is happy for others to know. We may discover, for example, that he wants to tell certain people, such as the other parent or grandparents, himself. Asking a child about this matter not only shows respect for him and his wishes, it also indicates clearly that the success is his to use as he pleases, not ours.

'Good Enough' Success

A mother spoke to me with some shame about an incident with her son some 10 years back. He had entered a regional debating competition and was through to the final. She had coached him for the last leg, played devil's advocate and covered all the possible challenges and angles. She then went to watch him perform. Sure enough, the predicted difficult challenges appeared, but in her view her son fluffed his replies. Nonetheless, he won. When she met him afterwards, her first comment was to criticise him for his errors. He was incensed. He left the room, silently fuming, did not return home that night and has not forgiven her to this day. She wanted him to be perfect when his performance was good enough to win.

'Good enough' success is not a cop out. It does not mean being content with second best when there is room for further improvement, or giving up before crunch time, an examination or other moment of public accountability. It does not mean being lazy, using the excuse that other things have importance in a balanced life, true though that may be. Good enough success is, instead, the protection against external and internal pressure – against demanding parents and children's self-imposed perfectionism.

Referring back to the last chapter which presented a model of learning as circles of competence, acknowledging good enough success allows a child to spend unpressured time in the area of overlap between circles before moving on to the next challenge. It gives time and space to breathe, relax, savour the achievement, strengthen self-belief and adjust self-image. Applying it also to the model of motivation in Part One, good enough success is an achievement which takes us to the target selected, and no further; to the final stage of the motivation journey when we are allowed to kick off our shoes, rest a while and feel proud of the distance travelled, even if it took us one or two days longer than we planned.

Pulling This Together

This understanding is summarised in the following two diagrams. Diagram 15.1 shows how effective motivators prepare for and respond

Diagram 15.1: CARE: the essence of effective motivation

The effective motivator's input and response to success

Child		Child sees success as:	CHILD FEELS:
Accepted (unconditionally)	Efforts appreciated, approval not dependent on success	Neutral – it tells the child what he's done right	● accepted and appreciated
	Encourages self-management		● pleased with himself, because he is allowed to 'own' the success
Realistic	Each success is, for the time being, good enough	Positive – it show the route to further success	● encouraged to continue his efforts
Expectations			

Diagram 15.2

The ineffective motivator's input and response to success

			CHILD FEELS:
Non-, or only conditional, acceptance	Approval conditional on continued success, or success ignored	*Child sees success as:* Essential – it is his own way to get approval	• self-denigration, because seeking perfection
Inappropriate or unrealisic expectations	Controls, pushes, manages Success seen by parents partly as a result of their efforts	Negative – pressure to 'succeed' can lead to failure through opting out	• empty, because parent has 'taken ownership' of the success • pressured and discouraged, by need to keep up the standard and by fear of 'failure'

to their child's success. The effective motivator 'cares'. CARE stands for Child Accepted unconditionally, with Realistic and balanced Expectations. Acceptance and approval are not dependent upon success. Realistic expectations mean that successes are frequent but have value. The child feels happy and fulfilled both because he is successful and because he is allowed to own and keep the success. He therefore feels encouraged to carry on working for his personal satisfaction, not to please or prove anything to others.

Diagram 15.2 shows how success can lead to failure when parents step in unhelpfully, demand and control too much, make their love and approval conditional on success and apparently walk away with the glory and credit, leaving the child empty.

Action Points for Managing Success

Is this something you could do for your child? Try to:

- accept and approve of him for who he is, not what he has done
- have realistic and balanced expectations
- make it safe to make mistakes
- see success as feedback, part of the learning experience, and ask him what he has learnt from this, about what he is doing right
- accept his judgement wherever possible. If he thinks he has achieved something to be proud of, that is enough. If you think he could have done better, raise this next time a target is selected
- let him experience a range of genuine challenges so success feels real
- value different skills, not just those commonly applauded
- let him be proud; acknowledge and share in your child's successes
- let him own the success
- practise good enough success

16

Silver Linings:
Managing Failure

All children experience failure – lots of it. A child will almost certainly fail at his first attempts at standing or walking, and yet he tries again. He won't master buttons on his first fumble, tie shoelaces straight away, or ride a two-wheeled bike immediately, and yet he is prepared to have another go to master the skill. Why do these early failures not make children give up, even though the frustration can be intense, while later ones in other spheres of learning can stop them in their tracks and throw them into the depths of misery? What is the important difference?

The uncomfortable truth is that adults are often responsible for the change. How parents see 'failures' inevitably influences how children define and experience their own 'failures'. Later on, friends, teachers and other adults will also affect their attitude. Parents cannot protect their children from the harsh outside for very long but how we start makes a difference. Part of the problem is the current emphasis on celebrating success. When we place such a high value on success, and make such a fuss of it, we automatically define failure as shameful by comparison. The more we reward success to help a child feel proud and appreciated, the more we have to hide failure because of its negative consequences. If we can promote a neutral and constructive attitude to both success and failure, and nurture each child's self-esteem, we will increase resilience both to setbacks and to the wounds inflicted by others. The crucial objective is to keep alive a child's self-belief and knowledge that he can correct the problem and move forward.

Another part of the problem is that, too often, we confuse two things which should be kept separate. The first is us and our child. Our child's failure is his, not ours. If we feel lessened by his shortcomings, we are more likely either to punish or to ignore them inappropriately. The second common confusion is our child and his failure. Just because he has failed to achieve something does not make him a failure as a person.

Another explanation for an increasing sensitivity to failure is the growing trend in measurement and comparison against others. If we allow and encourage this, we can end up with a child who, despite a string of small successes, still considers himself a failure.

This chapter sets out the silver linings approach to failure. It considers:

- failure as a neutral concept and an essential part of learning
- the need to separate the failure from the person
- effective responses to failure

Be Positive

Failure, like mistakes, tells us something. It provides useful feedback. But that information will only be useful if the failure is acknowledged, if it is inspected for the lessons to be learnt and if those lessons are taken on board and processed. Failure, therefore, can be the route to success.

What Failure Can Teach

Through particular failures, parents and children can learn a great deal. For example, if the mistakes leading to failure are of the 'careless' type, in other words, arbitrary slips, the failure can show that the child understands the principle or process being applied but was not concentrating. We then have to ask: what stopped the concentration? Was it the television being on; was it boredom, because the task involved repetition of something already mastered; or was it because the child's mind was focused on something else – on a problem, an exciting idea or the next event of their day? If the mistakes followed a pattern, failure might show some more fundamental problems with understanding either expectations or procedures, such as how best to 'carry' numbers in adding and take-away sums, or difficulties with a particular tense of a verb in a foreign language. Failure might even show that a target was too ambitious for this point in time. A child can see from the feedback what he needs to concentrate on, what he needs to understand a little more fully.

Through the general experience of failure, children can learn:

- that they don't have to be good at everything to be liked, loved or accepted, so it can actually strengthen their sense of security if the reaction is right
- that failure is not the end of the world, that it can be survived and therefore risked in the future
- to sharpen determination to conquer a problem, so failure can increase motivation
- new skills and develop existing ones: such as study and planning skills, problem-solving skills, reflection and increased self-awareness

Separating the Failure from the Person

No child, whatever his age, should be told he is 'a failure', or on a certain road to an empty future. Words which send similar messages are 'idiot', 'thick' and 'useless'. These are all terms that convey a negative, no-hope self-image. Worse than that, they are fixed labels that appear to lock a child into that role. There can be nothing more de-motivating than to be described as a no-hope idiot.

We can all be nasty. We have no problem finding the phrases used to put a child down. Perhaps they were said to us when we were young. Perhaps we heard our teachers say them to others in our class. Perhaps we have read them, or even used them ourselves. 'Can't you think straight?', 'You're as thick as two short planks' or 'Don't be so dumb' are commonly heard. It was not so long ago that schoolchildren who made mistakes were given a dunce's hat and made to stand in the corner.

These words and actions are a form of punishment and induce shame and humiliation. Shame makes us cringe and feel like curling up inside our protective shell, like tucking away under the bedcover, or hiding in a cupboard. Contrary to some people's view, shame and humiliation are rarely spurs to renewed effort. Instead, they inflict emotional wounds which fester and leave scars in the form of anger and resentment. Yet learning requires confidence, flexibility, openness, trust, self-belief and the ability to let go of ourselves and relax. Shame results in the opposite – it makes us tense up, cut off and doubt ourselves. Shame and humiliation, threats and degradation, disempower children. They are the tactics of people who exploit and abuse the superior power which they have.

Failure and Punishment

Parents who are inclined to punish failure, either physically, or emotionally through humiliation or rejection, should realise where this can lead. Their child might be tempted to:

- lie about the marks he is getting
- cheat to get higher marks
- continue to work at the level he feels he can manage easily and not risk extending himself for fear of failure and the disapproval that will follow
- invest all of his time and effort seeking perfection in one sphere, at the expense of either a normal social life or extending himself and developing a healthier spread of interests and skills
- boast about receiving good marks to receive the approval he craves but end up only annoying people, being disliked, and thus needing to prove himself even more

In the wise words of educational therapist Gerda Hanko, concealing failure adds 'the strain of pretence to the strain of failure and further saps confidence'. She continues, 'Failure becomes something to hide when you can't accept the whole of yourself, or when you fear the judgement of others, or both'.

Punishing a child simply because he has failed does not help. It:

- entangles the child with the failure, so that the child can believe he is being punished for who he is, not what he has done
- amounts to double punishment – because the failure can, in itself, be seen as a punishment
- causes guilt and distress. A child who is punished for failure will feel eternally guilty for the disappointment that he causes his parents. It also creates scope for emotional blackmail
- ignores how hard he might have tried. It is one thing to punish a child because he never bothered to train or revise, or whatever the appropriate preparation might have been. It is quite another to cause pain and injury when he did his genuine best to succeed, and when his self-respect will already have suffered a heavy blow as a result
- may not involve a·relevant 'consequence'. Not being selected for the team because training sessions have been missed is a relevant punishment. Being physically assaulted or grounded will have no association with the failure and is likely to cause anger, resentment and a decision not to do what parents want again

How Effective Motivators Respond to Failure

Punishment and humiliation may, possibly, work short term, but they will not be effective for long. They will certainly not encourage that all-important self-motivation. In these cases, the target can become the avoidance of punishment which is certainly not a valued end in itself. If we do see the need to intervene when our child fails, it is appropriate and effective only if it reinforces self-motivation and nurtures self-belief, self-efficacy and self-direction. We need to respond constructively, sensitively and genuinely.

Responding Constructively

Failure, we have noted, can be highly motivating. Handled appropriately, it can be seen as a problem to be solved – as a challenge to be met. In Dr Howard Hall's experience, failure can make people 'roll their sleeves up and apply more effort. They realise that the only way to overcome their difficulty is to take control. They realise that their self-esteem is inherently controllable through their own efforts. . . It is self-evident that each individual outcome is not the be all and end all of life, but for some people at the time it seems so.'.

At these times, any reassurance of the 'don't worry, you can try again' or 'I think you did very well' variety will have no impact. The appropriate response to mistakes and failure which knock someone backwards is to put him back in control. Encourage him to understand what went wrong, to identify what needs to be changed and to agree an action plan, a detailed and staged programme for improvement. Sports stars will often study video footage of their debacles to identify their errors.

Responding Sensitively

We shouldn't always believe the front our child presents to us. Failure can be upsetting, however much he may try to deny it, especially if he had really tried, very much wanted to succeed and was not expecting to fail. Failure can make all of us feel disappointed, frustrated, ashamed, anxious and sometimes sad. It can undermine our confidence. It can sap our courage, rock our self-belief, sometimes to such an extent that either we pretend it has had no impact, or we don't even try to do well so we can pretend that if we had tried, we could have succeeded.

Sometimes it won't be the failure itself causing the sadness but what flows from it. For example, a low mark, a poor placing, a bad audition may mean our child being in a different group from friends. Or the root worry may be being teased. If we can get to the source of any distress, it will help our child feel understood and accepted despite the failure.

When children experience failure occasionally and constructively – in other words the accompanying lessons and feelings are explored – it helps them to understand more about themselves. The better their self-knowledge, the more aware they can be of their strengths and limitations. It helps them to be well-calibrated – to have good self-judgement and accurate self-awareness. On the other hand, running away from failure, or being punished for it, increases fear, distances children from reality and leads to distortion and pretence. Nothing is impossible for the person who does not have to face up to reality.

When a child has a significant disappointment, we can:

● accept and understand his feelings, and let him talk about them. We should not deny how he feels or declare the problem is not as bad as he thinks
● try to reduce the amount of 'failure' experienced elsewhere; for example, go easy on him at home for a while
● help him to have some successes to balance it out. Make him feel competent and useful to you in practical ways

- explain that failure is a cloud that always has a silver lining. Ask him what there might be to learn and if he can see any compensations
- make it clear you love him nonetheless and that you are there for him if he needs to talk more

Responding Genuinely

It can be difficult enough to give praise and encouragement when it is clearly deserved, but it is even harder to be supportive and constructive in the face of poor effort or work. As a result, we – just like managers and teachers – can find ourselves in quite a muddle over what to say when our children do badly. We do not like to rub our children's noses in 'failure' – at least, most people don't – but equally we feel a fraud pretending that something is fine when, in our heart of hearts, we know it's not true. Identifying what children have done wrong without discouraging them is a skill. We know that praise and encouragement are important. How, then, can we comment on poor performance in a straightforward and helpful way?

Quite apart from this, we often go out of our way to avoid upsetting or inflating the egos of any other children in the family who might be within earshot. If we tell one child he has done really well, will another child think he is not favoured if we have not similarly praised him? If we tell one that he really has not done himself justice and could have done better, will that cause a brother or sister to tease and gloat? We are therefore very tempted to send mixed, half, or even counterproductive, messages to children. We find it hard to mean what we say and say what we mean. However, receiving accurate, detailed and speedy feedback on performance so it can be regularly monitored is vital to helping anyone develop and improve, as we have already seen. Our weasel words, spoken for the best of intentions, in fact make it much harder for children to take proper charge of their learning and development.

Conclusion

When faced with failure, effective motivators put the child back in charge, show the way forward and leave the child with enough self-respect and self-belief to have another go. Effective motivators empower children by responding constructively to failure. We can:

- encourage our child to 'own' and take responsibility for his failure
- help our child to arrive at the answers through his own thinking process and show him a way ahead
- put him in touch with his own power to monitor and evaluate himself
- have realistic expectations

- accept our child unconditionally, regardless of how successful he is at any task
- help him to feel comfortable with his feelings – of disappointment, frustration, sadness and loss of confidence – so these are not buried and allowed to fester and undermine confidence

In other words, failure should be tolerated and managed, not punished. Failure becomes debilitating to a child only when:

- it is linked to a judgement about him as a person
- it reinforces deep negative 'self' beliefs already held by the child
- he feels irresponsible and impotent: there seems to be no way forward, no way or need to change the situation or to improve
- he is not encouraged to take responsibility for his errors or misunderstandings
- we feel the need to hide it, for this sends the message that failure is shameful
- when our child is permitted to ignore it

The following two diagrams are similar to those in the previous chapter on managing success. Diagram 16.1 summarises the steps we can take to preserve motivation when a child experiences failure. Diagram 16.2 shows the opposite: how, often unintentionally, we can make things worse.

Diagram 16.1

The effective motivator's response to failure

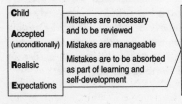

| Child Accepted (unconditionally) Realisic Expectations | Mistakes are necessary and to be reviewed Mistakes are manageable Mistakes are to be absorbed as part of learning and self-development | Child sees failure as: Neutral – it tells the child what to do next Positive – it shows the route to success | CHILD FEELS: • accepted and understood • that he 'owns' the failure and has the responsibility for making improvements • his self-belief is intact, so he retains the courage to try again |

Diagram 16.2

The ineffective motivator's input and response to failure

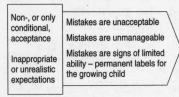

| Non-, or only conditional, acceptance Inappropriate or unrealistic expectations | Mistakes are unacceptable Mistakes are unmanageable Mistakes are signs of limited ability – permanent labels for the growing child | Child sees failure as: Shameful – it tells the child he is no good Negative – it's the sign of a future life of failure | CHILD FEELS: • worthless, punished and rejected, because parent blames child • unwilling or unable to 'own' the failure therefore to correct mistakes • self-belief is undermined, and is unwilling to try again |

17

Curiosity Rules! Handling Questions

Human beings have a fundamental need to make sense of their world, and it starts from the beginning of life. Very young children want to learn. They need to learn. They start from their first days by copying and by being curious. Babies don't stay lying on their backs for very long. They are absolutely determined to taste, touch, sit up, crawl, explore, stand up and walk, feed and later dress themselves. It takes great confidence to explore the unknown. Curiosity, about both the world and what we ourselves are capable of, is the springboard for life-long learning. How is it that the natural curiosity, confidence and determination of the infant so often becomes dented? This chapter suggests ways to keep curiosity alive through to adulthood.

Curiosity means a desire to know, an eagerness to learn, inquisitiveness. It might get us into scrapes, but it keeps us asking and keeps us open to new information. It is an energy that fuels and feeds a lively and growing mind. It is a formidable self-motivating force. A motive is a reason, and what better reason can there be for doing anything than because we want to know? It is a self-generated reason which means we own it. And because it comes from within ourselves, it is more likely to be long lasting.

It is vital that we foster children's curiosity. However, as all parents know, this is sometimes easier said than done. The first thing that stalls an inquiring mind is the widely accepted notion of the 'good child'. We send clear messages that we approve of 'good' children who do not challenge or make trouble. The second thing that stifles curiosity is our intolerance for all types of questions, not just the challenging ones.

'Good' Children Don't Rock the Boat

All children need to be noticed in an approving way. In her two-year study in Oxfordshire closely observing children in their home, nursery and school environments, Rosemary Roberts found that 'babies and young children urgently need approving attention; that they begin learning very early to behave in ways that will please their 'important' people. For a child, learning to be good means grown ups will be pleased with you. But learning to be good also means you might not learn so much.' (*Times Educational Supplement,* 2 February 1996).

Roberts asked parents when they felt most negative towards their child. Most of them said it was when their child protested verbally: contradicting, complaining, whinging and crying. Having to argue with their child was not pleasant, but they felt more negative when their children fought with each other, and felt most rejecting when their children protested outside the home and therefore showed them up in front of others. Children commonly whinge and cry when they want to be noticed. The other verbal protests, such as contradictions and complaints, show that a child is thinking and questioning. Roberts pointed out that when we ask children to 'be good', it usually means they should not ask questions, or argue; should not risk failure; should not make their own plans, or talk about their successes and mistakes. Answering back is one of the hardest things to tolerate. But protest is an essential part of communication. It is the substance of debate and discussion which is increasingly encouraged in education as children mature. Without protest, children cannot form their ideas or learn to resolve conflicts. Children who learn to say only what they think we want to hear become mere reflections of us and are certainly not exploring themselves. But, once again, there is a balance to be struck. They do need to be able, eventually, to defend their corner in a polite, constructive and well-timed way. However they also need to realise there are times when it is appropriate to retire gracefully. They need to accept different boundaries and be able to bite their tongues when required. And we need to learn not to view their protests as a personal attack and react defensively and provocatively.

Why is 'Why?' So Difficult?

There is a strange saying about curiosity: that it killed the cat. I don't know where it came from – except that it is an American proverb – but irritated parents have trotted it out happily for decades to stop their children battering them with questions, wanting to be told secrets, or generally 'being a nuisance'. Today, we are more likely to say, 'Stop asking so many questions' or 'Leave me alone. Why do you want to know that?', or we might respond 'Just because'. These answers are, incidentally, far more directly insulting to a child than the traditional response, and far more likely to kill curiosity than ever curiosity is to kill a cat.

Children's questions can be irritating, intrusive, threatening and certainly demanding and tiring. More than that, they sometimes show up our own ignorance which can be uncomfortable. It can be easier to say, 'Go away' than 'I don't know'. Questions do not always stem from genuine curiosity. Children ask questions for all manner of reasons. We don't have to answer all of them with the same degree of enthusiasm, or at the exact moment they are asked. For example, when very young children ask 'why?' so endlessly, it is frequently because they have discovered it as a way to control and direct conversation which adults have totally dominated until then. Through questions, they can get attention. In their hands, questions are a powerful tool of self-management, just like 'no' was before them, as well as a way to find out about things that puzzle them. We should not ignore these whys, but it is useful to understand the reason they come so thick and fast at particular stages of development. At two-and-a-half, children ask 'What?' and 'Who?' questions, such as 'What is the doll's name?'. At three, they ask 'Where?'. At four, they ask 'Why?', 'When?' and 'How?' – questions that involve more abstract ideas.

Responding to Questions

Certain questions will, then, need different types of responses from others. If we understand the different types of questions children ask, we can be a little more selective and sensitive in our responses and preserve our sanity at the same time. For example, we are entitled not to be hounded by questions demanding something we have just refused if we have already explained our reasons and listened to their case. If questions seem to be thrown at us just to get us involved and talking, perhaps we should think about spending more time actively doing something with our child so they get the attention they seem to need. Once children are old enough, the most useful general rule when answering a question is to respond in a way which helps them to answer it for themselves. This hands the initiative back to them and, in the case of questions which challenge and demand, it also encourages children to think ahead and learn to read situations and people. What sort of questions does your child ask most, and how might you answer them differently? Here are some examples:

Probing and Searching Questions
Why were the Egyptian pyramids built in that shape?
That's an interesting question. I don't know the answer. Have you got any ideas where we might look it up or suggestions for answers? What made you think of that question?

Trivial or Attention-seeking Questions
What are you doing now?
I think you might know the answer to that already. What do you think I might be doing?

Personal Questions

How many boyfriends did you, you know, have before you met Dad?
There are some things parents are entitled to keep private. I don't need to answer that question.

Embarrassing or Difficult Questions

What would you do if I got a girl pregnant?
That deserves a thoughtful answer. I need a little time to think about how to say it. Come back in five minutes and you can tell me what you thought I was going to say.

Demanding Questions

But why can't I go round to Mick's house?
I have already given you three reasons why you can't do that now. Tell me what you have heard me say.

I think you can guess my reasons already. Can you tell me what you think I will say?

Dependent Questions

I can't do this. Come and help me!
Got to a sticky bit? Have another try and you'll probably surprise yourself. If not, I'll come and help you.

Assertive and Challenging Questions

What would you do if I refused to do it?
You may want to do that, but I don't think you will. If you do, you can find out the hard way!

Encouraging Curiosity

When dealing with 0–3 year-olds:

- let them explore and play
- answer their earliest questions
- get them involved with a computer if you have one at home. Special software exists to exploit children's willingness to experiment with its use in a very hands-on way, even with very young children

When dealing with 3–8 year-olds:

- encourage experimentation: 'What would happen if. . ?' Simple science books for children suggest little activities which can be tried at home
- introduce them to non-fiction books. Many are available in a 'fascinating facts' format designed to feed children's sense of wonder and curiosity. These are often particularly popular with boys who seem to drop fantasy play before girls
- model curiosity. Ask questions yourself about things which puzzle you: 'I wonder why. . ?' Show that it is okay not to know things but to want to find out

When dealing with 8–12 year-olds:

- encourage self-help – using reference books or CD-rom encyclopae-dias when they want to find things out. These can be expensive, so trips to the library, family or neighbours can offset the cost
- develop their independence gradually and let them begin to explore their neighbourhood with friends
- ask if they have seen anything on television which has interested them and which they might want to try

When dealing with 12–17 year-olds:

- the challenge for us when our children become teenagers is likely to be curbing their curiosity rather than feeding it

Adolescent Curiosity: Exploration and Exasperation

Adolescence can be an exasperating time for parents. Even if we accept that it is normal and healthy for teenagers to confront, be curious and experiment, it can feel distinctly uncomfortable to have the certainties of our life challenged. But teenagers' curiosity must be understood and respected. Most people agree that, at whatever age, life is richest when curiosity is allowed to roam. It is the sign of an active and reflective mind, without which we stagnate.

Curiosity stays, or should stay, with us for our whole life. Teenagers, typically, are curious about such things as:

- rules and boundaries: How far can I go? What can I get away with?
- adult relationships: Can I make my parents disagree? Can I split them or manipulate them? If they argue over me, what will happen to them or to me?
- their future: What courses will I take? What job will I do and, more fundamentally, what sort of a person am I going to be?
- their security and safety: If I experiment and explore and challenge, will my parents still be there for me and stop me from going too far?
- the strength of their own ideas, values and powers of argument and how this changes their relationship with people such as parents and teachers: Why can't they see things my way? Why don't they do it this other, better, way?
- their growing independence over their body: How much can I drink before I get drunk? What does it feel like to kiss? What will I look like with a different hairstyle?

There is a great deal to be gained from a teenager's different approach to the world. It keeps parents up to date and it can be fun.

The teenager's friends often add further perspectives. Provided you make sure they are well-informed about the pitfalls and dangers of experimentation, you should see the benefits of their confidence to explore. It is part and parcel of an open-minded attitude to life which will help them to go on discovering their potential throughout their adult years. They may make mistakes in the process; it is virtually inevitable that they will. With their greater freedom, the scope and scale of mistakes is greater than before, so the potential for feeling threatened and let down by the mistakes when they happen is greater. Nonetheless, the message within Chapter Ten remains valid: that you should make it safe for them to make mistakes provided they are prepared to acknowledge and accept the personal lessons contained within them.

18

Golden Threads: Making Connections

Self-motivation depends on being able to see and make connections in a range of different ways. We need to be able to see the connection between our effort and the result. We need to be able to think creatively, making sometimes unusual links to solve an unexpected problem. We need to feel secure in ourselves and about the future, through having a thread linking us to our past and a connection to someone who believes in us. This chapter looks at practical ways in which we can give our children the valuable golden threads which help us to make the most of ourselves.

Creating Continuity Between Past, Present and Future

Younger children love nothing better than to hear us tell them stories about 'when they were little', especially if they make us laugh. They have an almost insatiable appetite for such stories, wanting to hear them over and over again. They love to see photographs, too, not just of themselves but also of us and others in the wider family when we were all children – until, of course, they reach the age when anything to do with families and their childhood becomes embarrassing.

This sharing of family stories has a very useful purpose, as well as being fun. It helps to deepen children's sense of where they have come from and where they belong.

Each of us has a past, a present and a future. As we have seen, past experiences have a strong influence on who we feel we are and on our attitude to what lies ahead. Motivation requires us to face the future optimistically, believing that we will be safe there and there is a chance that we will succeed. Children who cannot do that will live in and for the moment, which does not move them on. The future will be safe when past experiences have been broadly happy, or at least faced, thought about and understood. Being able to move back and forward in their lives will help them to feel grounded and secure. If, however, there is a part of their life they would rather block out because it was difficult to understand or was painful, the block acts rather like a lost piece of a jigsaw puzzle. Without it, they are not quite complete. Each block is the result of fear and uncertainty during times when they were stranded emotionally. It breaks the thread. If there are several such incidents, the missing bits can jumble the whole picture so they won't recognise who they are. How can we help our children feel connected to a continuous thread so they can use it to find their way back or take them forward when they feel the need?

Approaches to Try

As well as telling childhood stories, we can keep some items from their past – such as a favourite jumper or toy, or a special school report. Soft toys are sometimes kept for years, especially if they represent a valued memory. Keep one or two drawings, pieces of work, certificates or other symbols of their creativity and success as well. If we do decide it is time to clear out bedroom or family cupboards, even teenagers can be told it is understandable if they are not yet ready to discard certain items.

'Growth charts' can mark each child's changing height, and a photograph pinned next to each mark is even better though this takes planning and organisation.

Finally, talk about possibly stressful events as openly and honestly as possible.

Continuity Through Adolescence

Adolescence is a time of great change. As teenagers change and mature, the challenge for parents is to help them feel connected, to the family as well as to their childhood. Tolerance and patience are important. At all times they need to feel loved and accepted even if we cannot accept or understand some of their values and reasons for doing things.

The changes that take place are physical, social and emotional. They can generate anxiety and confusion. Although teenagers stay the same person, they can feel a need to reject the old before they build the new. Adolescence can, therefore, be a time of emptiness, when there is great scope for outside influence as they try themselves out and experiment with who they are going to be. Ellen Noonan, a counsellor who works with adolescents, has written in *Counselling Young People*: 'The task of adolescence is not to kill off the child in a self-mutilating manner. Rather, it is to leave the child in the past as a memory, and at the same time to retain modified capabilities and qualities which were originally developed in childhood. Those qualities – imagination, curiosity and the capacity to lose oneself in play – are essential to learning, sexuality and achievement as an adult.'.

Leisure Interests and Past Times

In adolescence, interests often change and multiply. Previous interests may be given up, but new ones usually take their place as new possibilities are explored. Teenagers can be very creative and adventurous. Schoolwork often takes up more time, particularly GCSE course work, but this frequently offers students scope to explore a personal slant. Teenagers may want to take a part-time job or have more time to themselves and with friends, so are tempted to drop previous activities.

Research shows that people feel more fulfilled and are better balanced as adults if they have a variety of interests outside work and the family, so it might not be a good for your teenager to drop everything at once if he has no plans to do anything else instead. Although adolescence is a quest for a new self, we can suggest either exploring any room to negotiate a more acceptable commitment, or dropping the activities in stages, not all at once.

We can help our teenagers to feel connected if we:

- stay strong enough to acknowledge their different outlook and ways, and continue to accept them and be there for them
- keep to the same house rules and boundaries, adjusted for their age
- show that, within your boundaries, you trust them with what they want to do
- try to accept some of their plans: 'I'll support you in that but not in this'
- maintain a united front with the other parent if there are any arguments
- keep the lines of communication open

Making Mental Connections: Creative Thinking

Creative thinking is important. It expands our horizons and opens our eyes to new ways of doing things. It helps us to feel capable and confident because, if we are creative, we know we will find a workable solution to a problem even if we are not sure what is expected. It is fun, because it uncovers surprises. It is the thinking that generates jokes and cartoons and is the launch pad for innovation. Creative thinkers are original and flexible thinkers. They have to have the confidence to think the unthinkable and the flexibility to see unusual connections between events, theories, or products between one field and another. For example, the stethoscope was created when its inventor remembered tapping out messages to his childhood friends on a hollow log.

Children are born creative and resourceful. Many people believe they are more creative than adults because they have not got locked into set ways of seeing things, the pressure to conform or the constraints of logic. I recall asking, on different occasions, each of my children when still quite young to eat some item of food more 'normally'. One was eating a biscuit, the other a piece of toast. They both explained that their bites changed the shape each time and they were holding it up to decide what to turn the food into next. Edward de Bono, the writer famous for his work on creative thinking, has produced a book called *Children Solve Problems* which shows clearly how creative children can be. He presented children with a number of practical problems and invited them to draw pictures and plans of their solutions to avoid being limited by language. Some examples of the creative challenges he set are 'improve the human body', 'invent a sleep machine', 'design a fun machine' and 'create a bicycle for postmen'. Any child can be invited to do the same, and the results will be as delightful and funny as those in the book.

Brainstorming

Brainstorming is a successful technique for generating plenty of creative ideas and solutions. In a brainstorm, four rules operate. These are:

1 Suspend judgement: every idea is accepted without criticism
2 Free-wheel: 'normal' assumptions should be ignored
3 Work on quantity: develop as many ideas as possible
4 Cross-fertilise: build on other people's ideas

Helping Children to be Creative

Encourage games and activities which develop creativity and flexible thinking: imaginative play, painting and drawing, word association or word choice games such as I-spy and alphabet games and crosswords. For older children, using IT and graphics packages, role-paying and fantasy games, dressmaking, cooking, carpentry, textile or CD cover design, technology projects and GCSE course work will all help creativity.

Model flexible thinking so they will follow your example. Talk to them about any connections you see between objects and events. 'That reminds me of. . . ', 'That makes me think about. . . ' or 'Does that make you think of anything?'. For example, it is quite easy to make connections between children's songs or story books and their everyday experiences.

Young children can get frustrated by the constraints of handwriting so cannot always write down the complex stories which are in their heads. You could either let them dictate their story to you or suggest they speak it into a tape recorder. This is a good idea for long journeys.

Tolerate some messiness while the thoughts are flowing. Free thinking cannot occur when we are worried about being told off for chaos or mess. I prefer to use the word 'busy' instead of mess when children have been productive and well-occupied. The aftermath must be cleared up, but it will not help to fret about it before they have finished exploring and experimenting. Even better, think ahead and lay down protective paper or put a waste bin close by to stop you getting anxious.

Encourage younger children, or older ones who are strongly visual to problem solve on paper, using pictures instead of words. Give them the chance to use their ingenuity. Tell them what the goal is, and how long they have got to reach it, but not precisely how to get there.

Always value creativity. Kitty, the girl in Bel Mooney's books of the same name, failed in her attempt to build a plastic model ship because she was too eager to start and would not read the instructions. Undaunted, she added shells and an anchor to the collapsed version which she produced, and instead created a shipwreck.

Help your children to become aware of the time and place they think most creatively, then they'll learn when to get the best out of themselves.

Don't expect them always to conform. If they are happy to be the odd one out, that should be okay. Don't dismiss or criticise an idea as silly. This may put children off being creative. Instead either ask how they expect this idea to work or ask them for three more ideas, inviting them to select the most practical one from all those suggested.

Co-operate to Motivate

Motivation is frequently marred by conflict. Of course, arguments are part and parcel of family life. It is not easy to live closely with other people in perfect and constant harmony. Children inevitably assert their independence and difference and compete against each other. There are different interests to satisfy. Children want things there isn't the money to buy. Parents often have different approaches which can add to the tension. We can all say things clumsily and provoke defensive replies. While it is normal and healthy for people to express different views, even to tease and banter, families which are in constant conflict hold children back. The challenge is not to wipe out conflict, but to avoid unnecessary battles and manage the rest without leaving a trail of simmering resentment. It is interesting to note that 'grievance' is linked to the word 'grief', which comes from the Latin *gravis*, meaning heavy. When we feel resentful, or 'aggrieved', we bear a heavy sadness about losing something – usually an important person's support and understanding.

Who Does What?

Take a moment to write down the things that cause the most friction in your home. It might be clothes, bedtimes, staying out late, watching too much television, what your children eat, messy bedrooms, table manners, not washing up their coffee mugs, poor school results, not telling you about comings and goings, generally getting into trouble. If you have several children and a partner, write a separate list for each one. When compiling your lists, think about the following points:

- Try to prioritise. Which is your biggest gripe, then next biggest? The less you argue about, the more co-operative everyone will feel. Rather than argue about everything and get nowhere, choose the two or three things that niggle you most, and go for change.
- Be specific and positive about the changes you want. Looking at your priority areas, write down what, precisely, you expect, or would like, to happen.
- Be reasonable. Write down two good reasons why you want it that way – to check that you have a good case and to justify your request if challenged.

- Make it practical. Is your child capable of reaching your target (e.g. putting used clothes in the wash basket)? What might he or you need to do to manage it better (e.g. put a special bag outside his room)? How might he do it (e.g. develop a nightly routine)? If your child is not old enough to think up a strategy for himself, you will need to suggest one and get him to agree to it. Would a simple reward scheme help to get the habit established?
- Identify room for compromise. It might be a good tactic to show flexibility, so think about this before you start talking (e.g. having his own laundry bag in his bedroom instead of using the main one in another room).

Now present your plan for a more peaceful life. State your aim positively. You are trying to create a more pleasant life for everyone. Don't just tell them they are driving you mad.

If your children are old enough, and you feel brave enough, you could invite them to do the same. When you are all calm, everyone's lists and priorities can be discussed, and joint targets and compromises, with tolerance and patience, agreed.

Conflict Over Homework, Television and Leisure

All arguments at home disturb children, especially those between parents or parents and partners. What affects motivation more obviously and directly is conflict over homework, television and commitment to activities such as sport and music practice. Here are some guidelines and tips.

Homework

Children are more likely to do the work that school expects if it is treated seriously at home. The need for time and space should be respected, with homework fitted into the family routines. Too much opportunity to avoid it, or not finish it, and they may not learn the lessons of commitment, application and perspiration. Though homework is important, it does not help to argue about it. Arguments about homework are usually about four things: where it is done, how it is done, when it is done (and if it is done), and who should do it.

Where it is Done

Anywhere your child feels comfortable and the work is of an acceptable quality. Some children like to work on the floor, others at a table. A regular place helps to set up a routine. A flat surface is usually necessary for legible handwriting, using rulers and so on. Apparently

Prime Minister Tony Blair always works on a soft sofa, never at a table.

How it is Done

Within reason, this is up to them. Some like total quiet, others like company or some background noise. Short breaks may help to keep up concentration, but others may lose the thread if they stop too often. It's your child's work. School needs to know what your child does not know. Keep criticisms to a minimum. Don't look at it and think how you would have done it. If you see any mistakes, suggest they check it through again; or let the teacher do the teaching.

When it is Done

Although some people work better under pressure, leaving everything until the last minute is not a good habit to get into. Rushed work can be careless work. Routines can help to take the tension out of wondering when they will get round to doing it. As children get older, they have to do it their way. Homework books provided by the school should tell you whether there is work due, whether it has been done and, sometimes, whether it was satisfactory. Ask to see it.

By Whom it is Done

It should be done by the child. Homework helps children to learn to work on their own. The more you interfere, the less they learn self-management. Children need to be able to rely on themselves. If you take it over, you imply they can't do it properly and arguments are more likely. Research has shown that children can stop seeing work as their own if someone else does even a small part of it, especially if that involves writing on their work. If children are unclear about how to do something, try to lead them to the right answer through asking them questions rather than simply telling them the answer, so they learn enough to do it for themselves next time.

To sum up, we should:

- treat homework as important. Make it a high priority
- try to establish good homework routines
- offer some choice about how, where, when, so they feel in charge of it – provided it gets done, of course
- agree a suitable place – where possible quiet, somewhere with a flat surface
- show confidence that they will manage it well
- be there to talk about it or look at it if they want you to
- let the teacher do the teaching, if, when you try to help, it leads to arguments
- co-operate to motivate

Television

Television and computer games are great for filling empty times and for keeping children out of harm's, and parents', way; but clear rules are needed about the time spent if children are not to get 'glued' to the screen, ignore their work and, more important, miss out on chances to do other things and find out more about themselves. Worries about children's viewing and playing habits usually concern how much time they spend in front of screen, and the content of what they see and do.

Issues of Time

Children need our time and attention. Time spent in front of television or computer screens is time not spent talking to us (if we are around), getting evidence that we enjoy their company and are interested in what they think and feel. Many children like to wind down after school in front of the television, but they can seem to get stuck there. Research has shown that children's arousal levels can get so low after half an hour's television watching that they become over-relaxed – not a good mental state for homework. A television guide will help them to select programmes and limit their viewing themselves. Invite them to write down their choices and their plan for the afternoon or evening's viewing. Research has also shown that children who watch a lot of television tend to have low self-esteem, be more antisocial and have poorer language development, so we do need to be careful about how much they watch. The more we talk to children, the better their language and learning skills become.

Issues of Content

Many parents worry about the suitability of certain programmes for children. They fear that unpleasant news items will make younger children fearful or anxious and lose their innocence or trust in adults. They fear that violent and sexually explicit drama may lead to copy-cat behaviour, desensitise children and reinforce a macho-style, anti-education culture which boys, in particular, seem to pick up. Research that has tried to identify a clear link between watching violence and violent behaviour is considered inconclusive. Nevertheless, many people remain convinced there is a link. Television companies all agree to schedule material that is not necessarily suitable for family viewing after nine o'clock in the evening. This is called 'the watershed'. Preventing young children from watching after this time will be the best way to safeguard their development. Always remember that your own attitudes and values will have greatest long-term impact.

To sum up, we should:

- try to agree rules about when and for how long, and bring the total number of hours down bit by bit
- help them to think of other things they might do, as nagging is not usually effective
- sometimes watch television with them or, even better, do something else or play with them
- make sure they get plenty of physical exercise too, as this sharpens the mind
- use television to develop imagination, judgement and other learning skills – discuss the programmes; follow up on activities shown on screen; invite them to think up an alternative ending to a drama; encourage other computer-based skills if game-playing seems to dominate
- offer a balance of activities, as children develop best when they do a number of different things

Extra-curricular 'Homework'

Children learn many different things outside the classroom which require extra commitments beyond the actual lesson time, such as sports training and music practice. Children often see these as boring and wish they were not necessary. The more arguments there are, the less a child will enjoy the activity and may ask to give up. How can these commitments be managed so they stop being such a bone of contention, yet get done?

A child's age, personality, interest and natural talent will affect the rules and expectations. Some children will willingly do what they are asked, while others fight every inch of the way, especially if pushed. Teachers and coaches usually make clear the tasks for the week and how much time they expect a child to spend on them. If the week's work is not expressed in terms of targets for improvement, there is a tendency to ask for a time commitment that will ensure a measure of progress – probably more than a child feels is necessary. Rather than push to the point of breakdown, it is far better, first, to try using some incentives and then renegotiate the child's commitment in discussion with the teacher if the incentives fail. The last resort before considering that a child stop the activity altogether is to change the teacher.

Arguments over these extra commitments usually cover how often and how the practice gets done.

How Often

Be guided by the teacher. Little and often works better than one or two longer sessions. With musical instruments, three times a week is usually the minimum to ensure progress. Younger children can be given incentives, such as pennies or sweets put in a 'practice jar', emptied every two or four weeks. This can be enough to get children over a difficult period. Record sheets can work well, and help everyone to agree on what was done when. Regular practice is certainly valuable. It encourages stickability, demonstrates a useful lesson that effort produces results, makes the lessons more enjoyable and productive, and if it takes place at a set time, it reduces the scope for conflict. However, some children will apply themselves better if they feel in the mood. If they have enough self-motivation to be trusted with the flexibility, this is fine.

Practice Quality

This is the teacher's responsibility. Ask your child whether he wants your help. Sometimes he may, sometimes not. If he invites you to listen or watch – do just that: resist the temptation to comment or criticise.

Giving Up

Consider whether your child has given it his best shot. Whose idea was it to start the activity, yours or his? Would the money be useful if he stops? Is there something else he wants to do instead? Might you try a different teacher first? Might he like a break and then go back later?

To sum up, we should:

- let the teacher do the teaching and don't expect too much; practice may make perfect in the end, but not every time our child plays
- remember that praise and encouragement go a long way, so notice his efforts
- agree a commitment, about how many times a week and for how long, and try to keep to it
- let him say what is manageable for him, if there's a dispute, and keep him to it

Lazy Listening and Careless Talk

An American researcher, Stanley Coopersmith, monitored the development of 1,760 children for seven years and identified three aspects of their lives which seemed to make a difference to their self-esteem. These were:

1 A caring, positive and supportive environment
2 Structure, consistency and predictability
3 Someone there who listens

Lazy listening not only harms self-esteem, it also fuels conflict. How can we avoid lazy listening and careless talk, and instead foster co-operation and understanding, not confrontation?

Lazy listening:

- misses the message
- forgets the feeling
- closes the communication
- starts and ends with the listener, not the child

Careless talk:

- is directive
- is deflective
- is destructive
- is dismissive
- disempowers the child

Listening that 'Hears'

Various terms have been used to define listening that 'hears' and registers what is being said. These include effective listening, reflective listening, sensitive listening, active listening and attentive listening. Paul Greenhalgh, in his book *Emotional Growth and Learning,* defines real listening as when the person speaking is 'being heard from the point of view of [his] own experience'. In other words, real listening respects and accepts the world of the person speaking. Greenhalgh concludes that 'effective dialogue is aided when the adult communicates that she has accurately understood the young person's frame of reference, which requires responding with empathy'.

Communication works when an adult:

- wants to understand
- mostly knows what the child means
- usually senses feelings
- appreciates how the experience feels to the child

Listening involves paying, or giving, attention. We have to give something of ourselves. 'Attention' means consideration and care. 'Attentive' means observant. Attentive listening could therefore be defined as listening in which the listener is careful to pay attention: is observant, shows consideration and seems to care.

All the different terms used to define productive listening entail important aspects of the whole listening process. So, for example:

- attentive listening refers to attitude, being observant and considerate
- effective listening refers to results, whether they address the problem expressed
- reflective listening refers to the process of confirming we have understood

- active listening emphasises that the activity entails effort and is not passive
- sensitive listening refers to the need, sometimes, to look beyond the words to identify the feelings and intended meaning behind them

Listening, we can now see, is therefore a multi-staged process:

1 Stop what you are doing. Mentally prepare; let go of yourself, empty your mind of your thoughts and imagine you are standing in the space between you and your child.
2 Apply yourself to listening, concentrate. Turn to face your child, look at him, and stay looking at him even if he turns away.
3 Receive the message; hold on to the words, hear them repeated in your mind, and mentally file them somewhere.
4 Think about what has been said, and reflect it back, using, for example, 'So you didn't like what he said to you. . . ' to confirm you have heard.
5 Check, through your child's response, that your understanding is accurate.
6 Absorb the implications, for you and others, of what you have heard.
7 Act accordingly, taking on board what has been said.

This staged process can be summarised in the six-letter word LISTEN.

L stands for 'let go', of ourselves, to enable us to focus on the other person.
I stands for 'intent', we actively intend and are committed to listen, hear and learn.
S stands for 'soak up', or absorb and understand, the message that is being sent.
T stands for 'transmit', our understanding of what has been said back to our child.
E stands for 'echo', to check if our understanding resonates with what he intended.
N stands for 'non-judgemental', which is what we must be when we absorb the implications.

Poor Listening in Adults

The above account clearly identifies how we can improve our listening skills. Greenhalgh has grouped the signs and reasons for poor listening in adults. His three groups are 'not managing oneself' listening, 'getting lost in the feelings' listening and 'losing the story' listening. Below is an edited description of each group, with some other comments and examples added.

'Not managing oneself' Listening

This occurs when people dip in and out of listening; jump to conclusions, and then switch off; only listen when the message is one they want to hear; constantly return the conversation to their preferred topic; pretend to listen but become lost in their own thoughts; tend to compete, saying they know it, have experienced it or have thought it too; or express a judgement about what has been said, based on their own view or opinion. In other words, the listener is unwilling to 'let go' of himself, as described in the LISTEN scheme above. The exchange starts and finishes with the listener who is very 'self' focused.

For example:

Child   Mum, Mr Regan asked me to read my story to the class today.
Mum   Really? That's good. That used to happen to me quite often.
Child   It was a story about a baby being naughty in the supermarket.
Mum   That's funny. I was just thinking, what would you like for tea today?
Child   Not bothered. (Walks away, disappointed.)

A better approach would be:

Child   Mum, Mr Regan asked me to read my story to the class today.
Mum   Really? It must have been good. Well done. What was it about?
Child   It was about a baby being naughty in the supermarket.
Mum   Ah! I bet you had fun writing that. Did it make the class laugh?
Child   Yes. That made me feel great.
Mum   Was there any of you in the story?
Child   Yup. I was the baby!
Mum   I thought as much! Has your shopping trip given you any ideas for tea?

'Getting lost in the feelings' Listening

This happens when people react emotionally and impulsively to the unconscious feelings aroused in themselves; focus on the symptoms, instead of thinking more deeply about what they might mean; or think only about the feelings they usually have when they relate to the other person – which is another form of 'self' focus.

For example:

Child   Dad, I don't want Grandpa coming to watch me play football today.
Dad   What do you mean, you don't want him to come? I can't possibly put him off. He'd be so hurt. You know how he loves to watch you. It's rude and I'm disappointed you're asking me to do that. I've talked to you before about how you speak to him!

Instead, Dad could have said:

Dad   You know that will upset him so you must have a reason.

Child   Yes. You see today a talent spotter is coming from the grown-ups' club to watch us. I want to do my best and I think too many people watching me will put me off. Actually, I'd rather you didn't come either. Do you mind?

Dad   Of course not. I'm sure Grandpa will understand. I'll take him somewhere else so he still gets an outing. And don't worry if you're not picked. You're doing well and there's plenty of time to get better.

'Losing the story' Listening

This happens when the listener focuses on the facts or detail, instead of the whole experience, perhaps to avoid any feelings which he himself finds hard to manage; or fails to notice surrounding non-verbal messages conveyed through body language, facial expression or tone of voice.

For example:

Mum   (Hears a crash, a yell and rushes out to see her son in a heap at the bottom of the stairs) What have you done?

Child   (In tears) I slipped. Can't you see?

Mum   (Offering no comfort) How many steps did you fall down? Were you carrying anything? What's hurting?

Child   My foot.

Mum   Is it your toes, your ankle, your heel or what?

Child   It just hurts.

Mum   Is it the left one or the right? Let me see it.

Child   (Still sobbing) No, I can't move it.

Mum   I've told you so many times not to walk around in socks. It's asking for trouble. It can't be that bad. Try to get up. See if you can walk on it.

Instead, Mum could have said:

Mum   (Cuddles to give comfort) You're obviously hurt. Is the pain bad?

Child   Right now, yes.

Mum   (Stays quiet with child) When you ready, tell me what's hurt. I'll get some ice. Poor you!

Lazy listening makes children feel ignored, misunderstood or wrong, instead of feeling accepted, supported and encouraged. It creates a resentful and withdrawn child, and draws us into careless talk, which makes things worse, especially for their motivation.

Watch What You Say

This book has emphasised the importance of 'mastery' – helping children to be actively involved in their learning and successful at it: how we should, at every opportunity, encourage our children to manage things for themselves, and to see and trust themselves as capable. Careless talk does the opposite. It ignores or denies a child's feelings or view of the problem. It directs a child and prevents him from sorting something out for himself. It devalues things a child sees as important. It tells him he cannot trust his judgement. In so doing, it diminishes, disempowers and demotivates him.

If we try to make a child's feelings go away, or if we disapprove of any feelings he has, he will believe he is wrong to have them. If we tell a child how to manage his feelings, he will not learn how to accept, process or take responsibility for them himself.

We should try to be more careful. Here are some examples of unhelpful and helpful ways to talk.

Ignoring a Child's Feelings or View

Challenging
Why are you so worried about that? It's an easy problem to solve! (Can you tell me what you find difficult about these sums?)

Reassuring
Stop fussing. You'll have forgotten about it by tomorrow and I think you're doing just fine. (It clearly matters to you that you came third today. Was there a special reason you wanted to do better?)

Shaming
Don't be so sensitive. You've got to toughen up. (It's hard when our feelings are hurt.)

Minimising
It's really not that important. Come and have a biscuit. (This seems important to you. Would you like to tell me more about it?)

Blaming
I told you you'd twist your ankle if you wore those shoes. Go and change them now. (That must have hurt. Which shoes will be comfortable for you now?)

Directing and Preventing a Child from Sorting Out for Himself

Advising
If you're so worried, go and do some more practice That's what I'd do. (What would make you feel less worried?)

Rescuing

I'll give you an outline for your essay and then you'll have something to write about. (What's the problem? Is it the plan, your main argument or the first paragraph?)

Manipulating

You could do it that way. But, really, this way is much better. Are you sure you want to do it like that? (You might like to try it your way first, and mine next time. Then you can decide which is best for you.)

Directing

Look. Do this now and then you'll have time to play on the computer later. (Make sure you plan your morning so the important things get done too. Here's some paper.)

Devaluing Things a Child Sees as Important

Excusing

You may see it as unfair, but I don't think she meant it. I wouldn't take it to heart. (I can see your point. Do you think she meant it that way, or was she under pressure?)

Dismissing

I don't know why you're so upset. It's not that big a deal. This happens to children every day of the week. (This has upset you a lot. I can tell.)

Deflecting

Why are you so upset about not being picked as class monitor? You're great at football and will probably have the glory of being in the team. (You wanted that job badly, didn't you. Can you tell me why?)

Careful Talk

If we are careful about what we say and how we say it, on the other hand, we can help our children.

Accepting Difficulty

Those French irregular verbs are hard to remember!
It takes a long time to get on top of all the times tables, doesn't it?

Acknowledging Feeling

You're very disappointed we're going to be away for Vijay's party, aren't you?
It's given you such a thrill to be asked to do the introduction for the school play, hasn't it!
I know there are times when you hate your brother.

Providing Encouragement to Succeed
Lots of people are anxious about learning to drive. You say you're not co-ordinated but good driving is about thinking ahead which you know you're good at. If twelve-year-old tear-aways can drive, so can you!

Allowing Autonomy
'What do you think about it all now?'
'I've got myself in a mess, haven't I?'
'Mmm.'
'I think I should have told my teacher about the problem a month ago.'
'Yep.'
'I'll go and explain it all now. It won't happen again.'

Final Tips on Managing Conflict

Try not to take any dispute personally. Just because we feel it personally does not mean they meant it personally.

Show you understand what it means to them. 'You're going to be disappointed in my answer, which is no.'

Keep it in proportion. It is easy to make yourself sound strong and tough by raising the stakes, but it is not helpful. 'If that's your attitude then I won't bother to cook for you any more!' Try, instead, something like, 'That's not helpful and is not acceptable. I asked you to do this because it needs to be done. Please think again.'

Try to respect things that are important to them, such as friends, how they look, what they like to do. Rubbishing them creates distance that become ever harder to bridge.

Try not to blame them for things that have gone wrong when you are, in truth, responsible. 'If you had not had your music on so loud, I wouldn't have forgotten to go to the school meeting.'

Try an 'opt out' with no questions tactic. Any phrase can be chosen to be used when either side feels they've gone too far and want to end the argument without losing face. When the phrase is used, the subject must be dropped instantly and not mentioned again. The tactic can be used with young children too. My daughter chose the phrase 'white rabbits' and it got us off many a hook. Make sure you let your child use it first.

Remember, it usually takes six weeks to change behaviour.

PART THREE

REDISCOVERING MOTIVATION: GETTING THEM BACK ON TRACK

'Neither people nor problems fit moulds, and the very act of doing so can create its own problems', writes Mark H McCormack in *What They Don't Teach You at the Harvard Business School*. Nevertheless, there are some common situations which are known to sap children's energy to do their best and undermine their motivation. If these are understood, we will be able to make our support and involvement more relevant and therefore effective. Some of these more usual situations are discussed in the following chapters. If none of these seems to explain your child's state of mind, the concluding chapter ends with a summary trouble-shooting guide which may give you other ideas and solutions. The guide follows the stages of the motivation journey as set out in the model in Chapter Two.

PART THREE

REDISCOVERING MOTIVATION: GETTING THEM BACK ON TRACK

The Impact of Stress

Motivation is affected negatively by stress, depression and uncomfortable emotions. Children who suddenly lose interest and direction in activities which previously absorbed them, or who seem to get stuck on a plateau and make no progress, may be reacting to situations and events which they find hard to accept.

Contrary to common belief, stress is not something suffered only by adults. Even those who work with children can make this mistake. Usually associated with events such as divorce, redundancy, problems at work, marital disharmony and even difficult children, which happen to us only as we grow older, stress is frequently seen as a consequence of adult responsibilities: burdens which we know children do not have.

We also link reactions to stress, including depression, with adults. Excessive drinking, dependence on tranquillisers, staying in bed all day and, at the extreme, suicide, are things we cannot conceive of young children doing. The idea that children suffer from stress and depression can seem far-fetched. If we do hear of older children abusing alcohol or drugs, we tend to see it as experimentation or rebellion. But, as Philip Graham has indicated in his booklet *So Young, So Sad, So Listen,* the reality is that rebellion itself can be a distress signal.

Symptoms of Stress and Unhappiness in Children

It can be hard to realise that a child has a problem, especially in the early stages. Like us, children have different moods, good days and bad days, go on and off people and activities, and sleep better or worse for little apparent reason. However, if we ignore the early signs we can be faced with far more serious consequences later. We need to be able to recognise when both older and younger children begin to feel out of sorts.

Common Signs of Emotional Distress in Children

Some of the commonest indicators include:

- a sad, unhappy mood that lasts for more than two or three days
- becoming withdrawn, showing little or no pleasure in ordinary, everyday activities or getting unduly immersed in television or computer games

- different sleep patterns – waking in the night or finding it hard to drop off
- appearing to be tired for no apparent reason
- different eating and drinking patterns – tummy aches, feeling sick, losing appetite and needing more drinks to quench a stronger thirst
- refusing or being reluctant to go to school: irritable and slow to dress in the morning and wanting to get back home again quickly after
- bedwetting, nail biting, renewed thumb or finger sucking
- becoming more uncooperative and aggressive at home and at school, including physical and verbal abuse, with both parents and siblings
- phantom aches and pains in limbs or head and neck aches caused by tension
- being more dependent and clingy
- stealing, particularly when the items stolen are hoarded
- finding concentration difficult, becoming inattentive and easily distracted
- retreating into fantasy and make-believe, to a world where they are back in control
- demonstrating low self-esteem; self-criticism, suicidal thoughts or behaviour; or striving for an inappropriate perfectionism

Different children react differently to problems depending on their personality and age, so this list covers a wide range of behaviour, even some complete opposites. Extreme behaviour at either end of the range indicates distress. Most children will display one or another of these symptoms at some time. We should take special note if:

- changes in behaviour are unusual and out of character
- this behaviour is inappropriate given the child's age
- several of the above symptoms appear at the same time

If there are grounds for concern on this basis, we can then look for a possible cause.

What Children Find Difficult and Stressful

The events that cause stress and depression in adults can be hard to bear because they contain certain features that all of us, whatever our age, find difficult to manage. Knowing what these features are will give us an insight into events that can destabilise children. These features are:

- separation from those close to us – as a result of, for example, death and divorce
- changes to our status and self-image – following marriage, birth, illness or a new job

• changes to our routines – such as holidays, religious festivals, house and school moves

Some of these changes are predictable and within our control; others happen without warning. Change, in itself, can be hard to cope with, but when we are caught unawares we will feel our lack of control more acutely.

Potentially stressful events, then, are those which impact on our key relationships, through which we understand ourselves, and our feelings of security, by introducing change and uncertainty.

In summary, stress changes how we look at ourselves and undermines our self-esteem. It makes us feel out of control and unstable. It undermines our trust in ourselves and the future. No wonder it can stop us in our tracks.

Children, of course, do not have jobs, so cannot be made redundant. They are not responsible for family finances, so do not have money worries. They do not have husbands or wives, so cannot experience first-hand marital problems such as infidelity or sexual difficulties though, of course, they are inevitably involved when relationships break down. However, not only do children pick up on the stress and depression of adults close to them, they also have their own experiences which they find stressful, independent of family problems. They therefore get a double dose. Add to this the reality that children have less experience of life and themselves to trust that 'normality' will resume, and we can see children are more likely to be confused and disorientated by stress than adults, not less.

Looking at the three categories of stressors, we can be more attuned to the experiences children will find difficult.

Separations

Death of a Family Member

When a child loses a parent, grandparent, brother or sister through death, many feelings are awakened. These will include fear, because someone else close might also be taken away, anger, confusion, disappointment, isolation and emptiness. Never seeing that close and treasured person again, they will miss the warmth, the support and the acceptance and identity that the now eternally absent person provided. Of course death is traumatic. Moving house and away from special friends can have a similar effect.

Death of a Pet

Children get close to pets because they are warm and safe. Losing one is like losing a best friend. The death of a pet can also make children realise parents can die too, and make them feel insecure for a while.

When Parents Split Up

When parents decide to stop living together, most children will feel profoundly sad. They will know that something important has ended and will have a sense of loss. They will also feel shattered, and perhaps torn, because the two people who made them and have supported them are taking that support away and going in different directions.

Short- or Longer-term Absence of a Parent

When children are young, parents are their safety net and are always in their mind. Children depend on them for daily support. When a parent moves out, or goes away or into hospital, even for a few days, a child can feel worried and vulnerable.

Losing or Falling Out with Friends

Friendships become increasingly important as children grow older. Close friendships make us feel wanted and special. They help us to feel acceptable and that we belong somewhere. When a child loses a special friend, either through a school move or an argument, it will almost certainly undermine his confidence. He will feel isolated and rejected. To respond 'Don't worry. You'll find another one soon' will not meet the concern or heal the hurt. Instead, we can say, 'If you are lonely at break-time now Vijay's decided to play with others, would it help to take a toy or game in to play with?' or 'It takes time to make new friends, often because others don't realise you're free to play. Is there someone you'd like to invite to tea?'

Change in Status and Self-image

School Changes

When children start school, they can no longer see themselves as a baby. When they move from infant to junior, or from junior to secondary school, they change from being one of the oldest children in the building to being one of the youngest.

New Family Members

The arrival of a new baby automatically changes the status of existing children, particularly the youngest. They may also have to accept new responsibilities, ready or not. At least in this case they will have a clear place in the family pecking order. Acquiring instant stepbrothers and sisters can produce considerable role confusion.

Illness and Hormonal Changes

Any kind of prolonged illness will change a child's self-image. Puberty involves physical changes which force children to see themselves in a different light.

Bullying

Anyone subjected to prolonged bullying will have their self-respect shattered. This subject is covered in greater depth in Chapter Twenty-three.

Work, Exam and Parental Pressures

These can turn a youngster who once felt strong and capable into someone who feels uncertain and incompetent.

Changes in Routines

Children like to know where they stand. They feel safe with routine and familiarity. It helps them to predict and to feel in control of their lives. Changes to routines can be unnerving, especially to children who already feel vulnerable. I once knew a young child whose family had two televisions. He regularly watched the black and white one in the family's kitchen-breakfast room. The second set was a colour one kept in the smart front room for the adults. When the kitchen was due for redecoration, he was told that he would be eating, playing and watching television in the front room for the duration. Instead of jumping with glee at the thought of watching his favourite programmes in colour and having access to the grown-ups' domain, he became quite disturbed and threw a tantrum. He wanted the regular television and his regular ways. This shows how a child's perspective on change can be radically different from an adult's.

Adult Stress Impacts on Children

Family stress can be the root of children's motivation problems. Stress makes us preoccupied, withdrawn, moody and certainly less patient. We are less available and more unpredictable. We forget things, including things that our children want us to do for them, which makes them feel forgotten. Children detect changed moods and don't like it when life becomes different. They will often seek reassurance through attention-seeking behaviour to receive a sign of continued love. This behaviour is usually 'difficult', otherwise it will not have the desired effect. It can easily be misinterpreted and lead, instead, to more apparent rejection. Very young children will simply behave badly; older children may stop working or go out more. They may change their eating habits or style of dress. If, after trying several times, they don't get the reassurance they seek, they will try to protect themselves by cutting off.

How Many Children are Affected by Stress?

No one can be absolutely sure, partly because it is difficult to agree on definitions in a field concerned with states of mind and partly because children can suffer without anyone knowing. Nonetheless, there is wide agreement among those working in this area that mental health problems are relatively common in children and young people. Young Minds, the children's mental health charity, estimates that up to 20 per cent may require help at some time. This amounts to nearly two million children under the age of 16 in England and Wales. Seven to 10 per cent of all children have problems which are moderate to severe, and as many as two per cent suffer from severe mental health problems. Dr Stephen Scott, consultant child psychiatrist at the Institute of Psychiatry at the Maudsley Hospital, suggests that about 10 per cent of children have problems that are significantly disabling. For Scott, these are problems which 'stop children and adolescents doing the normal things, being able to make friends, go to school, function productively. . . persistent problems lasting for a year or more which really handicap the ability to be happy'.

There is mounting evidence to suggest that problems at the severe end are growing. The following figures are those used by Young Minds and are quoted in the booklet *So Young, So Sad, So Listen* written for parents and teachers.

- Eating disorders are on the increase, among younger children too. Between one and two per cent of teenage girls now suffer from an eating disorder: the incidence is one in 100 in private schools, one in 500 in comprehensive schools and one in 55 in universities. Nine out of 10 sufferers are girls but the incidence among boys is growing. In 1984, the Great Ormond Street Children's Hospital saw two children with anorexia a year. Now it sees four new cases a week.
- In 1992, two young people aged 15–19 committed suicide every week. Every year, one in 100 12–16 year-olds attempts suicide. Suicides among young men are rising significantly. In 1996, it was the second most common cause of death among people aged between 15 and 24.
- Five per cent of teenagers are seriously depressed. Two in 100 children are seriously depressed.
- The number of children and young people admitted as psychiatric inpatients in hospital is growing alarmingly, albeit from a small base. Over the last five years, admissions of children aged under 10 have increased by 50 per cent.

It would be safe to say that these statistics represent the tip of the iceberg. For each of these cases, there will be many more where young people came close to not coping but were able to hold on to normality. These statistics also relate mostly to older children whose problems will almost certainly have taken root much earlier.

How Stress Disrupts Motivation

We all have a point beyond which pressure and challenge stop being exciting and manageable, and we crack. The more we have to manage, the less we are able to cope. Like weights added to one side of those old-fashioned, seesaw scales, it can be an apparently insignificant issue, the smallest weight, that upsets the balance and tips us over into feelings of failure and panic. At this point, even normal tasks seem difficult. We lose confidence and we lose self-belief. We lose energy and can become intensely preoccupied with our problems and failures.

A child cannot learn unless he feels at ease with himself. This means that pleasant and unpleasant emotions have to be faced and managed. Only then can he relax comfortably and concentrate. Most parents are able to understand that if a child is preoccupied with a problem and feels swamped with the emotions it brings in its train, he will not be able to clear his thoughts sufficiently to focus on anything else. But this is only part of the picture.

Fear, of failure, success, or the unknown, prevents children from opening up and trying. Anxiety keeps children in suspension, and makes them unwilling to commit to answers, opinions or actions. Anger makes children boil; it takes them over. Jealousy can be the spur to outdo someone else but it can also preoccupy. Resentment makes children uncooperative, cut themselves off and want revenge on those who have hurt them. Hatred causes children to withdraw cooperation. Children can hate because they feel let down; because their trust has been abused or they feel used. Hostility is closely linked to depression.

Emotions and Self-esteem

These feelings occur in situations which are likely to damage a child's self-esteem, which adds a further twist to the dynamic of underachievement. If we hate, it is because someone has been unpleasant to us and we might believe we deserved that treatment. If we are jealous, it is because we fear that another person is liked better ourselves. If we are envious, we covet something which somebody else has and feel incomplete without it. Resentment grows when we feel someone has ignored our interests or exploited us. Anxiety relates to a belief that we can't, or won't be able to, cope. We don't feel in charge and our competence is threatened. If we are angry, it is usually because we are frustrated and feel powerless. Yet motivation requires inner strength and good self-belief. It is not just strong, negative emotions that interfere with motivation but also the situations that give rise to them.

Getting Them Back on Track

We can support children through their difficulties. We can try to listen to what children say, and be sensitive to their behaviour. If they:

- raise something important, wherever possible we should stop what we are doing and give them our full attention
- behave out of character, we should try to attune ourselves to their needs by watching and interpreting their behaviour
- stop talking and listening to us, it may be because things are too strained. In these cases, it can be helpful to alert another adult who knows our child well and suggest he or she creates an opportunity to talk

Encourage Children to Talk

It can be hard to start a discussion about sensitive matters, especially with older children who may be defensive. Instigate a conversation at the appropriate moment, saying something like 'You don't seem to have been yourself recently. I don't like to see you so down. I just want to let you know that I am here for you whenever you want to talk', lets them know we are aware and concerned but hands the initiative to them.

If you want to try to get children to talk, choose a quiet place when there is plenty of time. With a younger child, it can help to look at a children's story book that covers the same or similar situation and feelings he is experiencing. With an older child, spending more open-ended time together may create a moment when he feels able to take the initiative. One teenage boy of divorced parents I met told me his father used to ask him how he felt about the divorce when driving him home after weekend visits. It was a short journey and the son felt insulted not only because the time available was so limited but also because it came across as a convenient 'quick fix' that demonstrated little genuine concern.

Acknowledge and Accept Feelings

Let them know we realise they are feeling something that is normal and understandable. Telling them they have no reason to feel that way will not reassure them. Encourage children to express their feelings in acceptable ways – through painting, drawing, music, imaginative play, sport, or creative design, especially if they are too young to talk or are finding it hard.

Take away any guilt they might feel. When things go wrong in families, even when someone dies, children can feel it is their fault. We can help to remove any self-recrimination they feel if we can explain clearly that they are not responsible or to blame in any way.

Help Them Feel Secure

Keeping as many routines going as possible through any changes will provide some continuity, security and comfort to offset any difficulties. Any other changes that are not essential are best kept to a minimum.

It can help our children if we actually tell them we love them and if we try to be around a bit more.

Boost Their Self-esteem and Self-belief

Show them that you accept and love them for who they are. Try to understand them and their feelings. Give them plenty of time and attention. Children who are depressed or not doing well at anything could be feeling insignificant. Talking and doing things together and being around more will help them to trust your love, feel wanted and therefore feel and cope better.

Create some 'motivation momentum' by letting them know you think they are good at things. Avoid criticism. Give them chances to try new activities so they can discover new talents.

If they have few friends and don't go out much, try to encourage them to be more sociable. Joining a club or an activity group can open up social opportunities, though older children may refuse this point blank.

Attention-seeking behaviour is attention-needing behaviour. Don't let bad behaviour be the only way to get attention.

Keep Them Informed

Tell them what is happening as far as possible. They will know something is different, and they will be able to understand it at their level. Try to answer their questions honestly and take their worries seriously.

If there are family rows, we should try not to confide in our children, ask them to take sides, or require them to keep secrets. The responsibility and divided loyalty this causes is very hard for children to manage.

Offering them some choices about events surrounding the happening, provided these are appropriate, can help children to feel respected and included, not left out and ignored.

Look After Yourself

Children who are feeling insecure need much more attention, but it is usually only possible to give this if you feel strong and confident yourself. Where difficulties stem from home, it is very likely that you will also be feeling vulnerable. Looking after yourself will help you to help your child.

Think about what helps you to calm down, relax and feel better. Build it in to your day or week. Reduce the pressures on yourself. Drop unnecessary jobs when you can. Jobs seem less overpowering if you list them in order of importance. Make it clear to the family what you need. You are entitled to have some time alone, for example, provided it still leaves room for them.

Listen and talk more. Understanding how each person sees the problem is the first step to sorting things out – so talking and listening to others in your family helps. So does sharing problems with friends.

It really does not help to feel guilty. And it will certainly add injury to insult if we pass on that guilt in the form of blame, making it appear as if they are responsible. Raise your own self-esteem by listing your good points and your successes. Do this with a friend if it will help.

Peer Pressure: Friends or Foes?

Friends are important to children, whatever their age. When your child's friends 'fit' your family, it gives you a lovely feeling. Not only do you feel warm, proud and relieved that your child is accepted by others as a whole human being and is able to be a friend to others, you are also grateful that your family boat is not being rocked by unwelcome influences. When you don't have to worry, friends are great to have around. The situation is far less rosy when children 'get in with the wrong crowd', when friends subvert your plans, challenge your values and cause problems.

Peer pressure is almost always understood negatively. We use the term when our children want us to buy the 'right' kind of clothes and shoes that usually cost more than we want to pay. We use it when we are pressed to acquire the latest craze toy, when we know it will be a passing fad and forgotten as quickly as it was grabbed. We use it when our children are persuaded to behave disruptively at school and take their eye off the learning ball. And we use it when we are bludgeoned with requests to allow later bed or homecoming times, trips to raves or visits to rock concerts. The tensions caused by peer pressure can, then, start early, despite being commonly associated with the teenage years. To add to parents' frustration, peer pressure usually comes well-laced with values different from our own.

If we are to have any success in encouraging our children to achieve a different balance in their lives, to stay true to themselves rather than be lured and diverted by the call of others, we need to understand why peer pressure can be so hard to resist.

Why Friends are Important

Children like to have friends. With friends, they feel they belong, they feel liked and likeable. Friends validate them, and match their current needs and interests. They help to define who they are, giving them an identity: 'I am friends with this sort of person so I am also like this'. Friends help them to fill their time and have fun, to become sociable and learn to be part of a group. They give them confidence to do things they would be reluctant to do on their own – both desirable and less desirable – and they provide safety in numbers. Friends can offer new ideas and interests, adding to experience, and can provide a relevant, moral framework. Real friends will offer support and care, volunteer loyalty and provide a safe haven when things go wrong. Friends become, quite simply, part of themselves; which makes it very hard for us to persuade them to change course.

Friends can be 'satisfying and growth-producing', or they can be the cause of distress and be 'growth-destroying', to quote Mary Pipher in her excellent book, *Reviving Ophelia,* on adolescent girls. Peers are not the same thing as friends. Not all peers are friends, and not all friends are peers, though they usually are. Children themselves can get confused between the two. It is a useful distinction for parents to bear in mind, as we shall see shortly. Peers are all those of a similar age who share their world – geographical, educational and social. The peer group will be broader than a friendship group, and influenced by more widespread values. Friends can be single or grouped. Though influenced by peer values, friendship groups will usually have more specific interests and attitudes in common.

Are They Really Foes?

Parents can become almost tribal in their defensive reactions to the changes which the outside world foists on their children. I remember very clearly my daughter coming home from primary school not just with a different way of talking picked up from the playground but also with clothes smelling different – a mixture of school dinners and disinfectant. I did not like it. I wondered if she was going to stay like that. In the same way, friends who introduce 'foreign' values can be difficult to accept. However we do need to try to keep things in perspective. Conflict over friends is likely to drive children away and reduce our influence still further, so it is important to keep our views and interventions for those times when it really matters. Here are some factors we can consider if we think our child's friends are exerting a bad influence.

First, our children may be entering a time of change. They have to experiment with their developing selves, and it is common for them to try themselves out with different friendship groups. They were going to change anyway. Trust them to settle with friends who reflect their earlier family experiences – or let them be different if they are not at the same time jeopardising their future opportunities.

Second, it is inevitable that our children live their lives differently from how we lived ours as children. It may seem threatening, and we may regret lost innocence, but this is the world they live in.

Third, a wider variety of experiences, handled responsibly and within clear limits, will prepare them well for a future full of choices and temptations.

Fourth, as children grow, they need to get up to mischief, make mistakes and pay the price for these. In general, we are far more aware of what our children get up to these days. Worry about alcohol, drugs and crime can encourage us to overreact and become overprotective.

Preserving Their Self-respect

So when should we start to worry? Some children do go seriously off course. Whether this is directly and solely the responsibility of their friends is something we have to ask ourselves. Sometimes, it is wise to start looking closer to home; working, first and foremost, on giving them a strong, positive identity that they can feel proud of and which will help them to stay strong and safe.

Children's sense of self, and their self-esteem, is tightly bound up in their friendships. The stronger their sense of who they are, the less they will get seduced by the pull of an unhelpful peer group. The more they learn to trust their own judgement, and can practise saying 'No', the more likely they are to recognise trouble in the making and have the confidence to walk away. The more they see themselves as unwanted, feel a failure or find it hard to please, the more they will seek status in alternative, and possibly illegitimate, ways.

We often hear about friends who think it is not 'cool' to study, but occasionally, peer pressure encourages children to strive too hard. Especially in academic, girls-only schools, the tide of competition can drive children to try to achieve an undue perfection, typically sucking in eating problems along with it.

If we feel the need to redirect our child, it is tricky to achieve this without undermining him, showing insensitivity to his needs and damaging his trust in his judgements. Whatever tactics we choose, we should ensure that they preserve his self-respect and protect his self-belief and self-esteem.

Getting Them Back on Track

As children choose friends to meet various needs listed above, try to make a list of the things your child may be getting from the group he is currently friends with. Can any of these needs be met in other ways. Try to talk to him about what he expects from a friend. Respect for his point of view, reliability, the ability to understand and compromise might be features raised. It will be up to him, then, to consider if his current 'friends' are really people who deserve his loyalty. It is dangerous for you to say they are no good.

If you feel that work or other, genuine, interests are getting crowded out by the temptations of new friends, perhaps you could discuss together what his various commitments and interests are and seek ways to meet them all. Speaking to the other parents involved to consider the scope for a shared set of rules and expectations may help. Consider if there are any clubs to join or new sporting or other activities to take up to widen the circle of friends available.

Acknowledge and welcome the changes that come with growing up so he can be proud of these, but suggest that we always move forward with some of our old self still in place. We are like snakes, shedding a skin but with our existing body intact. Which bit of his old self is still there, that he can still explore to maintain continuity and stay in touch with himself?

Explain that he does not have to sell his soul to be popular. He can want to be liked, at the same time as be unwilling to make the compromises necessary. It is strong, not weak, to stand out against things, such as treating other people badly or breaking the law, that the group likes to do. Make sure he knows it is okay to say 'No' when something is really important to him, and that it is okay to make mistakes.

Allow him to redefine himself in an accepting atmosphere. Try to reduce the amount of teasing, carping and criticism. Be as encouraging, supportive and non-judgemental as possible. Try to keep your worries to yourself. Predicting academic, sporting or social failure will only undermine his self-belief and it could drive him away. Accept and love him for who he is. Give him space, responsibility and the chance to be useful to you so he can find out more about what he can do. Try to compromise more to avoid too many clashes, but hold firm on a few important issues to you so you retain some authority and respect.

If you have room at home, invite his friends round, so you appear to accept them and can learn more about them than first impressions ever allow. Also spend more time together as a family, and include a friend or two from time to time if that is possible. Consider if any of your friends have children of a suitable age, and if you could invite them all over.

Try to speak optimistically about the future and his role in it, to give him hope. Encourage him to mix with other age groups if possible, perhaps within the family, so he gets another perspective on life and relationships. At the same time keep yourself in touch with his world, without currying favour, aping it or taking it over. Read his magazines, be prepared to listen to his music, talk to other parents, show interest in his school and out-of-school interests. Try to have some meals together so you can chat about his view of things.

And remember: friends can work as well as play together. They can offer mutual support and motivation.

22

The Dejected Child – 'I'm Just Useless!'

Most children will go through times when they feel out of their depth. This is natural, because learning is a constant process of pushing against the frontiers of knowledge. There are new skills to learn and longer time frames to manage. Some children sail through, but not many. Children who have no problems making progress in one aspect of learning may have difficulties elsewhere. Some children surge forward in every sphere for a while, and then find things hard going. Learning is not linear; it takes place in fits and starts. But when problems loom, they can loom large. Self-judgement can become punitive. When children are really low, they will feel useless all round. They will tear up or deface work which they believe is not good enough, and they may have difficulty completing projects, giving up before they have really tried. Success elsewhere, or at other times, will make little impact – 'that doesn't count', will be a typical response when they are reminded. This is because what we are good at, we find easy; and when it is easy, we find it hard to value any success in that sphere as an achievement.

Why Might They Be Feeling this Way?

As was noted in Chapter Two, children can get lost at different stages on the motivation journey. They can be confronted with, or choose, an inappropriate target at stage one. They can fail to assess their skill level sensibly, and fall by the wayside at stage two. They can jump in the deep end, forgetting the need to plan their approach to the target at stage three. They can wilt under the strain of boredom or setbacks at stage four, and find it hard to sustain the commitment necessary. Or they can simply be too hard on themselves, having standards that are too high, which prevents them from recognising when they have done well and arrived at stage five.

The root of the problem can lie deeper, in self-doubt, in which case we have to ask why they feel this way. It can be linked to:

- the drip, drip effect of negative labelling from others, including us, telling them they are 'useless', 'a loser', 'a hopeless case' or 'a dumbo'

- the fact that they tried extra hard this time and it still made no difference
- someone saying something careless, such as 'You had your chance and you blew it' or 'How long is it going to take you to get this right?'
- comparing themselves with a more able child
- realising that, however hard they try, they will never be as good as a particular person they admire or are competing against. Research has shown that, until children are 10 or 12, they believe that good performance is the result of trying hard, and is within everyone's grasp. At about 12, they are able, developmentally, to realise some children have natural talents and will always be better, regardless of how much training, work or effort they put in
- something has happened in their wider life to affect their powers of concentration, memory and listening so they not only start to fall behind but also feel insecure
- their personality – they are that sort of child. But beware that explanation; children are not born incompetent

Watch What You Say

When children are vulnerable, you have to be particularly careful how you respond. What you say has to be real – there is no point saying that something is wonderful when patently it is not – and sound acceptable to them. You have to find the way through their heightened sensitivity to criticism. The danger is that their self-denigration will make you feel impotent and frustrated and more likely to respond insensitively.

What We Tend to Say

We are easily tempted into offering instant solutions which minimise the problem because, as we saw in Chapter Nineteen, many parents consider they have neither the time nor the emotional energy to manage such intangible problems. We would prefer to wave a magic wand and make it all better. That way, we can also avoid feeling our child's pain and despair. At the harsh end of typical responses are, 'You're not the best, but you're not that bad either. Stop feeling sorry for yourself and just get on with it' or 'If you only listened in class, perhaps you'd understand it'. Less critical, but equally directive and unsupportive, are comments such as 'You're not useless. You came third last week. I don't want to hear you do yourself down', 'You'll feel completely different next week' or 'What's wrong with a B+?'. In each of these cases, the child's feelings are being denied. This will simply convey to a child that there is something wrong with him if he feels this way. It will not help him to rediscover his confidence and courage.

Chapter Nineteen also looked at how parents and other adults can respond carelessly to children's feelings and anxieties, denying, excusing, dismissing them. The guidance given there applies especially to the dejected child.

What We Should Try to Say

Dejected children need, instead, careful talk. We have to use language that is wholly encouraging and untainted with judgement or qualification. We must avoid the mixed messages typical of back-handed compliments ('You did pretty well, given your slow start'); references to past failures ('You played that beautifully this time, but why couldn't you play like that last week?') or requests for further improvement ('If you train even harder, you could come first'). As we have already seen, there are a number of components to careful talk which must be adhered to.

First, we should listen, attentively and effectively, to what our child has to say, without interruption. We can then accept the problem as he sees it, and acknowledge his feelings. When it comes to discussing what might be done to improve things, we can ask, not tell; and allow him to come to his own conclusions. Instead of offering advice, we can ask relevant questions. 'What do you think brought it about?', 'How long have you been feeling like this?' or 'Do you have any ideas about what would make it easier for you?'. Finally, we can leave the door open for further discussion. This shows him that you are there for him when he needs it. 'If you get low again, remember that I am here to listen whenever you want.'

When Praise Does Not Work

When children are very low, they often reject praise, the first thing we do to help. First, it will take time for them to accept any view of themselves that is different from their own. Second, they will be very sensitive to sincerity and intention. If they feel manipulated by the praise, they will ignore it. If they feel judged, they may trust their own judgement more than a parent or teacher's. If they are encouraged to try again, or harder, without addressing the source of their anxiety, they may feel they are simply exposing themselves to more failure. Hanko and Hall both state, from their different standpoints of education and sport, that we need to start from the child's anxiety, the underlying feelings and reasons for it, and allow the child to take himself forward, at his own pace. He has to feel in control. As Hanko writes, by finding out from a child how he views a problem '("Do I know what this task is about?" "Do I know how to go about it?" "Am I able to complete it?")', we can then encourage him to assess his own progress, '("How are you getting on?" "Is it as hard as you thought?" "What were the difficult bits?" "Why do you think you did so well?")'.

Getting Them Back on Track

Dejected and discouraged children need help to rediscover their capable selves and to see new possibilities. Although their problem is their own, not ours – they have to reframe and redefine themselves, to their satisfaction, and only they can they reinflate their self-belief – parents can be an important source of strength to children during such times.

We should accept our child for who he is, which includes his fears, anxieties, strengths and vulnerabilities, by listening, and giving time and attention. We can keep all criticisms and judgements to a minimum, especially in relation to those skills which our child feels he lacks. We must listen to, understand, accept and validate his feelings, and avoid belittling, denying or ridiculing these, even if we feel frustrated or irritated by them, or feel inadequate because we believe our child is incompetent and unconfident. If we reflect back to our child his feelings of inadequacy, it will help him to feel understood. It does not mean we agree with him.

We must give him experience of success by giving plenty of praise, lowering our sights and expectations and valuing a range of different talents. If we reduce the risk in what he does and learns by giving clearer instructions, making things slightly easier for a time or by just letting him rest for a while in the comfort of what he can manage, this will help. Appreciation of anything he has done which we like, such as clearing up after himself, will boost his self-belief.

Our child will need help to assess himself in a less negative way. In response to cries of 'I'm just useless', we can say: 'Hang on a moment. Let's just sit down and list those things you are good at. Don't write yourself off just because one or two things aren't going well at the moment!', 'How bad was it, really? Did everybody else do brilliantly and you were the only one who flunked?' or 'Take it step by step. What is the first thing you think you need to do to turn things around? If you can't answer that now, come back in 15 minutes and tell me'.

If we help him to judge how much of a problem he has, using a technique explained by Hall, we can help our child reassess his competence. Draw a line, and explain that the left-hand end of the line represents knowing nothing, while the right-hand end represents knowing everything. Then invite your child to mark the place on the line where he thinks he falls. Although he will exclaim in absolutes ('I don't know anything!'), when pushed to represent how much he knows he will be more realistic.

We can encourage him to identify things he is good at. Use the list in Chapter Seven to come up with suggestions and areas. Remember, such attributes as social skills, sporting skills, kindness to others, and knowledge of natural history all count. This will help to put him in touch, in Hanko's words, with his 'untapped or negated resources'.

A child has to be in charge of something if he is to feel capable. If we give him plenty of useful, practical things to do to help us and others he will feel depended on and therefore dependable.

Positive thinking is essential so we must model more positive self thoughts. If we constantly do ourselves down, this becomes a pattern that a child will copy.

23

Good Times, Bad Times: Problems at School

School is a major part of a child's life. When things go wrong at school, through bullying, work pressure or personality differences with the teacher, the problems cannot be parcelled up and forgotten. They invade, intrude and impede children's thoughts, feelings and actions at night and during the day, when working, resting or playing. We must take these problems seriously, both to prevent them from getting worse and to protect our child's self-esteem which, if damaged, could begin a downward spiral of underachievement, friendship difficulties and more permanent demotivation.

Bullying and Friendship Problems

Social and relationship difficulties at school cover a wide range of problems. They include being isolated and alone, ignored rather than excluded, pestered by a clinging friend, teasing, name-calling, being kept out of games or being jostled, and more serious taunting, destruction of belongings, extortion and physical and verbal aggression. Bullying, as a useful NSPCC leaflet called 'Stop the Violence' explains, is deliberate, sustained and intended to frighten or hurt. It is usually done by one particular individual, or by a group organised by a particular person.

Where a child is victimised and intimidated for a long period, the result can be devastating. Even milder forms of teasing and taunting will force children to question themselves. Their self-belief will be, at the very least, dented. Only the strongest will continue to value themselves to the same degree as before in the face of such prolonged hostility. Serious bullying can destroy self-respect, lead to serious depression and, rarely, suicide. It would be very surprising if any child could remain on task and motivated during the dark days of self-doubt resulting from humiliation, isolation and rejection at the hands of others.

If your child suddenly loses direction, and bullying – mild or severe – is the reason, it is important to act swiftly. This may be difficult.

Parents are often the last to know, because children can find it hard to talk about their troubles and own up to what they see as their personal weakness. There are telltale signs to look out for. The list of symptoms of stress in children on page 187 is a useful starting point. Look out particularly for any change in behaviour and attitudes in relation to school. Your child might be withdrawn in the mornings and reluctant to get ready to go, shed tears or have disturbed sleep at night, or suddenly lose confidence in his work and himself. Any of these events will indicate the time is right to talk and discuss with him ways that will bring it to an end.

Getting Them Back on Track

Put your child's mind at rest. Reassure him that it is not his fault; that there's nothing wrong with him and nothing to be ashamed of. Listen attentively to what your child says takes place, and believe it. Tell the school, and talk to other parents about their children's experiences.

Talk to your child about useful strategies. Teach him games you played as a child, and together discuss phrases he will feel comfortable using which will make him sound and feel stronger. 'Would you like to play with me?' is stronger than 'Can I play with you?'; 'That looks a good game. Can you teach it to me?' sounds better than 'Can I play too?'. Saying something like 'Bullies are weak. I think I know why you need to do this' or 'I don't like it when you pull my jumper', before walking confidently away, is assertive; withdrawing, looking hurt, shows the bullies they have won.

According to the reports of some adults who were bullied as children, hitting or hurting back sometimes works. It calls the bully's bluff. Nevertheless, physical violence is not something that parents should recommend. First, it teaches that violence is the right way to solve even minor problems, which it is not. Second, any response not made confidently and convincingly will be ineffective and liable to make matters worse.

Suggest he makes a friend of anyone else on his own, as children in groups are less likely to be picked on. Also, help your child to compromise, problem solve and take turns at home to reduce potential clashes at school.

If possible, involve him in children's groups outside school so he can lose the 'victim' label and regain social confidence.

More generally, try make him feel loved and accepted. Help to build his confidence by letting him know he is good at things, and give him lots of praise and encouragement.

Exam and Work Pressures

Work and exam pressure can become intolerable and intensely stressful for children of any age. ChildLine, the children's telephone help line, has produced a pamphlet called *Stressed Out: what children tell ChildLine about exams and work pressure*. It reports findings from a survey of children in school and the telephone calls it receives. Many older children feel that their whole future hangs in the balance at times of key examinations. 'They described feeling out of control, panic-stricken, overburdened and overwhelmed, often saying they could not cope any more and, occasionally, they were suicidal. Many said they had little support and that they felt unable to confide in those around them.' In their own words: 'Everyone expects too much of me.', 'I'm just stupid and abnormal.', 'Mum and Dad just don't realise I'm not as clever as my brother.', 'I feel stuck, as if there's no way out.' and 'I feel like I am in a box, shouting at them to listen.'.

So much depends now not simply on passing exams but on passing well enough to gain a competitive edge. Schools are even adding to the self- and parent-imposed pressure. League tables, parental choice and the way the size of school budgets is calculated mean that each school has a vested interest in their students' performance, even at aged seven. Their future depends on it. Children feel they are under a spotlight which is becoming laser-intense.

It was reported in a newspaper recently that the South Korean government is to gaol parents who put too much pressure on their children. New legislation aims to stop what is described as 'academic slavery', following a spawning of private cramming schools which two-thirds of the country's children attend after daytime school from primary age upwards. 'My school life,' reported an 18 year-old who is forced by his parents to study from 7.30 am until midnight, 'is a constant battle against sleep.'.

We have not gone that far, but some children suffer intensely from the pressure their parents place on them. One 15-year-old ChildLine caller was doing nine GCSEs and also had a part-time job. Her mother had very high expectations of her, demanding straight As. The girl was threatened with leaving home if she failed to get the grades necessary for her to follow her chosen course. She was very distressed and finding it hard to eat.

Getting Them Back on Track

Try to be sensitive to the early signs of problems. The more stressed children are, the more they need to feel secure emotionally. Try to make them feel important to you, and keep family conflict, with them or with others, to a minimum. Let them know you accept them for who they are, not what they can do. They must work for themselves, not to please you.

Give them support, by getting them drinks and snacks while they work, by listening, by asking them if they are finding anything difficult, by finding a family friend or neighbour who may know more to talk to them about anything they are stuck on. Help them to plan their revision or studying. Breaking the task down into bite-size chunks makes work more manageable. Remember the 80:20 rule – working 80 per cent harder to do 20 per cent better is not an efficient use of time.

Let them study in the way that suits them best. Each child is different: some like to work late at night; others like to get up early. Some prefer to work in short bursts; others for longer stretches before then taking a complete break. Social life or part-time jobs may be compatible with their work commitments so let them decide, after discussion with you if possible. Try to trust their ability to do well without pressure from you. Pressure demonstrates lack of trust; it is a form of power. And what are the two rules of misused power? The more you use it, the more you lose it; and you bring about that which you fear.

If you think you may be asking for a lot, try to reassess your expectations. Ask yourself what is really important and realise that there are many different ways children can lead fulfilled and happy lives.

Personality Clashes – 'My Teacher Doesn't Like Me!"

Children often lose interest in a subject or activity because of personality differences with the teacher – either they do not like the teacher or they believe their teacher does not like them. The two are often linked. Either way, children rarely pull out the stops for a teacher they don't feel comfortable with.

Few teachers will say to a child's face that he is disliked. If your child believes it to be true, it is his interpretation. It might be true, because teachers, like the rest of us, find it hard to hide their real feelings and children are canny creatures; but it might not be true. Just because a teacher shows, perhaps, a passing irritation does not necessarily mean general dislike.

Of course, some teaching styles and personalities work well with certain types of learners and not well with others. However, it is worthwhile exploring with your child what, specifically, has made him decide he is not liked. Perhaps he feels picked on.

Talking to the Teacher

When a child is unhappy, for whatever reason, his work, friendships and behaviour can suffer. It therefore helps to tell someone at school, or anyone else who works closely with him.

Even when we accept that telling someone may help, it is never easy to decide when, where and how to do it. It often takes particular courage to approach the school, especially if we think the school is at fault. There are several reasons for this. We might expect that, somehow, we'll get blamed. We might feel what we say will be kept in a file and be held against us or our child. We might prefer to keep this information private, wishing it were none of the school's business. We might fear being labelled pushy – or overprotective, or getting angry. Even parents who are teachers can find themselves turning to jelly when reaching for the telephone or walking up the corridor. There are ways to make communication easier.

To achieve a comfortable, non-confrontational meeting, remember to:

- make an appointment. It's not advisable to go in when you are feeling very upset about something
- say what you want it for when the appointment is made. For example, 'It's a personal matter' or 'My son's not happy at the moment and I want to talk about why'
- prepare yourself. Think ahead about how something is best said
- prioritise what you want to discuss and deal with the most important point first. Don't start with the least important one just because it seems 'safe', otherwise the matter you have really come for might get forgotten. Think twice about listing all your points in an introduction, especially those that may seem confrontational, as this may put the teacher on the defensive
- avoid getting side-tracked. Have a written list of things you want to raise and don't be afraid to refer to it
- avoid apparently telling teachers what to do, by explaining what has worked at home. 'Tom seems happier to read when he sees he can manage the first page' is better than 'The books you give him to bring home are putting him right off.'
- translate any complaint or verbal attack from the teacher into a worry: 'It sounds as if you are worried that Ben won't. . . '

It is important to remember that our child's health, happiness and future should come first, above any personal discomfort and embarrassment. The child should be the school's priority too. Having the same aim should help both sides to problem-solve together. We should certainly expect information to be exchanged, in a two-way process. This is what home-school partnership means.

It is usually better to approach the class or form teacher first, and only take it to the headteacher if you do not get satisfaction. Always bear in mind that you are the expert on your child, and that you have a right to be concerned and to follow up any worries you have.

When you go in, think carefully about whether you tell your child. Sometimes it is better to keep it to yourself. More often, though, children value being told the truth and given a chance to influence what you are going to say. This makes them feel involved, not worried or suspicious.

24

The Gifted Child

Gifted children and their parents are usually considered extremely lucky. The very term 'gifted' implies this. If the talent is seen as a gift, it must be desirable. The child can feel proud of himself. The parent does not have to worry about whether his or her child succeeds. People may be surprised, then, to discover a chapter devoted to gifted children in a book on motivation, and especially to find it in a section dealing with problems.

Yet educational, social, behavioural and emotional problems are quite frequent among gifted children – at least until their ability is recognised and responded to. Why? And if highly able children experience problems with underachievement and poor motivation, where might this stem from and what can parents do to help them get back on track?

Characteristics of Gifted and Able Children

These questions are easier to answer if we understand something about what very able and gifted children can be like. Sometimes, the very characteristics they have as gifted children – the way they are – can provoke others to respond and react in ways which undermine the child, causing him to feel misunderstood and dejected.

What are these characteristics? Perhaps frustratingly, there is no agreed, simple definition for high ability or giftedness. There is wide agreement, though, about the sort of abilities and ways of thinking and doing things that set these children apart. Very able children probably constitute about five per cent of the child population, and the term 'exceptionally able' is usually taken to refer to the smaller number, about two per cent, who are capable of functioning at a level several years in advance of what is considered normal for their age group.

In the United States, educationalists use different versions of a similar typology which describes the difference between a bright child and a very able or gifted learner. It is useful for highlighting the relevant characteristics that can cause problems. An example of this typology appears in a booklet published by Westminster Education Authority entitled 'Working with Very Able Children'. It is selectively reproduced below.

Bright Child	Gifted Child
Knows the answer	Asks the questions
Is interested	Is highly curious
Is attentive	Is involved
Has good ideas	Has wild, 'silly' ideas
Reads and writes well	Enjoys the use of language, especially its use in humour
Learns with ease	Often looks for hidden difficulties
Listens with interest	Shows strong feelings and opinions
6–8 repetitions for mastery	1–2 repetitions for mastery
Understands ideas	Constructs abstractions
Well-presented work	Messy presentation because thoughts are rushing ahead
Enjoys peers	Often prefers adults
Absorbs information	Manipulates information

Why Gifted Children Can Lose Motivation

Gifted children can become demotivated because they:

- are inadequately challenged
- are put down for being themselves – exposing their talents and knowledge
- wish to conform – underperforming so they can appear 'normal'
- feel frustrated because their ideas are ahead of their ability to carry them out

Verbal Fluency

From the list of characteristics above, it can be seen that gifted children will often be very good with words, which means that they will talk fluently and at length, but their written work will not always be up to the same standard. Schools naturally look at the quality and the speed of written work for 'proof' of a child's exceptional ability. Frustration, boredom and learning to fill the time available with extraneous thoughts can lead these children to work slowly, so the 'proof' is not forthcoming.

Case Study

A parent felt that his five-year-old son, who began to read when he was three and was a fluent reader on starting school aged four-and-a-half, was not being stretched. At the regular monthly session with the teacher, his father asked if he could be given more challenging work. The teacher replied that she could not agree with this assessment of his ability level. The lad took ages to complete simple work sheets, so clearly had a problem with concentration, and frequently got sums wrong. It was her policy not to move children on until every answer was correct. She was unmoved by the father's account of long chess games with him. Unfortunately, she had already moved from the school when, one month before his seventh birthday, he was assessed as having a reading age of 12.

Verbal fluency also means a gifted child may prefer to talk to an adult than to a classmate, someone who is more likely to comprehend his latest schemes and ideas. Desperate for a soul mate, he can easily come across as irritating, and his pestering as an attempt to curry favour and brag.

Quick to Understand

The gifted child will be a quick learner, who does not need to practise much, if at all, in order to understand new concepts. Repeating tasks will be boring, and may even lead to careless mistakes which many adults will read as proof that *more* work or practice is necessary. If a child takes the initiative to move his own learning forward, or shows that he already knows the next stage, he can easily be reprimanded for being arrogant or for stepping out of line.

Case Study
A child, aged six, was grouped with four other 'bright' children in the class for occasional 'extension' work. One day, she came home complaining that a teacher had put some of her work in the waste bin. Already able to tell the time, and bored with the task of marking only the hour and half hour positions on printed clock faces, she had decided to fill in some alternative times. The support teacher took these sheets from her and threw them away, saying that Mrs X would not like to see that she had not stuck to the task at hand.

Curiosity and Humour

Gifted children can be creative and abstract thinkers with a pronounced curiosity and an unstoppable sense of humour. Always asking questions, always wanting to take the discussion and explanation further, offering wild and apparently silly ideas, and frequently cracking verbal jokes, it is easy to see how the constant disruption to carefully constructed explanations would interrupt the concentration of the class and be disapproved of. Being strong on imagination and the ability to concentrate, gifted children are inclined to become frustrated without a real challenge and to pursue other, more absorbing thoughts. Yet the problem is usually defined as an inability to concentrate.

Know-alls

Very able children may come across as irritating know-alls because they often have a good memory, wide general knowledge and surprisingly deep understanding and excitement about some particular field of interest which they want to share. Where their wide knowledge is combined with a tendency to express strong feelings and opinions and an enjoyment of logical argument, their assertiveness can be perceived as verging on the insufferable.

Case Study

While at infant school, a young boy was already reading widely. His excellent memory meant he was developing an extensive general knowledge. It was only after he left that he told his parents the older children used to queue up at break time to put test questions to him, to see if they could find something he could not answer. Although this was done in a good-humoured way, it inevitably made him feel different, and very self-conscious about his knowledge which was an entirely unintended consequence of his love of reading and wide interests, and not remotely cultivated to impress.

How it Might Feel to Be Different

There is a saying in Japan, where conformity is highly valued, that if a nail sticks up, hammer it back in. Although British education has been renowned for its encouragement of individuality and creativity, the classroom reality is all too often that excellence is frowned upon. You can be a personality, but you cannot outshine anyone else. Many gifted children will find themselves being hammered back in, either by their teachers, who should know better, or by their classmates who can feel threatened by someone who is more capable, or just 'different'. Sometimes, very able children will stamp on themselves, in effect hammering themselves back in, to stay 'normal' so they do not stand out.

Given all the above, how might a gifted child feel? He may feel put down, even punished, for being himself. He may feel disliked and see himself as a nuisance. He will also feel profound frustration and disappointment that he has been misjudged and misunderstood, and be confused about whether it is okay to be the person that he feels he is. He will often be made to feel different, as strange and freakish rather than special, though it may not be intended. He may therefore feel quite isolated, cut off from the other children around him: not quite a child but in a child's body. In these circumstances it will be hard to stay comfortable with himself.

If he decides to conform, either to please adults or to get closer to his peers, he will be unable to relax. He must manipulate what he thinks and says constantly to ensure that he does not show himself up. He has to underachieve, and in so doing loses touch with himself. He may even forget what he can do, and spontaneity disappears. He can never experience any pride in an achievement, unless he produces different quality work in the privacy of his home, which is what many such children do – for their own self-respect.

Gifted children will also find it hard to be true to themselves in two further ways. The first is that their enthusiasm, depth of understanding and ideas will often encourage them to set targets for themselves that are simply not attainable without great application or adult support. Plans for projects or ideas for stories are not so much grandiose as over-ambitious for the child that they are. Usually reading at an advanced level, this is the prose they hear in their heads but cannot always put into words – let alone actually write on paper. Yet they desperately want to write – a book, an in-depth school project or similar ambitious scheme. For those who want to do rather than write, they can also be tempted by the stimulating research projects they have encountered to set themselves unreal standards. It will be hard to sustain their commitment without a degree of adult input that will itself endanger the future of the project because it dilutes the child's sense of ownership. Half-finished, madcap schemes litter the lives of many creative children. The frustration, disappointment and confusion caused will eventually sap motivation as they recognise the pattern and lose faith in themselves.

Getting Them Back on Track

Taking each of the possible 'causes' mentioned above in turn, do these suggestions contain something you can consider?

Inadequate Challenge

Find challenges for him in other areas, outside school. Some hobbies and interests can be followed at home if you have time and space to let him experiment. Introduce your child to someone who is knowledgeable about your child's special field of interest who might be able to spend time with him.

Local museums, libraries or other places of interest often run special days for children. Explore whether there are any special activities for very able children available locally; for example, Explorers Clubs organised by the National Association for Gifted Children, GIFT workshops or groups organised by Children with High Intelligence (CHI).

Being Put Down

Nurture your child's self-esteem and self-worth. A child who feel 'hammered in' will have a greater need to be accepted at home. Accept him for who he is, not for what he can do – his special abilities – so that if he is teased for this talent, he has some self-esteem remaining.

Try to value him for his humour. Early humour is painful, but without those early attempts, no one will become skilled. Practice makes perfect.

Encourage relationships with other sympathetic adults. Feeling comfortable with a parent when the world outside seems so difficult can make a child quite dependent and untrusting of others.

Underperformance

Give him the space and freedom to work at his natural level at home, but try not to make too much fuss about what he achieves. He is doing it for himself, not for glory. Try to avoid showing the astonishment your child finds so tedious from others; let him feel normal. Let him keep ownership of this work.

Research ways in which your child can spend time with like-minded children, and even like-minded adults, with the same passions.

Frustration

A gifted child will become frustrated because his ideas run ahead of his ability to carry them out. Discuss more realistic targets, and then help him think through ways to achieve them. This will encourage stickability, develop planning skills and put the fast flow of ideas so typical of very able children to constructive use. Helping him to experience success and pride, not failure and frustration, will prevent him from never really fulfilling his promise – the 'busted flush' syndrome.

Try not to take his project over. The safest approach is to ask, not assume, that our help will be welcomed. 'Is there anything I can do that you would find helpful?' will give him the choice about how much support he accepts.

A Note of Caution

To be happy in life and relationships, children need social skills that help them to fit in; but often gifted children don't fit. Parents of gifted children have the difficult task of finding a balance between allowing the child to be himself – perhaps insistent, impatient, sounding bossy or arrogant – and preparing him for the sometimes harsh world which finds such characteristics difficult to stomach.

It is a balance that some will not be very interested to achieve. Those who feed off their very bright child to fuel their own self-worth, may need to encourage the talents that set their child clearly apart to 'prove' and constantly reinforce his difference. The further danger is that he may then become one-dimentional, and value himself exclusively through his talent. Pandering also to a parental need for status and to his need for parental approval, he can become almost a pastiche of himself as he acts out the role of the gifted child. Professor Joan Freeman, a writer and authority on gifted children, calls these youngsters 'the career gifted'. It is easy, then, for such children to slip into a permanent role as a 'one-off' eccentric. Yet we have seen that personal success depends on much more than raw IQ. Employers increasingly demand team players, not loners and eccentrics. Personal relationships require compromise and empathy if they are to last and be fulfilling.

Gifted children, who start their lives with such a potential asset, need support to gain insight about their impact on the world. If they are to capitalise on their talents, they will need to become sensitive and adaptable at the same time as retaining the important bits of who they are.

25

Conclusion: Helping Children to Help Themselves

Writing about motivation is like writing about the human condition. It is difficult to know where to start or stop. So many factors influence how we behave, what we want for ourselves and how we respond to challenges it is hard to select any single one as a universal truth let alone translate it into practical strategies. Concentrating solely on detailed tactics can also be unsatisfactory. You cannot be absolutely certain what will work. Some tactics succeed for some people with some children but not for others. Some approaches are great for children of a certain age, but not for those who are older or younger. Each of us has to decide what we feel comfortable with, starting from who we are and the personality of our child, applying the understandings and insights covered in the previous pages that seem most relevant to us.

This book has raised many issues from many different perspectives. The conclusion is therefore a good place to summarise the central ideas and principles before bringing it to a close.

Children are people, not possessions or puppets. Each one is a creative, talented human being with hopes, fears and feelings who deserves to be cherished for who he is and not for how clever he is at this or that. We have to nurture the whole child. A broadly based and positive sense of self is their main spring. It gives them the courage and determination to explore their uncharted capabilities in a risk-filled and changing world; but this sense of self is vulnerable. Children look first to us and then to others for affirmation and confirmation. From relationships that are emotionally safe and richly rewarding, they gain the strength to project themselves and the confidence to trust both themselves and others. If, on the other hand, they grow up in emotional poverty without trust, without anyone showing interest, support or commitment, or with continuous messages that they cause pain and disappointment rather than pleasure, they will lose their sense of direction, cut themselves off and stop trying. Children believe in themselves when someone else believes in them. If we want our children to be self-starters, we have to think carefully about the negative messages we send both when we criticise them and when we kick start them into action every time. When they leave home, they have to manage alone. Offering close help, guidance and support when children are young is, of course, crucial. Being available to give the same to older children when it is needed it is also important, provided this is withdrawn once they can manage without it. Children who grow up constantly propelled by ambitious parents never get the chance to discover or direct themselves.

At the beginning of this book, I suggested there were some tried and tested principles that could help to maintain that difficult balance between doing too much and doing too little. I also wrote that it is possible, from the start, to establish practices which create a safe and sound motivational climate for children within which they are encouraged to try themselves out and learn to apply themselves happily and effectively. Of course, children are unpredictable. They can develop in surprising ways. They sometimes even set out to prove parents wrong. Friends or teachers can say the wrong thing at the wrong time and undo years of work. However, using the 14 principles set out in Part Two and and the five stages of motivation in the model which appears on page 18, will help you decide when and how to intervene or, alternatively, when and how to withdraw.

To recap, the most favourable motivational climate for children is one in which adults:

- encourage a spread of interests and skills, academic and non-academic
- value and reward a range of achievements
- nurture curiosity, creativity and imagination
- establish flexible but recognisable routines and habits for work and personal care
- develop self-knowledge and self-awareness
- expect, model and reinforce responsible behaviour
- show a commitment to quality learning and self-development
- have time – to be interested and for family fun
- respect everyone's need to relax or switch off

If, at the same time, we apply the central principles: accept our children for who they are; help them to feel good about themselves, but keep it real; provide practical and moral support and encouragement; set clear targets and give quick, accurate and constructive feedback; let them own and learn from their success and failure; help them to help themselves and put them in charge wherever possible; listen, understand and work to co-operate, we shall be doing our best to foster self-motivation. At all times, we should preserve their self-belief and give them hope in themselves and their future.

Children have their own way of looking at things, of course. They will compare themselves against others and they will compete. Yet – we now know that children are less prone to anxiety, more resilient during setbacks and ultimately more self-motivated if they are 'learning', or 'task oriented' – if their sights are set on improving on their last best personal performance – instead of being 'ego' or 'performance oriented' – that is, bent on beating someone else or proving themselves in the eyes of others. If any competitive urge can be directed inwards rather than outwards, towards mastering a task rather than performing to impress, there will be less pain and disappointment at setbacks and more sense of control over meeting the goal. When children are successful, therefore, we should beware of basking in their reflected glory and comparing them favourably with others. Instead, we should welcome their success, delight in their development and remind them they have nothing to prove to us because they are lovable as they are. Safe progress is about self-development, not 'self'-improvement.

Where there seems to be little competitive urge, and no desire to develop, tactics help. A well-timed incentive, or series of incentives, can help a child complete a boring or difficult task and encourage stickability. The occasional sharp word or tough choice can be used with effect. Support at the planning stage can make a goal more accessible. Putting them on daily report to you or to the school can rein them in when they have strayed. Applauding one skill can create the confidence to achieve elsewhere. The Troubleshooter's Guide, Diagram 25.1, at the end of this chapter contains further ideas. However, if too much time is spent tweeking and oiling, it is probably time to go back to square one and focus on the fundamentals. We will set children off on the right road if we work to build their self-belief, self-efficacy and self-direction and actively engage younger children, especially boys, in reading and talking to develop these essential passport skills.

Relationships Matter

Children are most likely to develop a positive sense of self, and develop good social and communication skills, within healthy relationships: relationships in which children are noticed, given time and space, praised and enjoyed, listened to, respected and where emotions are discussed and understood. Money and possessions are no substitute. Children do better when they are relationship rich and possession poor, rather than possession rich and relationship poor. They are most disadvantaged when they feel insignificant, isolated and insecure, which can happen when they feel unsafe, uncetain, unloved and excluded.

Parents need neither qualifications nor wealth to help children flourish. Formal qualifications are not necessary to show delight in their achievements, ask how things are going, give plenty of praise and encouragement and have the time and commitment to support them in school. Money is not an essential to help children find out about themselves, learn how to make plans, solve problems or develop regular routines – though some money does help for extras such as outings, holiday courses or local activities. Children might not like to hear it, but most of them would benefit more long term if the money spent on designer clothing or computer games was instead spent on trips and talent-developing activities.

We are living through a time of great change and uncertainty – political, economic and social. Many people, aside from parents, have a vested interest in understanding the dynamics of motivation. Employers should realise that the more they demand from parents, the less they may get from the next generation. Government has a duty to provide jobs that have to be the ultimate incentive, and to reflect on where pressure for 'educational excellence' may lead. There is one certainty: if we do not become more sensitive to the needs and interests of our children, we will all lose out in the long term.

Diagram 25.1: Troubleshooter's Guide

	Signs of motivation difficulties	Possible reason	Possible action by parent
Stage One IDENTIFY THE TARGET	Unwilling to commit to a target Unable to decide what to aim at No aims or ambitions Inappropriate targets – too easy or too hard	Low self-esteem and belief, so assumes failure – future does not feel safe Poor sense of who he is Uncertain of what he wants or can do Personal or parental expectations too low/high	Make the future seem safe through a safer present Build his self-belief Find good role models for inspirations and example Help him to set more realistic targets
Stage Two ASSESS AND DEVELOP COMPETENCE	No interest in trying new things Thinks skills not worth improving because not good enough to start with	Low self-confidence. Feels generally incapable Fears change because uncertain of self Tendency to make or to be told about comparisons with others who are better	Encourage a variety of interests and talents Nurture child's self-esteem and confidence. Praise more, criticise, nag and punish less Show interest and pride in all his skills as they develop
Stage Three PLANNING THE ROUTE	Unwilling to think about creating a plan Plans tend to be impractical. Unrealistic expectations about what can be managed	Personal experiences have been unsettling Low trust in the ability to do anything well, and used to being directed Unwilling to take responsibility for effort made	Make home more predictable and secure. Provide routines and loving relationships Model planning skills – think ahead, make lists and break tasks down Make child responsible for his behaviour Discuss cutting down television and computer games
Stage Four APPLICATION AND DETERMINATION	Gives up very easily when problems surface Seems to run out of steam Leaves everything to the last minute so quality affected	Finds it hard to problem-solve, evaluate and alter performance Unable to concentrate, easily bored, target too distant or parent competing Poor time management	Make it safe for him to make mistakes. Discuss what goes right or wrong, and why, together Offer incentives. Make it fun. Show interest, encouragement and commitment. Don't compete Encourage routines, agree priorities and time plans
Stage Five SUCCESS	Success never good enough. Devalues own achievements Gives up just before the finishing line Invests everything in success in one field only	Striving for acceptance through self-improvement and perfection Fears responsibility for keeping high standard. Avoids the final judgement for fear of failing Feels accepted for achievements, not self	Let him own the success, and celebrate it to prove it's good enough Accept him for who he is, not what he can do Help him with the last push. Reward stickability Value many talents

Further Reading

Tina Bruce, *Helping Young Children to Play*, Hodder and Stoughton (1996)

Sally Burningham, *Young People Under Stress*, Virago/Mind, London (1994)

ChildLine, *Stressed Out: what children tell ChildLine about exams and work pressure* (1996)

Peter Downes and Carey Bennet, *Help your Child through Secondary School*, Hodder and Stoughton (1997)

Adele Faber and Elaine Mazlish, *How to Listen so Kids will Talk and Talk so Kids will Listen*, Avon Books, New York (1980)

Howard Gardner, *The Unschooled Mind: how children think and how schools should teach*, Fontana Press, London (1993)

Daniel Goleman, *Emotional Intelligence*, Bloomsbury, London (1996)

Philip Graham, *So Young, So Sad, So Listen*, Gaskell (1995)

Elizabeth Hartley-Brewer, *Positive Parenting: raising children with self-esteem*, Cedar, London (1994)

Charles Handy, *Beyond Certainty*, Arrow Business Books (1996)

John Holt, *Why Children Fail*, Penguin Books, London (1990)

David Lewis, *Helping your Anxious Child*, Cedar, London (1993)

Jennie and Lance Linden, *Help Your Child Through School*, Hodder Headway, London (1994)

Jennie Linden, *Growing Up: from eight years to young adulthood*, National Children's Bureau (1996)

Gael Lindenfield, *Self-motivation*, Thorsons, London (1996)

Nyberg, L and Austine Templeton, R, *How to Talk so Kids can Learn at Home and in School*, Simon and Schuster, New York (1996)

Young Minds, *Mental Health in Your School: A Guide for teachers and others working in schools*, Jessica Kingsley Publishers (1996)

Useful Organisations and Addresses

SELF-ESTEEM

The Self-Esteem Network
32 Carisbrooke Road, London, E17 7EF
Tel: 0181 521 6977

SUPPORT FOR PARENTS

Parent Network
Winchester House, 11 Cranmer Road, Kennington Park, SW9 6EJ
Tel: 0171 735 4596

The Parenting Education and Support Forum
National Children's Bureau, 8 Wakley Street, London, EC1V 7QE
Tel: 0171 843 6099
A variety of parent education and support courses are available nation-wide. Local libraries will usually have details. If not, the above organisation may be able to offer information on what is on offer in your area.

Trust for the Study of Adolescence
23 New Road, Brighton, East Sussex, BN1 1WZ
Tel: 01273 693 311

BULLYING PROBLEMS IN OR OUTSIDE SCHOOL

Kidscape
152 Buckingham Palace Road, London, SW1W 9TR
Tel: 0171 730 3300

COMPUTER-AIDED LEARNING

National Council for Educational Technology
Milburn Hill Road, Science Park, Coventry CV4 7JJ
Tel: 01203 416994

Parents Information Network (PIN)
PO Box 1577, London W7 3ZT

HIGH ABILITY AND TALENTED CHILD

The Support Society for Children of High Intelligence
PO Box 4222, London SE22 8XG

National Association for Gifted Children
National Centre for Children with High Abilities and Talents
Elder House, Milton Keynes, MK9 1LT
Tel 01918 673 677/8

SPORTING AND OTHER OPPORTUNITES FOR CHILDREN

The Sports Council
PO Box 480, Crystal Palace National Sports Centre, Leadrington Road,
London, SE19
Tel: 0181 778 8600

The Children's Theatre Association
6 Great Newport Street, London, WC2
Tel: 0171 836 3623

CHILDREN'S MENTAL HEALTH

Young Minds
102-108 Clerkenwell Road, London, EC1M 5FA
Tel: 0171 336 8445

The Association of Workers for Children with Emotional and Behavioural Difficulties
Allan Rimmer, Administrator
Charlton Court, East Sutton, Near Maidstone, Kent, ME17 3DQ

WHERE CHILDREN CAN GO

ChildLine
Freepost 1111
Tel: 0800 1111

Children's Express (Children's newpaper)
Exmouth House, Pine Street, London EC1
Tel: 0171 833 2577

Article 12
c/o National Children's Bureau, 8 Wakley Street, London EC1V
Tel: 0171 843 6000

Irchin (Independent Representation for Children in Need)
1 Downham Road South, Heswell, Wirral, Merseyside L60 5RG
Tel: 0151 342 7852

Advisory Centre for Education
Unit 1B Aberdeen Studios, 22-24 Highbury Grove, London N5 2EA
Tel: 0171 354 8318 Advice line: 0171 354 8321

Children's Legal Centre
University of Essex, Wivenhoe Park, Colchester. CO4 3SQ
Tel: 01206 873820 Advice line open 2–5pm

Bibliography

Adair, John (1983) *Effective Leadership* Pan, London

Ames, Carole (1992) Classrooms: Goals, Structures, and Student Motivation, *Journal of Educational Psychology.* **84** No 3 261–271

Ball, Christopher (1994) *Start Right: the importance of early learning* RSA, London

Blanchard, Kenneth and Johnson, Spencer (1981) *The One Minute Manager* Collins

Burningham, Sally (1994) *Young People Under Stress* Virago/Mind, London

ChildLine (1996) *Stressed Out: what children tell ChildLine about exams and work pressure* A ChildLine study

City of Westminster (1996) *Working with Very Able Children*

Csikszentmihalyi, Rathunde and Whalen (1993) *Talented Teenagers: The roots of success and failure* Cambridge Universtity Press, Cambridge

Davy, A *Playwork: Play and care for children 5–15* (1995) Macmillan, London

Dunn, J (1988) *The Beginnings of Social Understanding* Basil Blackwell, Oxford

Freeman, J (1991) *Gifted Children Growing Up* London, Cassel Educational Ltd

Gardner, H (1993) *The Unschooled Mind: how children think and how schools should teach* Fontana Press, London
(1983) *Frames of Mind: the theory of multiple intelligences* Basic Books, New York

George, D (1992) *The Challenge of the Able Child* David Fulton, London

Goleman, D (1996) *Emotional Intelligence* Bloomsbury, London

Greenhalgh, P (1994) *Emotional Growth and Learning* Routledge, London

Haldane, J M and Taylor, M, eds (1996) *Values in Education and Education in Values* Falmer Press. London

Hall, E and C (1988) *Human Relations in Education* Routledge, London
(1990) *Scripted Fantasy in the Classroom* Routledge, London

Hall, H K and Kerr, A W (1997) Motivational Antecedents of Precompetitive Anxiety in Youth Sport in *The Sports Psychologist* **11** 24–42

Hall H, Roberts G and Treasure D (1994) Parental Goal Orientations and Beliefs About the Competitive Sports Experience of their Child in *Journal of Sports Psychology*, **24**, 7, 631–645

Handy, C(1983) *Understanding Organisations* Penguin Books Ltd
(1994) *The Empty Raincoat* Arrow Business Books, London
(1995) *Beyond Certainty* Arrow Business Books, London
(1997) *The Hungry Spirit* Hutchinson, London

Hanko, G (1995) *Special Needs in Ordinary Classrooms: From staff support to staff development* Third edition. David Fulton
(1994) Discouraged Children: when praise does not help *British Journal of Special Education* 21 **4** 166–168

Hartley-Brewer, E
(1988) *Positive Parenting: raising children with self-esteem* Vermilion, London
(1996) *Cooperative Kids* Hartley-Brewer Parenting Projects
(1996) *School Matters, and so do parents!* Hartley-Brewer Parenting Projects

Health Education Authority (1995) *Expectations for the Future: an investigation into the self-esteem of 13 and 14 year old girls and boys*

Holt, J (1990) *Why Children Fail* Penguin Books, London

Hunt, J (1981) *Managing People at Work* Pan Books, London

Lewis, D (1993) *Helping your Anxious Child* Cedar, London

Linden, J and L (1994) *Help Your Child Through School* Hodder Headway, London

Linden, J (1996) *Growing Up: from eight years to young adulthood* National Children's Bureau

Lindenfield, G (1996) *Self-motivation* Thorsons, London

MacCormack, M H (1984) *What They Don't Teach You at the Harvard Business School* Fontana/Collins, London

Montuschi, O Howell, E with Kahn, T (1997) *Parenting Perspectives* Courseware Publications

National Commission on Education (1993): *Learning to Succeed* Heinemann, London

National Council for Educational Technology (1994) *IT Works, Learning Together with Computers*

Nierenberg, G I (1975) *How to Give and Receive Advice* Editorial Correspondents, Inc., New York
(1981) *The Art of Negotiating* Simon and Schuster, New York

Noonan, E (1989) *Counselling Young People* Tavistock/Routledge, London.

Pipher, M (1994) *Reviving Ophelia* Ballantine Books, New York

Pollard, A with Filer, A (1996) *The Social World of Children's Learning* Cassell

Russell, A and R (1996) *Information Technology for Parents* Piccadilly
    Press, London

Sylva, K (1994) The Impact of Early Learning on Children's Later
    Development Appendix C in *Start Right* RSA, London

Tizard, B and Hughes, M (1984) *Young Children Learning* Fontana,
    London

Vroom, V and Deci, Ed (eds) (1983) *Management and Motivation*
    Penguin, London

Young Minds (1996) *Mental Health in Your School A Guide for teachers
    and   others working in schools* Jessica Kingsley Publishers

Index